LANGUAGE, DISCOURSE, SOCIETY

C000050400

Editors: Stephen Heath, Colin MacCabe and Denise]

published titles

Stanley Aronowitz
THE CRISIS IN HISTORICAL MATERIALISM
SCIENCE AS POWER: Discourse and Ideology in Modern Society

John Barrell
THE BIRTH OF PANDORA and Other Essays

Mikkel Borch-Jacobsen
THE FREUDIAN SUBJECT

Norman Bryson
VISION AND PAINTING: The Logic of the Gaze

Teresa de Lauretis
ALICE DOESN'T: Feminism, Semiotics, Cinema
FEMINIST STUDIES/CRITICAL STUDIES (*editor*)
TECHNOLOGIES OF GENDER: Essays on Theory, Film, and Fiction

Mary Ann Doane
THE DESIRE TO DESIRE: The Woman's Film of the 1940s

Alan Durant
CONDITIONS OF MUSIC

Jane Gallop
FEMINISM AND PSYCHOANALYSIS: The Daughter's Seduction

Peter Gidal
UNDERSTANDING BECKETT: A Study of Monologue and Gesture in the
Works of Samuel Beckett

Peter Goodrich
LEGAL DISCOURSE: Studies in Linguistics, Rhetoric and Legal Analysis

Piers Gray
MARGINAL MEN: Edward Thomas; Ivor Gurney; J. R. Ackerley

Paul Hirst
ON LAW AND IDEOLOGY

Ian Hunter
CULTURE AND GOVERNMENT: The Emergence of Literary Education

Andreas Huyssen
AFTER THE GREAT DIVIDE: Modernism, Mass Culture and Postmodernism

Nigel Leask
THE POLITICS OF IMAGINATION IN COLERIDGE'S CRITICAL
THOUGHT

Michael Lynn-George
EPOS: WORD, NARRATIVE AND THE *ILIAD*

Colin MacCabe
JAMES JOYCE AND THE REVOLUTION OF THE WORD
THE TALKING CURE: Essays on Psychoanalysis and Language (*editor*)
BROKEN ENGLISH

THE BIRTH OF PANDORA

and the Division of Knowledge

John Barrell

MACMILLAN

First published 1992

Published by
THE MACMILLAN PRESS LTD
Houndmills, Basingstoke, Hampshire RG21 2XS
and London
Companies and representatives
throughout the world

Printed in Great Britain by
Billing & Sons Ltd, Worcester

British Library Cataloguing in Publication Data
Barrell, John
The birth of Pandora and the division of knowledge. (Language, Discourse,
Society)
1. British culture, history
I. Title   II. Series
941
ISBN 0–333–48287–5
ISBN 0–333–48288–3 pbk

For
J. R. Hartley

Contents

List of Illustrations

Acknowledgements

When these essays were delivered as papers, more people than I could list or even remember commented on them, in many cases very helpfully, and I am most grateful to all of them. Especial thanks are due to those with whom I have discussed one or more of these essays in detail, often after they had read and annotated a draft version: Homi Bhabha, Peter de Bolla, Colin Brooks, Tim Clark, Harriet Guest, Nigel Leask, Marcia Pointon, Jacqueline Rose, David Simpson, Ann Wagner. My thanks also to Anne Rafique, for her watchfulness and patience as the book made its far from untroubled passage through the press.

Five of the essays in this book have already been published elsewhere, and I am grateful to all those who gave permission for their republication in this volume. Full details will be found in the footnote on the first page of each essay. I am grateful too to all those who invited me to give the papers that were later developed into essays. Some were given as papers on several occasions; for brevity's sake I have usually recorded only the first such occasion.

My grateful acknowledgements are due to the following institutions and individuals who kindly gave me permission to reproduce images and objects in their possession: Ashmolean Museum, Oxford, for Figure 24; British Museum, for Figures 22, 23, 25, 27, 29, 30, 32, 43, 46, 47; Crawford Art Gallery, Cork, for Figures 37, 44; Fine Art Society, London, for Figure 6; Huntington Library, San Marino, California, for Figure 5; Kunsthaus, Zurich, for Figure 33; Manchester City Art Galleries, for Figure 28; National Archaeological Museum, Athens, for Figure 26; National Gallery of Art, Dublin, for Figures 42, 45; New Brunswick Museum, New Brunswick, for Figure 38; The Oppé Collection, for Figure 36; Pinacoteca Nazionale, Bologna, for Figure 35; Royal Society of Arts, London, for Figures 34, 39; Terenure College, Dublin, for Figure 40; Uffizi, Florence, for Figure 12; Yale Center for British Art, for Figures 1, 2, 3, 4, 7, 8, 42. Figure 9 is the property of a private collector, who is also gratefully acknowledged.

xi

Foreword

A woman gesturing from an upstairs window; a sentence of interminable length; a painter struggling uphill against the wind; a pair of statues in the entrance hall of a country house; a man holding the lopped branch of a tree; imagining the king's death; a foot, a woman's or a man's, that seems to hang in the air. As I approach the question of what the essays in this volume have in common, it is ideas and images such as these that come first to mind. They have as good a claim to be regarded as the true starting-point of the essays as do the issues I officially address; and they seem to offer themselves as moments in a sequential narrative it would be easy enough to invent or to reconstruct. Fortunately, however, the decencies of cultural criticism – this is one reason why I write it – oblige us to look elsewhere for the coherence of an intellectual project, and it may be more appropriate to begin by saying that these essays, which are all concerned with the polite culture of the eighteenth century in Britain, were all written in the Britain of the 1980s. They have some of the coherence, I believe, of that very coherent decade, and not just in that they share, here and there, many of the intellectual preoccupations of the period: a concern, say, with writing and with images as discourse, or with the gendering of cultural objects and practices, or with the boundaries of public and private space. More to the point, they continually return to one question in particular, a question about the nature of knowledge and of representation in a society which is (or which is represented as) a distinctively *commercial* one; a society in which the values expressive of a concern for the public interest are challenged by, or are identified with, the values of an 'enterprise culture'.

The seven essays in this book, though they can all be thought of as essays in the politics of culture, are concerned with very diverse topics: with Thomas Rowlandson's comic representations of the rural poor; with a long, elaborate sentence by the poet William Collins, the 'Icarus of syntax', as Geoffrey Hartman once described him; with the ability to understand the composition of landscape as a metaphor for the ability to understand the public interest; with how to represent Venus, image of all that the citizen should both reject and admire; with how to represent the divided labours of commercial society; with high

xiii

treason, the rights of juries, and the diseases of the imagination; with the policing of the boundaries of gender and race in neo-classical history painting. But they all situate themselves, to a greater or lesser extent, within the terms of a range of specific discourses and discursive conflicts, and of conflicts between the class and gender interests that these various discourses both construct and express. The summary I am about to offer of those discursive conflicts will be much too brief, too much *one* way through a difficult terrain, too wary of saying too much, to satisfy anyone who knows much about the subject. But the aim of this book is to interest a wider readership than studies in the eighteenth century usually attract, and it seems best to begin with a sketch-map whose outlines can be filled in and corrected later.

The discursive conflicts I have in mind are mainly centred in the late eighteenth century, though I sometimes stray backwards in time, and sometimes forward to the opening years of the nineteenth century. For much of the century the discourse of 'civic humanism', of aristocratic and republican virtue, had been the most influential and the most fully articulated language of value, across a wide range of cultural practices, including government, polite letters, and the visual arts.[1] It was a discourse which defined 'man' – not man in general, as it sometimes pretended, but man as opposed to woman and even to most men – as a *political animal*, a man destined to find fulfilment as the citizen of a republic in which he was both ruler and ruled. It valued the various genres of literature and the visual arts more or less as they contributed to the education of citizens so defined. It divided cultural practices between a public and a private sphere – the economic was often represented as no less private a matter than (for example) the erotic – and it used the division to measure their relative importance and ethical value.

Throughout the century the discourse of civic humanism is to be found in relations of conflict, of collaboration, of mutual incroachment, of mutual appropriation, with a discourse more favourable to the values of commercial life, and one which – in terms of form, genre and style as well as of content – is coded as socially inferior. But what has always intrigued me, and other historians of eighteenth-century culture is a series of moments, mainly in the second half of the century, where this other discourse – whether as 'political economy', or as the discourse of 'the division of labour' – comes to be articulated in ways which posed quite fundamental questions to the authority that had accrued to civic humanism. Partly this is because it begins to find expression in a literary style which announces its own authority. Partly it is the result of its claim to offer a thoroughly systematic account of history and of economic and social organisation. Partly it results from the invention of a new account of what it is to be human – to be human is now to be an *economic*, rather than a political animal. And partly it results from a challenge to the claim of the independent gentleman that he (and he alone) enjoyed that comprehensive view of society which enabled him to see the interests of everyone, of the public. Either no one has such a view, it was now argued, or someone else has it, but it could by no means be the exclusive property of the aristocratic man of virtue. Might it not be necessary to have mixed more in the world of work – and in the modern world of commerce – to know what was in the interests of a commercial society?

The potential for this discursive conflict to be represented as a class conflict is clear enough; and the privilege of class was much more certainly the stake in the struggle at the end of the century, not over the authority, but over the very ownership, of the civic discourse. The same sentiments which, proceeding from the mouth of a gentleman, announced a concern for the virtues of aristocratic government, were nothing less than 'jacobinism' when mispronounced in a popular assembly. There is a moment in the trial for high treason in 1794 of Thomas Hardy, the shoemaker, where some lines of verse are read out in court. They are lines from James Thomson's poem *Liberty*; they offer a miniature civic homily on the virtues of patriotism and the dangers of corrupt and venal government; and they had been quoted in a document published by the London Corresponding Society, of which Hardy was secretary.[2] There was no suggestion that Thomson, the poet laureate of the civic republic, could have written anything treasonous; but there was a real question as to whether a shoemaker, the leader of a popular political reform movement, could have quoted the passage except with a treasonous intent.

Even before the 1790s and the arrival, real or imagined, of jacobinism in Britain, there had been signs of an unease with the civic discourse on the part of those with a claim to own it. For in combination with a democratic reading of Locke and of the language of inalienable human rights, it could be appropriated only too easily to represent all men – even women – as 'political animals', as capable of ruling as well as of being ruled, as capable of public virtue. Many of those who had earlier found themselves and their interests best described in civic terms began to look elsewhere for an account of those things, and in particular to a discourse which had earlier been represented as in many ways the opposite of the civic. For one symptom of that unease was an increasing interest, on the part of those with most to lose by the threat of advancing democracy, in the language of 'custom', of the 'customary'. It was this discourse which seemed able to give the most authoritative definition to the distinctive nature and value of the established constitution and legal system of Britain, and which provided the most effective language in which change – almost all change – could be represented as dangerous. This language was itself under pressure, however, and not only from the democratic movements, but from a new utilitarian approach to questions of law and government, as the trial of Thomas Hardy also serves to demonstrate.

These shifts of investment and interest, these renegotiations of allegiance and identification (I have offered only the barest simplification) are what constitutes for me the special attraction of the late eighteenth century. What has always fascinated me is the hybridity of the discursive formations that characterise the period, and the mobility with which different discourses and interests seem to change partners. That mobility, however, is not at all the same thing as historical indeterminacy; each change of allegiance or identification is an anticipation of, or a response to, another, and takes its course according to a recoverable trajectory and logic.

I hope these essays will seem to share a common approach as well as a common object, though I have no clear sense of them as belonging to a particular discipline. I can best talk about that common approach in terms of what they aspire to do, rather than of what they achieve. They are preoccupied with questions of cultural history, but they are not attempts to write a history of ideas, still less a history of real events, but rather of discursive representations. To say that is to say that they are necessarily as concerned with questions of meaning as of history. I try not to write, except sometimes as a kind of necessary shorthand, as if the meaning of texts and images is more or less immediately obvious, available or pre-given to the historian of culture; as if the hard part of the historian's job comes after the business of reading, in the attempt to define the order of texts and the relations among them. We should do this kind of history, I am suggesting, as literary critics do literary criticism, aware that we have no texts to discuss until, by our reading, we have produced them ourselves.

The problem of the literary critical model, however, is that too often it seems to propose an inverse relation between an attention to the detail of a text, its rhetorical economy, its ambiguities, its loose ends, and an attention to the discursive history in which it participates: the closer the reading, the more distant the history. I try therefore to be a historian among literary critics, and a literary critic among historians – and among art historians too. Whatever I bring to the history of art, it is not, I think, any particular sophistication in talking about images. But where my forays into the subject have occasionally attracted adverse criticism – I do not mean from critics concerned to deny that there is any such thing as a politics of visual culture, but from those who agree that there is – it has not been for my treatment of images, but for my treatment of writing about images; and what has been at stake, it seems to me, is conflict between a practice of reading that has characterised literary criticism, and a practice of reading which some historians of art have borrowed from the history of ideas, as it was done before the emphasis placed on the problematics of interpretation by historians as diverse as Michel Foucault and Quentin Skinner.

I said earlier that the essays collected in this volume were all written during the 1980s; indeed the first essay I ever published came out in 1982, ten years after my first book. With a couple of exceptions, therefore, the volume contains all the essays of any length that I had written by the end of the decade and that seem worth reprinting – that were not either cannibalised in writing a book, or written to summarise the argument of a book, or for some other reason best forgotten.[3] The first exception is an essay on Thomas Hardy – the novelist, not the radical – which seemed too remote from the essays on the eighteenth century to be included, and which in any case is soon to be reprinted elsewhere.[4] The second is an essay on William Blake, co-authored with Harriet Guest, which it would be improper to appropriate to this collection, as it was mainly written by her.[5] I have managed to resist the temptation to tinker with texts already published, except in so far as was made necessary by the need to adopt a consistent scheme of reference and annotation, and except where I could remove an unwanted ambiguity by changing a word or two, or a punctuation-mark. This therefore is the only place where I can say how much better the third essay would have been, had I not forgotten to discuss two pages of Mary Wollstonecraft's *Vindication of the Rights of Woman*. Anyone interested in extending the argument of that essay is urgently advised to look them up.[6]

1

The Private Comedy of Thomas Rowlandson

I

From the 1740s through to the 1770s in Britain, the comic was an essential resource in the painting of rural life, and particularly of the rural poor: the work of Gainsborough, in his Bath period especially, and the figures added by Hogarth to George Lambert's *Landscape with Farmworkers*, which I shall discuss shortly, are only the most striking instances of the representation of rural labourers as, typically, 'clowns' – the term from the literature of rural life makes the point exactly. But in the last decades of the century, the comic was deliberately and almost entirely expelled from the art, as it was from the poetry, of rural life, and the grinning swains of Gay and Goldsmith became the abject 'poor' of Crabbe, soberly described if not, alas, always sober themselves. The reasons for this expulsion are complicated, and I have discussed them at some length elsewhere;[1] but they can be summed up perhaps in terms of a demand for an image of the poor which is at once more repressive, and more concerned to solicit our benevolence, than earlier in the century. There is no contradiction in this: the literature of 1780 to the end of the century which considers the poor is continually anxious to take the problem of rural poverty seriously *as* a problem; it offers to take a more benevolent, indeed a more guilty attitude towards their sufferings, and prides itself on the charitable sentiments it evokes. But it is a determinedly selective benevolence: to earn the goodwill, and the alms, of the rich, the poor were to submit to their authority and discipline more abjectly than had been demanded by the literature, if not by the employers, of earlier in the century. And, similarly, to evoke a properly benevolent response from the buyers of pictures, the art of rural life tries in the last decades of the century to define, by a rigid code of artistic propriety, an image of the 'good' poor, of the poor worthy of the charitable consideration of the rich.

This essay developed from a paper first given at the Yale Center for British Art in Autumn 1981. It is reprinted from *Art History*, volume 6, number 4, December 1983.

This image is defined, for example, in the 'cottage door' scenes of Gainsborough's last years, and in those of Francis Wheatley, whose sequence of four *Rustic Hours* was painted in 1799 and exhibited at the Royal Academy in 1801.[2] In the third of these paintings, *Evening* (Figure 1), the central figure, for all her apparent youth, is I suppose the mother of the three young children who stand round her. She stares out of the picture, directly at the source of light, as she works her churn; and the time of day, as well as the usual iconography of such evening cottage scenes, would have indicated that she is expressing, in that wistful look, an eager concern for the return of her husband, the family breadwinner, who in the first picture of the series, *Morning* (Figure 2), had been depicted as about to set off to the fields. The two elder children, with expressions no more animated, are carrying tokens of their dutiful industry: the girl has a dish of cream or buttermilk, and is evidently helping her mother; the boy carries a bundle of faggots he has just been collecting. Another woman stoops to hang out some washing on the rough banister of the cottage steps, watched by the youngest child, the only one of those whose faces we see who seems particularly carefree.

A picture like this expresses most of what the polite wished to believe about the rural poor in 1800. The setting is domestic: the cottage is the safe centre of rural life, opposed (if not overtly here, then overtly in a good deal of contemporary writing) to its unsafe centre, the ale-house, where, especially at this time of day, the less responsible labourers of the village might congregate, waste the money they should be spending on their families, and discuss their grievances. Everywhere are tokens of industry, and also of that neatness which was the most visible badge of the good poor – here, the broom, the sparkling clean linen, and the spotless apron of the central figure. And the equally spotless, almost textureless faces of the cottagers themselves, wear expressions of a contented acquiescence, an improbable refinement, and an almost complete lack of animation. The only trace of an expression which seems transient, unfrozen, is on the face of the youngest child, and that is surely permissible because the child is represented as being so far uninitiated into the necessity and inevitability of labour, and so has energy to spare; but to depict surplus energy in the faces of the poor of working age was, in 1800, to suggest the possibility of a degree of inclination on their part not entirely subordinated to duty. The good poor are not part of the mob, the *mobile vulgus*, and thus their faces are immobile.

Except, then, in the faintly animated face of the youngest child, there is no room for the comic in an image such as this; for it is essential to comic art that it be able to represent transient expression, a flexibility of posture. In the comic art of the mid century a notable

1. Francis Wheatley, *Evening*, 1799. Oil on canvas 44.5 × 54.6 cm. Yale Center for British Art

2. Francis Wheatley, *Morning*, 1799. Oil on canvas 44.5 × 54.6 cm. Yale Center for British Art

example would be the figures supplied by Hogarth to George Lambert's *Landscape with Farmworkers* (Figure 3):[3] the delight here represented is almost unimaginable after 1780, when the faces of the rural poor may register, not delight, but only a cheerfulness which is almost the opposite of delight. Cheerfulness, in the late eighteenth century, is for the poor a duty, and is inseparable from the acknowledgement and performance of their other duties: the poor were to accept their station, their poverty, their labour, cheerfully. If delight is not quite opposed to the duty of cheerfulness, it is irrelevant to it, and to indulge that irrelevance is to pursue one's inclination with the energy that should be employed in doing one's duty. To sit in a meadow or cornfield at lunchtime, with a still expression of contentment, is to express a proper gratitude for rest – this is the subject, indeed, of the second painting in Wheatley's sequence, *Noon*, (Figure 4). But to horse around in a haycock, in the time prescribed for labour, and with gestures and expressions of active enjoyment, is to call attention to one's indiscipline, and to an energy that should have been expended in labour.

The celebration of energy surplus to one's tasks, of inclinations imperfectly subordinated to duties, is as I have said almost impossible to represent after 1780. But not for Thomas Rowlandson. Throughout the large number of drawings of the rural poor in Rowlandson's *oeuvre*, the image of them is unabashedly comic. This is most immediately apparent in Rowlandson's line, which even at its most delicate is never far from caricature, and this even when the tendency towards caricature is quite at odds with the usual treatment of the subject by other artists. The point will be clear if we put alongside Wheatley's *Evening* a drawing by Rowlandson which goes by the name of *The Cottage Door* (Figure 5),[4] and which has been dated to the earliest years of the nineteenth century, so that the two pictures are pretty well contemporary.

There is obviously a potential for comedy in such subjects as this, which arises from the fact that they may represent children too young to work, whose licensed idleness offered rural subject-painters a chance to relax the imagery of industriousness of which they usually make such a display. In versions of this subject by other artists around 1800, however, the comic potential offered by toddlers is always contained by the tender solicitude represented on the faces of the parents watching over them. The final effect is anything but comic: it is of a refined domestic Georgic which represents the upbringing of children as an important social duty. Something of that effect is aimed at in this drawing too: the mother, who may be drying her hands after washing something in the wooden tub, tilts her head and turns her eyes towards the children with an expression of infinite tenderness, as who should say 'a-a-a-h!', and the eldest daughter, as she seems

3. George Lambert and William Hogarth, *Landscape with Farmworkers*, date unknown. Oil on canvas 101.5 × 127 cm. Yale Center for British Art

4. Francis Wheatley, *Noon*, 1799. Oil on canvas 44.5 × 54.6 cm. Yale Center for British Art

5. Thomas Rowlandson, *The Cottage Door*, c. 1805. Pen and watercolour over pencil 18 × 20.5 cm. Huntington Library, San Marino, California

to be, looks much the same. And yet the picture doesn't quite manage to offer itself as a pattern of the contented, dutiful and loving family, for the rotund but energetic line seems to be on the edge of undermining the domestic virtues that might contain the comedy.

The drawing comes closest to caricature, of course, in the plumpness of the younger children: in the face of the nearer one, in particular, which is made almost into a figure of eight by his vastly swelling cheeks, and in the round little arm that embraces the puppy so determinedly; but it comes pretty close in the images of the older members of the group. The firmest line in the sketch of the mother, less full-bodied though she is than her elder daughter, is the jovial curve that gives a sensuous but still caricatural plumpness to her forearm; and if her sensuousness is not altogether out of key with a notion of what the good poor should look like,[5] the figure of her daughter is certainly more problematic. The almost aristocratic refinement of her profile – the arched eyebrow, the full-lidded eye, the columnar neck – is placed on top of a thoroughly comic, rustic body, much more than buxom, the enormous but sensuous plumpness of her forearm emphasised by the smallness of her hand. The joint of the elbow becomes a curve in the arms of both women, as Rowlandson manages to lose all angularity in rotundity, and this characteristic rotundity of Rowlandson's drawing everywhere suggests a sense of well-being which is rather animal than moral. In particular, the contrast between the refined angularity in the profile of the daughter, and the rustic buxomness of her body, seems to separate even as it pretends to link the enjoyment of life, represented by the body, and the dutiful living of it, represented in the expression. The two compete for the subject of the picture, which seems to celebrate the pleasures of an amoral physicality as much as of morality.

Now, if Rowlandson's images of rural life regularly offer – and I think they do – to preserve the comic in a tradition of representation from which it had been painstakingly expelled, and expelled for reasons which can only be accounted ideological, we may be tempted to read his images of the poor as implying a criticism of that irremissively sober, dutiful, industrious, refined version of rural life we discovered in Wheatley's *Evening*. If his line is always verging on caricature, even when it is not evidently caricatural, might it not threaten to unfix the inflexible attitudes and expressions that Wheatley attributes to the poor? It may shift that almost motionless but purposive activity of the mother at her churn in either of two directions, by relaxing it to the point of indolence, or by animating it into transient energy. In the image of the elder daughter, Rowlandson's line has relaxed the heavy, sensuous body, and allowed us to feel the weight of her naked arm. In the figure of the elder son it has done the opposite: this lad grasps his youngest brother (I think it is) and props him upright to try to engage his attention; he gazes at him intently, as if determined to provoke a reaction. He shows a degree of animation quite opposite to the staid, dutiful expression of the boy in *Evening*. And if the poor as Rowlandson represents them do seem to be on the point of bounding or of dropping out of the fixed positions assigned to them by contemporary notions of artistic and social propriety, what of the position of those who looked at this picture? Might not that too have been unfixed, as they tried to grasp at whose expense the caricature was operating – at the expense of the poor themselves, as it may have been in the comic art of the mid century? – or at that of the stereotype of the dutiful poor which the public themselves had so successfully demanded from other artists working on rural subjects?

But in fact it seems that no such dramatic questions need be asked. It does indeed seem true that Rowlandson's art is continually failing to comply with contemporary codes for the representation of the rural poor; but still it offers no challenge to the codes it seems to break. Quite evidently, it does not do so now: Rowlandson's rural subjects now seem to depict a relaxed and comic idyll of rural life which is in no sense disturbing, but then we aren't perhaps in the habit of reminding ourselves, as we look at them, that his drawings could include a range of gesture, attitude and expression which were excluded from other contemporary images of rural life. But again there seems no evidence – none of the evidence there is, for example, in the case of George Morland[6] – that his work was enjoyed in any less security, was found any more uncomfortable, in 1800 than it is now.

In a remarkable paper first published in 1935, Ernst Kris and E.H. Gombrich argued that the art of caricature is a product of a *security* in the artist, and is received in security by its public. The paper is too closely written to be summarised here, but a few quotations may suggest its main points: the 'playful, "artless" character' of caricature, they argue, must be understood as a renewal of 'infantile pleasure'; it is a 'controlled regression' into a 'scribbling style' which 'is only possible where representational skill determines the ordinary level from which the virtuoso can let himself drop without danger. The pleasure in this sudden relaxation of standards demands a certain degree of security.' For

> Caricature is a play with the magic power of the image, and for such a play to be licit or institutionalized the belief in the real efficacy of the spell must be firmly under control ... Aggression has remained in the aesthetic sphere and thus we react not with hostility but with laughter.   (Kris 191, 197–8, 201, 203)[7]

In what follows, I shall suggest that we must understand Rowlandson's comic imagery in a similar spirit: not as challenging the proprieties observed so conscientiously, for example, by Wheatley, James Ward and Richard Westall, but as somehow 'institutionalized', 'secure', and licensed to ignore them. I shall argue that the reasons for the survival of the comic in Rowlandson's images of rural life may be explained in the terms of social history, as well as (no doubt) in the psychoanalytic terms of Kris and Gombrich: in a consideration, that is, of the ideological site of the comic, and of informal graphic media, in the period of his work. On what terms, and in what places, was such a comic imagery permissible? What were the social functions of oil-painting, on the one hand, and of pen-and-ink, watercolour, and so on, on the other?

II

In the final book of *The Seasons*, James Thomson considers how a period of retirement in the glooms of winter might most usefully be spent. He produces different answers, according to whether it is the retirement of a private or a public man that is in question.[8] By a public man, I mean one who has the means and social station that enable him to expect to make a career in public life. The private man, on the other hand, is 'doomed' – the word is Thomson's – to repress the ambition to do the same. He must remain, suggests Thomson, in 'powerless humble fortune'.

This distinction is a familiar one in the social philosophy of the seventeenth and eighteenth centuries. In the eighteenth century, it may serve to characterise the situation of the man who, as a gentleman, follows no occupation, and – since occupations may be defined as interests – is therefore presumed to be disinterested, and to enjoy a comprehensive overview of the society he is, in a manner, detached from – a possibility not open to the private man who, usually following one or another specific occupation, has his view of the social world distorted and occluded by the interests of that occupation. The gentleman is supposed to be an owner of freehold land, a form of fixed property that attaches him to the permanent, and therefore the true, interests of the state, which his 'wide Survey' – that phrase too is Thomson's ('Summer' 1. 1617) – enables him correctly to assess; while the private man, whose property is often in money or movable stock, has no similarly stable ground on which to base his judgements, and thus has no right to a place in the councils of state. The notion of the 'public' is thus associated with a notion of responsibility; the 'private' is the site, not of irresponsibility exactly, but of condition of life which does not call for responsible public action.

In the remarks that follow, I shall use the terms 'public' and 'private' in relation to this essentially political understanding of the functions and potentialities of different classes of men; and not in the more psychological sense in which the distinction is often used to refer to those aspects of meaning in a work of art which are available to all who examine it, and to those which may be concealed from everyone but the artist himself, and often from him too.[9] When Thomson was writing, in 1730 or before, the revised version of 'Winter' in which the passage I have referred to first appeared, the distinction was a good deal clearer than it became later in the century: public virtues and public responsibilities were, as I have said, the concern only of public men, who could, however, also enjoy moments or periods of privacy. All other members of society were, in Johnson's words, 'idle and helpless spectators of the commonweal, *wholly unconcerned in the government of themselves*' (Johnson 1977 112). The virtues of such private persons were essentially different from those which the public man was expected to exhibit: they were known, indeed, as the 'private' virtues – industriousness, sobriety, an affectionate concern for one's family and servants, fair-dealing in the practice of one's trade, and so on.

Towards the end of the century, however, the distinction became more complex, as the health and unity of society came to be understood less in terms of a political model, by which society was composed of competing political interests which required to be united or balanced by the public man, the statesman, and more in terms of an economic model, by which the unity of society was created by the joint labour of men pursuing their own interests and those of their occupation. In this latter notion, there was less opportunity for the display of the old public virtues; and the health and progress of society depended far more on the exercise of 'private' virtues, by the merchant, the trader, the manufacturer, the artisan, and the husbandman – most of whom were, however, understood to be unaware of the consequences to public life of their willingness or unwillingness to exercise them. The virtues of the private man were, to him, still private, and he was persuaded to exercise them out of a consideration of the consequences to himself if he failed to do so; while those who did the persuading were conscious also of the consequences of his behaviour for society at large.

How is it, then, that according to Thomson the public and the private man can best pass the glooms of winter? The options open to the public man are unsurprising: he may contemplate the order of the universe, until his 'opening Mind' comprehends yet 'larger Prospects of the beauteous Whole', and until what appear to him to be discords in creation are revealed as 'diffusive Harmonies' united in 'full Perfection'. He may scan the moral world, secure in the faith that, if its plan and perfection are less evident to him than are those of the created universe, still it is impelled by the hand of Providence towards *'general Good'*. He may study the reasons for the rise and decline of states, and contemplate the careers of patriots and heroes, men of 'public Soul', and the patterns of the public virtues. The retirement, it seems, of the public man is largely to be spent in preparation for the resumption of his public duties.

The meditations appropriate to the private man require more comment. He may contemplate the importance of the private virtues, of value to him, it seems, principally so that he may live as quiet, as untroubled and smooth a life as possible, unconcerned and unvexed by public duties and anxieties. He makes a virtue, it seems, of his 'powerless humble Fortune': he is, says Thomson, 'even superior to Ambition'. But it is in no spirit of criticism of the public man that the private man regards ambition as a folly; that he is 'above' ambition is indicative only of his acceptance that he is 'an idle and helpless spectator of the commonweal': he is superior only to such ambitions as the private man may mistakenly indulge.

In what remains of his time, the private man may contemplate the happiness that awaits him after death, a familiar enough consolation to those 'doomed' on earth; and, when his thought is 'foil'd' by the immensity of such speculations, he may turn for relief to the pleasures of the imagination, or rather – for the phrase is crucial – to those of 'frolic Fancy', and the passage needs quoting in full:

> We, shifting for relief, would play the Shapes
> Of frolic Fancy; and incessant form
> Those rapid Pictures, that assembled Train
> Of fleet Ideas, never join'd before,
> Whence lively *Wit* excites to gay Surprize;
> Or Folly-painting *Humour*, grave himself,
> Calls Laughter forth, deep-shaking every Nerve.

The conversational and aesthetic pleasures available to the private man are, as we shall see, a long way from anything the public man could enjoy; for the private man may be delighted by a 'play' of 'Pictures', of ideas whose characteristic is that they are impermanent, and incessantly changing – 'fleet' ideas called up in 'frolic', 'rapid' pictures whose function is to excite, surprise, and produce laughter. The pleasures we may take in impermanence, in the instability of the comic – these are characteristically the pleasures of the private man.

III

A related division between the public and private is at work in the theory of the visual arts in the middle and late eighteenth century. For Sir Joshua Reynolds, for example, the rules to be imparted to students of painting at the Academy are all to be framed so as to impress upon them the public function of the art. The definition of beauty in terms of a stable nature recognisable to all men; the recommendation that the expressions and gestures proper to the representation of the human figure should be of the kind that can be *held*, and should not be mobile or transient; and the insistence on compositional structures which do not divide the attention or allow the spectators to choose how they will read the picture – all work to confirm a view of painting as succeeding when it identifies and engages that which we, as its public, are presumed to have in common *as* a public.[10] The works of art which observe these and other such rules make us aware of the grounds of social sympathy, and thus of social affiliation: they confirm our membership of society, of the 'public', by excluding whatever might permit us, as individuals, to experience them in a way at all different from how other people understand them. For James Barry, more alert than Reynolds to contemporary developments in social philosophy, one function of the representation of the human figure is to offer a model of the homogeneity of the citizens of a state divided by the separation of the arts and professions: it represents the ideal of the human frame, which in each of us has been variously deformed and distorted by the practice of our several occupations (Barry 1809 2: 219–25).

For Reynolds himself, landscape-painting and rural subject-pictures were not important branches of art, and the tradition of English peopled landscapes, concerned to represent a recognisable, local scene, or to depict the rural life of England in its contemporary dress and animated by the spirit of comedy, must have offended against his notions of the public function of art in almost every detail. They were full of the 'accidents' of nature; they did not offer that image of 'quietness and repose', of the permanence of an ideal and abstract nature, which we find in the landscapes of Claude (Reynolds 1975 69-70).[11] But in the last quarter of the century, as we have seen, paintings of the rural poor began to take on more of the image of stability, of immobility, that Reynolds had recommended for figures in the grand style; and that they did so was a condition of the popularity they began to enjoy in 1780s and through the following decades. Such paintings did not, of course, exhibit the public virtues, but because the private virtues to which the poor were expected to aspire were now understood to be essential to the health, not only of themselves but of society at large, the pictures came to take on some of the characteristics of Reynolds's notion of a properly public art. They became, indeed, public statements: their production an act of public virtue, and their exhibition a display of responsibility on the part of their owners.

At one moment, near the conclusion of his variously surprising eighth discourse, Reynolds suddenly encounters, and is seemingly excited by, the possibility that one source of pleasure an image may offer us is precisely that it *does* return us to ourselves as individuals, as men whose imagination is uniform, and who may take a singular pleasure in contemplating pictures which allow us a freedom of interpretation not permissible elsewhere in the *Discourses*. The point emerges in some remarks about sketches and preparatory drawings:

From a slight undetermined drawing, where the ideas of the composition and character are, as I may say, only just touched upon, the imagination supplies more than the painter himself, probably, could produce; and we accordingly often find that the finished work disappoints the expectation that was raised from the sketch; and this power of the imagination is one of the causes of the great pleasure we have in viewing a collection of drawings by great painters. These general ideas, which are expressed in sketches, correspond very well to the art often used in Poetry. A great part of the beauty of the celebrated description of Eve in Milton's Paradise Lost, consists in using only general indistinct expressions, every reader making out the detail according to his own particular imagination, – his own idea of beauty, grace, expression, dignity, or loveliness.   (Reynolds 1975 163–4)

The notion that we might have, and might be allowed to enjoy, our own particular ideas of beauty, when elsewhere in the *Discourses* it had been represented as no less than a public duty to make our ideas of beauty conform with the central, and public, form of it, could appear, of course, only in the discussion of what Reynolds certainly regarded as *private* images. These are images which the artist did not imagine would be viewed by posterity, and just as such a private poem as Gray's 'Elegy', a soliloquy, is not heard but overheard, such images as these are not looked at but overlooked.

That the pleasure of the indeterminate is allowable only in the private site occupied by the sketch is clear enough from the continuation of Reynolds's argument: the pleasures of indeterminacy are denied to the painter and spectator of images on canvas; a 'complete and finished picture' is obliged to follow the 'fixed rule' that 'everything shall be carefully and distinctly expressed' (Reynolds 1975 164). For an oil painting is an act of communication, as a drawing is not: its meaning must not be open to negotiation. It is an act of communication in another way, too, for its possession and exhibition tell us whether its owner is a man of taste, and so (in Reynolds's view) of virtue.[12] The ownership of pictures which, though produced in the more public medium of oils, do not appeal to that which we have in common with other men, or do so imperfectly, will threaten our status as public men. But that status will not be threatened by the ownership of such images executed in informal graphic media, which occupy a space in the system of art, and, as we shall see, in the house, where we may legitimately regard ourselves as temporarily released from our obligations to the public and to the state.

IV

Among works of art, the division between public and private was reinforced by the physical spaces assigned to the different kinds of works in the collections of the eighteenth century. This involved, in the first place, a division between the kinds of works to be hung on the walls; and the theory, if not always the practice, was that the appropriate place for large historical compositions was in the most public areas of the house – the staircase, the saloon – where formal portraits might also appear. Smaller paintings in oils – landscapes, still-lifes, 'subjects' – were described as 'cabinet pictures'; and just as Reynolds regards paintings in such genres as imperfectly addressed to the public *as* a public, so they were to be hung, primarily, in the 'cabinet' or 'closet', those private rooms into which, however, particularly favoured guests might be invited, on the understanding that there they would meet their host on more intimate, more private terms. That this division of paintings among rooms of the house was also to be understood as a division in terms of their moral character is pointed out by Fanny Hill: 'The greatest men, those of the first and most leading taste, will not scruple adorning their private closets with nudities, though, in compliance with vulgar prejudices, they may not think them decent decorations of the staircase, or saloon' (Cleland 10).

The division of oil paintings between the public and private rooms, or between those compatible with public decency and those, for one reason or another, less so, was not, however, a complete one, or one easily observed. It is not clear that the cabinet picture was understood by Reynolds, for example, as a private image, and not simply as an imperfectly public one. Many such pictures must have been hung in public rooms, particularly in town-houses, often too small for the exhibition of the larger paintings that were anyway unpopular with English collectors – for the reason, as Barry and Fuseli understood it, that they were preoccupied with the 'trifling particulars of familiar life', with the 'snug, less, narrow, pretty, insignificant' (Barry 1809 2: 306; Fuseli 3: 48). It was no doubt for such reasons as these that the cabinet picture was more subject to the standards of public art than an image understood as entirely private would have been; it may be, for example, that one reason for the increasing sobriety of the image of the rural poor represented in cabinet pictures was that rural subjects were finding a market among those who, unable to afford or to display larger pictures, required that those they could afford should be appropriate, in moral terms, for display in the public rooms of their own smaller houses.[13]

There was, however, a clearer division between all works in oils, exhibited in whatever rooms, and works in informal graphic media such as pen-and-ink, watercolour, pencil, chalk, and charcoal. Such works were not usually displayed, but kept in portfolios in the closet, or else in the living-room or library – rooms which, through the eighteenth century, became more regular parts of the topography of the house, and to which guests, if admitted, were admitted on terms of privacy and intimacy.[14] Dr Thomas Munro, the early patron of Girtin and Turner, is known to have hung, and even papered, his drawing-room with watercolours, but, as a particular devotee of the medium, he was certainly an exception from the general rule that, until the early decades of the nineteenth century, watercolours were not displayed (Clarke 125; Webster 112). He was not however an isolated exception: Rowlandson's pair of watercolours, *An English Review* and *A French Review*, exhibited in the Academy of 1786, were 'carefully framed for the Royal Collection' prior to the exhibition (Hayes 11). Among other devotees, however, Rudolph Ackermann kept his collection to be consulted in the library of his house (Clarke 125), and W.H. Pyne, who was delighted by the later practice of framing and selling watercolours as 'cabinet pictures', nevertheless repeatedly speaks of them as being kept in portfolios, and, by reason of the fugitive nature of the pigment, as only suitable for the portfolio.[15]

In the system of aristocratic government, issuing from the palatial mansions of patriotic statesmen, that was Thomson's ideal, only the private man could enjoy the pleasures of an informal, an un-responsible privacy; in the various versions of the bourgeois-democratic ideology[16] of Reynolds, Barry, Fuseli, all men – at least, all men of taste – were citizens, all of whom also enjoyed moments when they might put aside that public role. By the late eighteenth century, all might therefore enjoy, in the private spaces of the house or the culture, those 'rapid Pictures' which Thomson describes as diverting only the private man: images which are fleeting, unstable, transient, quickly produced and quickly enjoyed, taken out and put away again, and not, as the phrase is, 'on permanent exhibition'. What in the public media of oil and fresco might appear as private vices could, in more informal media, be regarded as simple sources of pleasure which raised no moral issues, for we enjoy them in those private moments when we, too, are not on exhibition, are not acting as citizens on the public stage. In Book IV of *The Task* (lines 267–310), Cowper seems to recall the passage from 'Winter' which we looked at earlier, and, in a mood of 'indolent vacuity', indulges the 'brittle toys' of 'fancy, ludicrous and wild': and it is exactly to the point that he does so in his parlour, which he is careful to contrast with the showily illuminated drawing-rooms of the great.[17] The distinction he is making is on the lines of that made by the *OED*: a parlour, 'in a private house' is 'the ordinary sitting-room of the family, which, when more spacious and handsomely furnished, is usually called the drawing-room'; it is something like the difference between family rooms and showrooms - 'the rooms' as the *OED* has it, 'in a large mansion which are regularly shown to visitors'.

The relations between the 'public', the serious or the 'decent', on the one hand, and the 'private' and the 'comic' on the other, may now be clearer. The first set of terms functions as part of a list which includes the 'stable', the 'permanent', the 'responsible', and the 'moral'. And to the second pair of terms we may add, in opposition to our first list, 'rapid', 'shifting', 'brittle', 'indolent', 'frolic', which along with the comic and the 'ludicrous' are appropriate to a space or condition of life where we are not required to act responsibly.

If there is a literary critic in this class, she will recognise in this latter list a similarity between my reading of the passages I have cited from Thomson and Cowper, and Stanley Fish's reading of 'L'Allegro', and of course both passages may themselves be readings of Milton's poem. But she may also agree that the enjoyment of a succession of discrete images and fancies, 'gaudy shapes', the 'brood of Folly', is not to be left as a flat datum of 'reader-response', as a 'mode of experience' simply to be identified: it is not merely susceptible to, it demands analysis as a political datum, as once it demanded a political justification. Fish writes as though he finds it puzzling that he should *need* to argue that the pleasures of 'L'Allegro' are simple, secure, and irresponsible; and the *need* is felt to be enjoined on him by the pressure of a 'Formalist', and apparently twentieth-century, critical practice which demands that texts (and, we could add, pictures) be interpreted responsibly, and which believes the proof of their having been so interpreted to be the production of an account of experience as connected, as coherent.[18] But when Milton, when Thomson, Cowper, Reynolds were writing, when Rowlandson was drawing, that demand was no less present: and if the private enjoyment I have been describing was to maintain a place among other modes of experience which threatened to appropriate or banish it, a space had to be negotiated for its survival – a *political* as well as a topographical place.

In the British art of the late eighteenth century, it was in the informal graphic media that a comic image of the poor could pass without condemnation, for in the private spaces of their lives the polite could allow themselves the pleasure of not always demanding of themselves that they judge the behaviour of the poor – though only, of course as imaged in pictures – in the insistently moral terms of the public world. In this aspect, the informal graphic media all partook of the character of caricature as defined by the *Encyclopédie* (or of 'private comedy' as described by Thomson and Cowper): 'une espèce de libertinage d'imagination qu'il ne faut se permettre tout au plus que par délassement' (quoted in Kris 202); though (as we shall see) in the early decades of the nineteenth century the development of 'watercolour painting' was to move works in that particular medium further towards the right-hand end of the spectrum composed of portfolio, cabinet or library, and saloon, and so further from relaxation, and nearer to responsibility.[19]

V

The permission which, in extending it to themselves, the polite extended to the artist also, was simply that – a permission, and not an obligation, to make use of the freedoms allowed by the graphic media; and while Rowlandson made use of this permission throughout his career, Wheatley, for example, almost never did. We do not know enough about who bought drawings by Rowlandson, or paintings or drawings by Wheatley, to explain this difference in practice, and so the difference between the comic imagery of Rowlandson and the sobriety of Wheatley, in terms of a distinction between their patrons, and certainly not one in terms of class. The prices of Rowlandson's drawings (especially after the 1780s) and of Wheatley's watercolours (which did not, in the 1790s, differ in the moral implications of their imagery from his oil paintings) would have put the work of both men within the range of even the less well-off portion of the middle class, though buyers of Rowlandson's drawings included, on occasion, the Prince of Wales and a couple of dukes; both men of course sold much of their work directly to printsellers (Hayes 11; Webster 111–12). In general, however, it does not seem to me that, as far as the representation of rural life is concerned, much distinction can be made, in the second half of the eighteenth century or the early years of the nineteenth century, between the tastes of the aristocracy, the gentry, and the urban middle class (Barrell 1980 7–8; Solkin 1982 23); and the difference between the image of the rural poor in Rowlandson's and Wheatley's graphic works is more convincingly explained in terms of the site they were produced to occupy, not the patrons they were designed to attract.

Let us compare a watercolour of 1796, *Returning from the Fields* (Figure 6), by Wheatley,[20] with a pen-and-ink and watercolour drawing by Rowlandson, known for some reason as *Harvesters Resting in a Cornfield* (Figure 7)[21], though it depicts haymakers resting in a meadow; it has been assigned to the period 1805–10. Put together like this, the two pictures seem perhaps to interpret each other: the haymakers in Rowlandson's picture, with only half the working day behind them, are still animated, still in good spirits, while Wheatley depicts a return from the labours of the day, the young lady looking sober and serious, as if chastened by those labours. But my only point in suggesting that sort of anecdotal contrast between the two pictures is to suggest also how far beside the point it is. Wheatley's soberly beautiful harvester wears the same refined and dutiful expression that his young women wear on every occasion; Rowlandson's haymakers wear expressions, and adopt atttitudes, characteristic of a time of life, not a time of day

– an energetic youthfulness that he celebrated so tirelessly, whether in the country or out of it (Paulson 1972 71–9).

The haymakers display, once again, a surplus energy; they communicate a sense of having the energy not only to do their work, but to enjoy more of life than just working. They take pleasure in each other's company, and it is an active and animated pleasure, not a morosely cheerful one.[22] The reaping-hook carried by Wheatley's young woman marks what she is, and she bears it firmly in front of her as a badge not simply of her occupation but of her virtue. The dignity of her figure and her other-worldly expression also mark her as a good woman, one of the dutiful, the good poor – a condition marked in the images of the period by a degree of refinement obviously inappropriate to their social position, and well understood at the time to be an idealisation, but a necessary one, for a less idealised image of the poor would of course be that much less a model of how the poor should be. This refinement makes necessary the exclusion of any expression or attitude surplus to its representation, surplus to that image of sober contentment this woman enjoys, not in spite of, but resolutely within her situation. Her face cannot show more animation, or her body more energy, because the aim of the image is to show how fully she has subordinated her inclination to her duty – and in this context it's worth glancing back to *Evening*, for in that picture it is entirely to the point that, far more than in the face of the youngest child, energy is exhibited in the figure of the dog; to be human, it seems, the poor must overcome that eagerness of the passions which the animal cannot help but betray.

Rowlandson's haymakers have a related eagerness about them; yet the picture would have challenged the proprieties acquiesced in by Wheatley no more than did *The Cottage Door*; and clearly, what announces that Rowlandson is here making use of a permission that Wheatley does not use, is the greater *casualness*, and informality, of his picture as compared with Wheatley's. For it is precisely the casualness, the 'off-hand' character of Rowlandson's work, so much of it dashed off, and the rapid facility of his line,[23] even in his more worked-up pictures, which invite us not to forgive, but positively to welcome its lack of seriousness, when to demand of it the sobriety demanded of a worked-up contemporary oil painting would be to demand of ourselves, the observers, a similar if less taxing subordination of inclination to duty as we demand of the poor.

For in the first place, the crucial distinction between the two pictures is one of method: Rowlandson's is a 'stained' or 'tinted drawing', while Wheatley's is a 'watercolour painting', relying far less on visible outline than had the more Rowlandson-like pictures of Irish fairs he had produced in the 1780s – like Rowlandson, I mean, in terms of

6. Francis Wheatley, *Returning from the Fields*, 1796. Watercolour 25.5 × 30.5 cm. Fine Arts Society, London

7. Thomas Rowlandson, *Harvesters Resting in a Cornfield*, date unknown. Pen and red ink and watercolour 20.6 × 28.5 cm. Yale Center for British Art

their technique and structure, for they are not comic.[24] The distinction
makes it apparent that, in the last years of his life, Wheatley was
beginning to work in what was coming to be understood as the more
elevated, as well as the more painterly manner of watercolour practice
which was to lead to the foundation of Society of Painters in Water
Colour and of other societies of watercolour artists, scornful of the
older method, conscious of themselves as members of a profession
and of their art as the most important British contribution to the
development of the visual arts, and some of them anxious to release
their works from the privacy of the portfolio, and to market them, in
gold mounts and frames, as cabinet pictures, for display, if not in
most public spaces of the house.[25] 'Painters' in watercolour were
hostile to 'sketchiness' in technique: they were concerned to emphasise
that their landscapes could satisfy the hunger of the most refined taste
for images of moral grandeur, of the sublime, of exquisite feeling; and
were anxious to assert that, however much the medium obliged them
to work with speed and facility, watercolour-paintings no less than
paintings in oils were properly the product of a long apprenticeship,
correct drawing, an adherence to academic standards, and a foresight
which minimised the degree of spontaneity the medium itself seemed
to invite.[26]

Rowlandson's practice, by contrast, would have marked him, certainly
by 1805 or 1810, as an artist whose work could not be accommodated
within this serious and elevated view of the art - a mark of whose
seriousness was also of course the abandonment of comic subjects and
(in the representation of rural life) a preference for images of the poor
as refined, as lacking in animation, or at least as too small, or too
much a *part* of the landscape, to be seen as anything else.[27] The
distinction, then, between these two pictures must again be understood
in terms of public and private: Rowlandson's picture seeks to occupy
an entirely private place in the system of art; Wheatley's is among the
first productions of a movement which will take the watercolour into
the relatively more public area of *display*: if not into 'halls of state', at
least into the cabinet, the 'breakfast-room', and even the modest urban
drawing-room (Clarke 123, 137).

VI

In this final section, I want to examine some aspects of meaning, or
lack of it, in the private, comic art of Rowlandson, and I can begin by
pointing out that though when I said that his line was always verging
on caricature, I was thinking of his figures, it is true of his landscape,

too. In *Loading Sacks into a Cart* (Figure 8),[28] the figures are clearly on the edge of being caricatured, but so too are the houses, the uprights of which waver in a happily casual exaggeration of their shapes, and their thatches seem to sprawl, to flop, to drip over the eaves in a manner which, calling attention to its humour, also calls attention to the fact that Rowlandson is not offering us an image of truth; and the same is true of the jovial pen-work of the trees. The lines, in announcing the informality of the scene, announce their own informality as well, and so their exemption from the code of propriety which demands, in oil paintings, an idealised image of rural life, which is also the image of a moral truth: an unambiguous representation of how the poor should behave. The picture has none of the distinctness of marking that Reynolds demanded of an oil-painting, by which the same truth would be impressed on all who looked at it.

And, related to this point, there is another aspect of Rowlandson's licence that I want to call attention to; the fact that it is entirely casual in its concern for the possible readings it may generate. A large number of his pictures seem to suggest, for example, that they have an anecdotal content: the actions and relations of the figures seem to invite us to put a construction upon them, and yet often fail to provide the information we would need to arrive at it. A convenient, though not a particularly striking example, would be *Loading Sacks into a Cart.*

8. Thomas Rowlandson, *Loading Sacks into a Cart*, date unknown. Pen and red ink and brown wash 16.9 × 24.8 cm. Yale Center for British Art

If we start with the woman who looks out of the window of the right-hand cottage, it seems that there is something to explain in the gesture she is making, and certainly in a contemporary oil painting such a gesture would offer itself to be explained. Her face, youthful and seemingly pretty, expresses the same sort of good humour we found in the haymakers. The gesture (the more salient as her hand breaks the line of the cottage wall) and perhaps something she says, have attracted the attention of the two young women beneath her, one of whom also gestures, perhaps enquiringly, at the group on the left; but nobody in that group pays any attention to the woman on the right. The situation seems unusually specific, its explanation oddly hard to specify from among the host of explanations we can all invent. Such signifiers work in contemporary oil paintings to announce the content of the paintings, to signify some thing; here they seem free, and yet, contained as the picture is by its evident informality, these drifting gestures cause no great unease, no puzzlement, no very urgent need to understand them.

A more striking example of the untroublesome ambiguity of Rowlandson's pictures which, without our bothering much about it, at once suggests and withholds an anecdotal, and in this case a social and political content, would be the drawing known as *A Group of Rustics* (Figure 9)[29], though three of the figures, carrying shotguns, are evidently farmers, gentlemen, or both. The mounted sportsman on the

9. Thomas Rowlandson, *A Group of Rustics*, about 1790–1800. Pen over pencil 16.5 × 22.9 cm. Private Collection

left is engaged in some stage business with the fat and comic rustic in the centre; the pretty young sportsman half embraces the equally pretty barmaid as she hands a quart of ale to the sportsman nearer the centre; on the right, unregarded by anyone, sits an aged beggar, his hat (or so it seems to be) upturned in his lap in an invitation the others ignore. If it were not for him, this drawing would certainly be a comfortable affair, an uncomplicated and low-key celebration of English country life as enjoyed by those favourably placed to find it enjoyable, and undisturbed by the fun had at the expense of the fat man, whose paunch, the stoutness of whose legs, and the irritation on whose face, all mark him out as a comic character but one whose grievances are not presented in such a way as to elicit our sympathy or guilt.

But what of the emaciated beggar? Is there a point in the fact that he is ignored? Is he also represented as a comic character, whose pointed ugliness is there as a foil to the good looks of the pair to his left? One can't be sure. Rowlandson's drawing, the graceful and easy exaggerations which seem almost wished on him by the facility of his line, is once again on the verge of caricature but may have stopped there: the beggar is not unambiguously comic, nor has Rowlandson insisted on his misery at the expense of the good-natured fun behind him. As a result, though the pictorial relation between the beggar and the rest of the group is clear enough – he serves as a *repoussoir* which locates the other figures in a three-dimensional space – the social relation between them is quite illegible – or rather, there is no relation, and we cannot know what to make of the fact.

This is particularly worth insisting upon, for in the 1790s, the period to which this drawing has been assigned, it was next to impossible to represent in oil paint such an image of abject indigence as this beggar, and to leave it unglossed by the anecdotal content of the rest of the picture. It could be done in landscape, where the beggar is the only figure; but at that time the problem of the rural poor was so present to the consciences of the rich that the presence of a beggar among a group of figures was always a call for moral judgement on their part, and on the part of the public. But here, if judgement is called for, there is no way of knowing what it would be; for the beggar hovers between being a comic creation and an object of benevolence, and nothing in the picture helps to fix him in either identity.

But the time I have spent discussing the drawing, the urgency I have tried to inject into the problem of reading it, even the suggestion that there is such a problem, all misrepresent its effect. It is exactly the point that in another medium this image would be problematic, or, indeed, that in another medium it could not have been made. Here, it is entirely contained by its medium, and by its genre – the unfinished sketch, an idea for a picture – where figures may be assembled quite casually, and where the moral expectations which the late eighteenth-century polite brought to public pictures may be suspended. The casualness of this image, however, is only an extreme of that casualness I have tried to suggest is a general characteristic of Rowlandson's images of rural life, and it ensures that they ask no questions, and make no statements, that have to be engaged in a public, in a political space. In a sense, these images have no public: they invited those who looked at them to put aside their responsibilities as members of 'the public', to lose their duty in their inclination, and to rediscover, as private persons, the anxious landscape of rural England as a place where public fears and public pieties could, for the brief period in which such 'rapid Pictures' could engage them, be forgotten.[30]

2

The Public Figure and the Private Eye:

William Collins's 'Ode to Evening'

This piece is a reconstruction of some remarks made *ex tempore*, punctuated by questions and observations from students and followed by discussion, in one of a series of classes on eighteenth-century poetry.

> If ought of Oaten Stop, or Pastoral Song,
> May hope, chaste *Eve*, to sooth thy modest Ear,
>   Like thy own solemn Springs,
>   Thy Springs, and dying Gales,
> O *Nymph* reserv'd, while now the bright-hair'd Sun   5
> Sits in yon western Tent, whose cloudy Skirts,
>   With Brede ethereal wove,
>   O'erhang his wavy Bed:
> Now Air is hush'd, save where the weak-ey'd Bat,
> With short shrill Shriek flits by on leathern Wing,   10
>   Or where the Beetle winds
>   His small but sullen Horn,
> As oft he rises 'midst the twilight Path,
> Against the Pilgrim born in heedless Hum:
>   Now teach me, *Maid* compos'd,   15
>   To breathe some soften'd Strain,
> Whose Numbers stealing thro' thy darkening Vale,
> May not unseemly with its Stillness suit,
>   As musing slow, I hail
>   Thy genial lov'd Return!   20
> For when thy folding Star arising shews
> His paly Circlet, at his warning Lamp

Reprinted from *Teaching the Text*, eds Susanne Kappeler and Norman Bryson, London (Routledge & Kegan Paul) 1983). This was a collection designed to exemplify the teaching practice of members of the English Faculty at Cambridge who in 1981 supported Colin MacCabe during what became known as the 'MacCabe affair'.

The fragrant *Hours*, and *Elves*
Who slept in Flow'rs the Day,
And many a *Nymph* who wreaths her Brows with Sedge, 25
And sheds the fresh'ning Dew, and lovelier still,
The *Pensive Pleasures* sweet
Prepare thy shadowy Car.
Then lead, calm *Vot'ress* where some sheety Lake
Cheers the lone Heath, or some time-hallow'd Pile, 30
Or up-land Fallows grey
Reflect it's last cool Gleam.
But when chill blustring Winds, or driving Rain,
Forbid my willing Feet, be mine the Hut,
That from the Mountain's Side, 35
Views Wilds, and swelling Floods,
And Hamlets brown, and dim-discover'd Spires,
And hears their simple Bell, and marks o'er all
Thy Dewy Fingers draw
The gradual dusky Veil. 40
While *Spring* shall pour his Show'rs, as oft he wont,
And bathe thy breathing tresses, meekest *Eve*!
While *Summer* loves to sport,
Beneath thy ling'ring Light:
While sallow *Autumn* fills thy Lap with Leaves, 45
Or *Winter* yelling thro' the troublous Air,
Affrights thy shrinking Train,
And rudely rends thy Robes.
So long, sure-found beneath the Sylvan Shed,
Shall *Fancy*, *Friendship*, *Science*, rose-lip'd *Health*, 50
Thy gentlest Influence own,
And hymn thy fav'rite Name![1]

The 'Ode to Evening', by William Collins, first appeared in 1746, in his *Odes on Several Descriptive and Allegoric Subjects*; though the text I have reproduced incorporates some later revisions presumed to be Collins's own.[2] Exactly what Collins meant by the title of his volume has been the subject of some discussion; in particular, it isn't clear what sort of a distinction he assumed between the allegorical and the descriptive – whether, for example, he thought of them as mutually exclusive, or whether an allegorical subject might also be a descriptive one. What agreement there has been among critics of Collins about his intentions as a poet has usually been based on those announced by his friend Joseph Warton, whose odes were at one time intended to be printed alongside Collins's but in the event appeared separately, also in 1746. Warton prefaced his collection with an advertisement in which he claimed for them an intention usually taken to correspond pretty much with Collins's own:

> The Public has been so much accustom'd of late to didactic Poetry alone, and Essays on moral Subjects, that any work where the imagination is much indulged, will perhaps not be relished or regarded. The author therefore of these pieces is in some pain least certain austere critics should think them too fanciful or descriptive. But as he is convinced that the fashion of moralizing in verse has been carried too far, and as he looks upon Invention and Imagination to be the chief faculties of a Poet, so he will be happy if the following Odes may be look'd upon as an attempt to bring back Poetry into its right channel.   (Warton 1746: 'Advertisement')

The emphasis Warton wished to place on invention and imagination, at the expense of the didactic and the moral, can be understood in terms of the process whereby poetry becomes, in the mid-eighteenth century, more concerned with the direct representation of nature – what I mean by 'direct' will become evident later; for you will notice that Warton seems to assume a close relation between description and the inventions of fancy. It seems to me that Collins's ode also invites itself to be read as partaking in that process, but not in such a way as to endorse Warton's preference for the descriptive over whatever it is – the moral, the didactic, or it may be the allegorical – that we might take to be inhospitable to description. Whatever Collins meant by the title of his volume, and I don't think that can be determined, I see this poem as one which enables a transition, back and forth, between an understanding of its subject as 'allegoric' and as 'descriptive'; so that if we were to construct a history of eighteenth-century poetry as a body of writing in which is effected a transition, among other things, from allegorical to more directly descriptive representation, I would like this ode to be understood as one which makes us aware of the value of both procedures, and which produces some sort of accommodation between them. To make this point, I shall have to discuss in some detail the syntax of the ode, for it is, I shall argue, largely by the structure of its sentences that the accommodation is effected. I shall not demand of you, however, any understanding of sentence structure beyond what you might have picked up, had you been candidates for English language at O level twenty years ago. Let me begin by asking a few of you to read aloud the first sentence of the poem, or its first five stanzas.

(Two members of the class then read the sentence, in such a way as to divide it up into three separate sentences, treating each colon as a full stop. A third read it most of the way through very tentatively, in a way that committed her to no decision about its overall structure, then stopped, and re-read it so as to indicate her understanding that the clause beginning 'Now teach me . . .' (line 15) was what answered the conditional clause in the first stanza.)

I'll try and frame what I have to say as a commentary on those readings, suggesting also some alternative possibilities which none of you came up with. As you'll have realised from the last reading we heard, the first five stanzas of the poem can be read so as to form one extended sentence of some complexity; so that if, on a first reading, we are concerned to understand the meanings of the sentence in terms of the relations proposed by its syntax, we are likely to pick our way through it with considerable care, as we search for a main clause to answer the opening conditional; and that main clause is held back, apparently, until the fifteenth line of a sentence of twenty lines. When we reach it, the structure we will have discovered could be summarised like this: 'If there's any music that will soothe you, while the sun sets and silence reigns, teach it to me now'; or 'If there's any music that will soothe you, now, while the sun sets and silence reigns, teach it to me.' But those summaries, while they can indicate rather baldly the shapes we have found for the sentence, conceal what the last reader evidently felt to be the problem of reading the passage; for in whittling down to four the seven clauses which precede the main clause (and for the sake of my argument I'll be content with a grammar which finds clauses only where it finds finite verbs), we largely get rid of the difficulty she experienced: that the main clause, on which the preceding seven are all directly or indirectly dependent, continually, as it were, fails to appear.

When she discovered a structure for the sentence, and read it again, she found herself continually prompted to indicate, by a succession of imperfect cadences at the end of each clause, that she was still waiting for the main clause, for the element in the structure that will answer the opening 'if'. The continual need to indicate, at the end of each clause, that the structure is still open, incomplete, is facilitated of course by the absence of rhyme, but still it makes the experience of reading or listening to the poem a much less placid experience than the vocabulary of the sentence – 'sooth', 'reserv'd', 'hush'd', and so on – suggests it should be. Now perhaps we could understand it as being precisely to the point that this anxious syntax is all that the poet can manage, unless Eve comes to his aid. But his description of himself, as 'musing slow', suggests that he is not at all anxious, and that Eve may have answered his request, to be taught 'some soften'd Strain', by the very manner in which he is inspired to make it; and this notion is not, we may feel, best communicated by being involved in such a long, elaborate and suspenseful opening structure of dependent clauses, so inappropriate to the hushed atmosphere of the evening. There are however a number of other ways of reading the sentence which may *seem*, at least, to reduce this difficulty, by treating the words in the ninth line, 'Now Air is hush'd', as a main clause or something like it. The first of these seems perfectly acceptable in terms of grammar, but is most unlikely to be opted for by any reader of the poem; the second is justifiable grammatically but not particularly intelligible; the third produces a sentence that is not well-formed, but it was the reading adopted, and with good reason, in two of the versions we've just heard.

We can summarise the first of these readings as follows: 'If there's any pastoral music that will soothe you, Eve, now's a quiet time (except for the sounds of bat and beetle), teach it to me now.' That summary reveals the advantage and conceals the implausibility of this way of reading the sentence in a way that's fairly instructive. For, by it, we allow the clause 'Now Air is hush'd' to stand in briefly as a main clause; to fulfil, temporarily, our desire to put an early end to the succession of dependent clauses, before we come to the main clause proper – proper, in the sense that it is the only one that will satisfactorily answer the conditional clause at the start of the sentence. But it's most unlikely that we'll find ourselves choosing this reading, and I've never heard the sentence read this way; partly, no doubt, because this structure is too informal for the solemnity of the poem, partly because the success of such a structure as this depends almost entirely on the brevity of the expression which stands in as a main clause. 'Now's a quiet time' is sufficiently brief; 'now's a quiet time (except for the sounds of bat and beetle)' is already uncomfortably extended; and the full six lines, from 'Now Air is hush'd' to 'heedless Hum', reintroduce into the sentence all the suspense that this reading, if we were to choose it, would have been chosen to allay.

The next two alternatives I wish to consider seem to make much less sense, at least in terms of syntactical relation, and yet both of them seem in some degree to be invited by the text. I can best introduce them by looking again at the clause 'Now Air is hush'd', and pointing out that, according to our third reader's understanding of the structure of this sentence, that clause was, as it were, co-ordinate with the earlier clause, 'while now the bright-hair'd Sun/Sits in yon western Tent': so that the two clauses could (for our immediate purposes) be summarised like this: 'While now the sun sets' and 'while now', or 'now that', 'silence reigns'. But of the two words that introduce the clause about the sun, the poem picks up – if you'll forgive me putting it this way – the wrong one, one which conceals instead of indicating the relation between the two clauses: not 'While Air is hush'd', or even 'Now that Air is hush'd', but, simply, 'Now'.

That there is something at stake here – how importantly at stake we'll be able to consider in a moment – is clear from the fact that, when the poem appeared in a 1758 edition of Robert Dodsley's *Collection of Poems by Several Hands*, 'Now Air' became 'While Air'. The emendation was made in Collins's lifetime, but not necessarily at his suggestion; and it has the advantage, or the disadvantage, of removing all the alternative readings of the sentence I am examining, and leaving us only the thoroughly well-formed and thoroughly complex structure we looked at first, and one other possibility, which we'll glance at in a while.

Clauses introduced by the word 'while' can only be dependent, but 'now' can also introduce a main clause, and it is as a main clause that our first two readers of the poem seemed to find themselves taking the words 'Now Air is hush'd'. If we read the sentence like this, we can do so in such a way as to produce two possible structures for it – the one we choose will be indicated by the cadence we employ in our reading of the last lines of the second stanza. We can produce, to begin with, a structure that can be summarised like this: 'if there's any pastoral music that will soothe you, Eve, while the sun is setting, now is a quiet time, except for the sounds of bat and beetle'; a reading which goes on to treat 'Now teach me . . .' as effectively introducing a new sentence. This is, I suppose, a perfectly grammatical reading – we have something that behaves like the apodosis of a conditional sentence but which, though it does something, does very little indeed to reveal how the opening conditional is imagined as being fulfilled. But what is lost to the sense of the lines is a gain to our sense of the propriety of this structure to the words of text, for there is now much less of the suspense which, in our original reading of the sentence, seemed so much at odds with its semantic content. We can, however, reduce the sense of deferment, of suspense, still more, by treating the first eight lines as themselves a complete sentence, though an ill-formed one – and if this seems an unlikely reading it is exactly the one produced by our first two readers, as it often is by those I can persuade to read the poem aloud. This is a version which is impossible to summarise, but which, by reading the lines 'With Brede ethereal wove,/O'erhang his wavy Bed' in the tone of a perfect cadence, behaves as though the opening conditional has been answered, the sentence is already complete, and then goes on to treat the next two sections of the sentence, 'Now Air is hush'd . . .' and 'Now teach me . . .', as each of them separate and complete sentences. The complex twenty-line sentence has now been divided into three short ones, allowing a far more measured, more hushed and solemn reading, than will any structure which attempts at once to be properly grammatical and wholly intelligible.

Both of these readings which treat 'Now Air is hush'd' as a main clause seem to be invited by the colon at the end of the eighth line. I make that point tentatively, for the conventions for the use of the colon were not much more clear in the eighteenth century than they are today; but one rule, at least, was pretty well established, if only to the satisfaction of grammarians. Here are three versions of it, from the beginning, middle and end of the century: 'The Colon or two points comprehends indeed an entire sense by it self; but yet such a one as depends upon, and is joined to another'; 'A Colon . . . marks a perfect Sense; yet so, as to leave the Mind in Suspense and Expectation of what is to follow': and, finally, 'When a member of a sentence forms complete sense, and does not excite expectation of what follows; though it consists but of a simple member, it may be marked with a colon' (Maittaire 191; Buchanan 51; Walker 35).

These three specimen rules don't agree on whether a colon should be used so as to excite expectation, at the end of 'a perfect Sense', of what follows; but they do agree that the clauses preceding the colon *should* make 'perfect' or 'complete' sense, by which phrase, as their examples make clear, they mean a well-formed sentence. Now, according to any reading of this sentence which seeks to represent it as well-formed, this rule is not observed by this text – no consideration of syntax will persuade us that the first two stanzas could thus stand on their own – and this is only one of a considerable number of occasions in the early texts of Collins's poems where the punctuation (whether it is his own, or the typesetter's) is so extremely rhetorical that the colon is used, with little regard for the convention of grammarians, to mark pauses, or structural divisions within the stanza; indeed, before the final stanza of this poem, we find even a full stop before the completion of 'a perfect sense'.

But these considerations don't dispose of the problem entirely; for the combination of the colon, and the fact that we cannot *predict*, certainly not on a first reading, the grammatical relation of the clauses before it and those that follow, may persuade us to do what our first two readers did, and to treat the first eight lines *as if* they made 'complete sense', and the lines that follow as starting a quite new sense-unit. For this seems to be exactly what happened to our first reader, whose tone of voice suggested that he was, almost until the end of the second stanza, expecting and looking for a clause to answer 'if'; but, apparently seeing the colon ahead of him, and seeing no obvious relation between what he was reading and what he was about to read, he dropped his voice on the phrase 'wavy Bed', to indicate that the sense-unit was, for him, somehow at an end. And if this colon persuades us that a perfect sense has been made, the next one may do so as well, though as we'll see there is another alternative.

But if we do read 'Now teach me . . .' as introducing a third unit of complete sense, then by dividing the sentence into three separate sentences we have managed, as I say, to slow it down, and to produce a concord between its syntax and the reticent vocabulary it employs. In doing so, we produce a syntax that is more musical than logical, whose function is to mark the speed of our reading, and to produce formal relations in the sequence of words which are not always consequential relations.

If, by one or the other of the readings I've just outlined, we do take 'Now Air is hush'd' as a main clause, whether as the apodosis to the 'if' clause, or as starting a new sentence, we quite change the nature of the poem as it was interpreted by our third reader, who read all twenty lines as one sentence with one main clause only. This ode, as I've said, comes from a collection of odes 'on several descriptive and allegoric subjects'; and I want to suggest that our third reader placed her emphasis on the poem as an allegorical ode; as an ode of address, that is, to a personification imagined as a figure of allegory; and that our first two readers, who divided that opening sentence into three, shifted the emphasis towards the poem as a descriptive one. Let me explain what I mean. If we treat these twenty lines as together forming one well-formed sentence, then it is the opening conditional clause, and the main clause, that carry most of the weight of our reading, and are ushered into the foreground: 'If there's any pastoral music that will soothe you, Eve, teach it to me.' 'If' excites expectation, 'Now teach me' fulfils it, and all that intervenes between them, as it defers the appearance of the main verb, is treated as secondary, as material to be *got through* on the way to that fulfilment. And if this is true, then the effect is intensified as we read down the page, approaching nearer to the main clause, but, in terms of the structure of dependence among the clauses, getting further away from it. Thus the clause 'Or where the Beetle winds/His small but sullen Horn' is dependent upon 'Now Air is hush'd', which can perfectly well be taken as dependent upon the conditional clause, which in its turn is dependent upon the main clause; and 'As oft he rises . . .' is still further removed from the main clause.

The longer the sentence is extended, the more the content of the dependent clauses, to be managed at all, must be pushed into the background of our attention, to enable the conditional and its answering main clause to reveal the structure as well-formed, and so to allow us to experience it as complete. The rest becomes the background, as it were, against which the transaction between Eve and the poet takes place; and it is the background clauses and phrases which hold the directly descriptive content of the sentence. In front of, and above them, rides the rococo personification of Evening – to whom, if we have read the poem before, we can attribute a good deal of identifying paraphernalia; the evening star which is the lamp she carries, the chariot in which she will ride, together of course with the vaguely classical draperies, and the wreath of sedge, myrtle or some other appropriately dusky vegetation which, as Donald Davie has pointed out of eighteenth-century personification in general, we may be sure a contemporary reader would have visualised as the accoutrements of such a figure as this without having to be invited to do so (Davie 40). We are offered an image of evening as an image of Eve – in a manner we may compare with this reproduction, which I'll circulate, of one of William Kent's frontispieces to James Thomson's *Seasons* (Figure 10),[3] where the main focus of attention is less the seasonal landscape than the sky, in which floats a host of attendants to a tutelary deity, who are clearly far more responsible for conveying the meaning of the landscape, and of the poem, than is the landscape itself. In just this way, these twenty lines, read as one sentence, offer an image of Eve as the tutelary goddess of a landscape which is much less attended to than she is herself; and prepare us for the next sentence, the next two stanzas, where we are invited to imagine Eve's attendants preparing the 'shadowy car' in which she rides across the sky.

By dividing the sentence into three, however, we shift all that background into foreground, and come to attend to the images of the evening itself at least as much as to the image of Eve. The effect is initiated in the first of the three sentences we produce, the ill-formed one, where the need to finish the second stanza in the tone of a perfect cadence gives an emphasis to the details of the sunset far greater than in the other reading; and it is secured in the second sentence, where no reference to Eve appears. Here the topic is simply the silence of the evening landscape, as it is at once broken by the sounds of bat and beetle and reinforced by the fact that, at evening, such sounds can make themselves heard. In this sentence the main clause is offered us straight away, so that we read through the clauses in which the bat and beetle are referred to with no sense (however pleasurable it might have been) of deferment, and are able to allow them much more of our attention. And the effect of these images of bat and beetle becoming more salient is now less evident to us than it would have been to mid-eighteenth-century readers, for such 'mean' images would then have called attention to themselves the more by the fact of their meanness, by the discomfort such objects could threaten to a sense of propriety. Such images had an appropriate place in satire, for example, but a less secure one in the diction of some other *genres* of poetry – even in Georgic, thought Joseph Warton, such words as 'horse', 'cow', 'ashes', and 'wheat' would 'unconquerably disgust many a delicate reader' (Warton 1753 1: 294). If their appearance in poetry neither satirical nor burlesque could be justified – and a beetle finds its way into Gray's 'Elegy', for example – it could be so most easily by virtue of their provenance in the works of Shakespeare and Milton, but only there in passages which might similarly have disturbed a mid-eighteenth-century sense of propriety, by suggesting that there might be an inverse relation between genius and taste. By one reading of the poem, such images are more easily admissible, as descriptive divagations from the main topic of the sentence; by another, they are pulled almost as uncomfortably close to the reader as the beetle is to the pilgrim, the evening rambler, who the beetle crashes into in mid-flight.

By the first of those readings, then, the poem introduces itself by its first sentence as primarily an ode of address to an allegorical personification; by the second, as a descriptive poem at least as much as an allegorical one; and in the mind of a reader concerned to discover a 'correct' structure for the sentence, and so aware also of the obstacles to its discovery, these readings will both be present, each able to be played off against the other.

At this point let me introduce one further possible reading of these lines which is relevant to the issue of what kind of poem we think we are reading. For if we find ourselves reading the first two stanzas as if they formed a complete sentence, we then have the option of reading the whole of the next three stanzas as a second complete sentence, of which 'Now teach me . . .' is the main clause: 'Now' that 'Air is hush'd' (except for and so on), 'Now teach me . . .' That reading seems to me to offer an intermediate understanding of these stanzas, between a version of them as primarily allegorical, and one in which the descriptive content is foregrounded; for it does not push the clauses in which the evening itself is described as far into the background, or pull them as far into the foreground, as do the other readings we're currently considering. And that will be particularly the case if, as might well happen, we launch ourselves into lines 9–14 without a clear understanding of their syntactical function, but then indicate by an imperfect cadence before the second colon that we have now discovered a function for them, as dependent upon the clause which follows.

I want now to suggest that, in thus negotiating between an allegorical mode and a descriptive one, the poem also negotiates between a conception of poetry as public statement, and as the expression of private, 'individual', or 'particular' experience. That this issue was an important one in the poetry of the mid-eighteenth century I hope has already been sufficiently established by earlier classes in this course, but perhaps I can remind you briefly of what the issue is. I have in

10. Nicholas Tardieu, after William Kent, frontispiece to 'Spring', from James Thomson, *The Seasons*, 1730. 20.7 × 16.2 cm

mind, for example, the sense we often find evinced in the poetry of the mid-century, that the range of poetry had been unduly contracted during the career, and by the influence, of Pope; that poetry, in becoming more concerned with public themes, and more didactic, had developed a range of concerns which excluded, and a language by which it was not possible to express, private or individual feelings and experiences, and by which the epigrammatic statement of conventional social wisdom had come to seem of more value than the inventions of a poet imagined as a man of a particularly refined and sensitive nature. The justice of these criticisms of Pope and of his influence is not at issue here; what I am pointing to is an explicit or implicit criticism of him (you can find it, for example, in the remarks I quoted at the start of this lecture by Joseph Warton, regretting the prevalence of 'Essays on moral Subjects') which prompts the experimentation with forms other than the heroic couplet, and with poetic languages other than Augustan – with blank verse, the ode, the elegy, the Spenserian stanza, the sonnet and the ballad, and with the versions of the language of Milton, Spenser or Shakespeare, of middle-English poetry or of the Anglican liturgy, of Celtic or popular poetry; all of which could be argued as attempts to recover the range that had been lost to poetry, and even to propose versions of an ideal, less complex society for the poet to operate in, where private experience was not inseparable from public, or not suppressed in favour of an abstract idea of the typical, the representative, the common.

In terms of this concern, personification can be understood as a figure which encourages an awareness of what is common in our experience, to the exclusion of what is private or individual; the personification of Eve, for example, has as its function to unite, stand for and replace the various images and ideas that as individuals we have of evenings here and there, in such a way as to produce a statement about Evening which we all recognise as corresponding with our own, or rather, perhaps, which is not so specific as evidently *not* to do so. It is, like the notion of what will appeal to our 'common humanity' propounded by Johnson, or like the abstract image of beauty argued for by Reynolds in his *Discourses*, a general idea which unites us as a public; and the more it can make the personification capable of being visualised, by the attribution, say, of lamp and chariot, the more it can satisfy our hunger for the concrete in such a way as successfully to efface the vividness of our individual and different experiences of evening. It is a figure which demands that we attribute no value to whatever we do experience as individuals which does not correspond with common experience; and to this generalised image, the particular and the specific are enemies, just because they proceed from individual experience.

It is in these terms that the 'Ode to Evening' seems capable of being read as a negotiation between a public and a private imagery: as far as it preserves, and emphasises, the conventions of an address to an allegorical figure, it addresses us as a public, or as readers it seeks to unify into a public; as far as it invites us also to read it as something like the opposite of that, it offers us images of evening itself too particular – for example in the image of the beetle colliding with the evening rambler – to be regarded as parts of a common experience, and too mean to form part of an idea of evening represented as 'above' the specifics of our experience as individuals. In doing so, it does not attempt to displace the public in favour of the private, but instead makes room for individual experience, as the experience of the particular, within the procedures of art, in a way more comparable with the practices of Romantic poetry. We could take as an example Keats's 'To Autumn', which also preserves the proper form of an address, while describing with a persuasive degree of particularity the figures to be encountered in an autumnal landscape; and it achieves this by treating the personification of Autumn as if it were continually migrating, and were thus able to be discovered in each of those figures in turn: the winnower, the reaper, the gleaner, the cider-maker.

This negotiation continues throughout the 'Ode to Evening': the next sentence, in stanzas 6 and 7, works to make more visible the figure of Eve which had been in danger, earlier, of being submerged by the details of the landscape, and it does this by attracting attention to the attributes and attendance of the deity; while the eighth stanza invites us, by images of considerable specificity, to attend to the evening more than to Eve – most notably in the image of the grey 'upland Fallows' reflecting the 'last cool Gleam' of the 'sheety Lake'.[4] The next two stanzas seem to offer to do the same, but instead find a way of uniting the experience of the poet as he imagines himself observing the landscape, with the image of Eve as its tutelary goddess. The effect is perhaps best described by attending again to the structure of the sentence that makes up these two stanzas, though I shall do so this time, you will be glad to hear, rather less minutely. I can introduce the issue by looking at how the transition is managed, across the stanza-break, from images of a rain-swept wilderness with 'swelling Floods', to the calm images which follow, 'Hamlets brown, and dim-discover'd Spires'. The contrast between these images would have struck an eighteenth-century reader, much more than it will us, as a contrast between images of sublimity, with the power to resist our ability to grasp the world as order, and others, which do not seem to threaten that ability at all. By some means or other, a transition is made between them in such a way as to comprehend the images of disorder within a landscape we finally experience as composed and harmonious.

In the first place, these images of differing power and tractability are held together by the innocent copula 'and', which accords them all more or less equal weight within a simple list of the objects of the poet's vision, or of the vision available from the 'Hut'. But the list of words and phrases linked by 'and' then seems to expand, apparently to include the clauses 'And hears . . .', 'and marks . . .', which are not a part of that list at all, but separate activities of the hut, which 'views', 'hears' and 'marks' the various aspects of the landscape. The last of these clauses re-introduces Eve, both as an object of vision, part of what the hut observes and organises, and also as herself an active agent harmonising the landscape; for the 'gradual dusky Veil' that Eve draws across the images of the landscape, by harmonising them to the neutral tones of a painted landscape of evening, blurs the distinctions between them. The main characteristic of evening becomes the ability to harmonise what, in the full light of day, seems discordant; and the harmonising action of evening is observed by the poet himself, as he organises by means of syntax the objects imagined as seen from the hut. But the inclusion of the 'Dewy Fingers' of Eve, among the images observed, works to validate, on the basis of his own imagined observation, the representative power of personification itself, and the harmonising process by which it produces similarity from difference.

The remaining three stanzas can therefore return the poem to one which is unequivocally an ode of address, and of address to a personification no longer in danger of excluding individual experience, because acknowledged by it. The handling of the personification becomes no less remarkable, however, for being thus, as it were, stabilised; for as Eve herself is now an appropriate subject for the descriptive powers of the poet, she is described, in a series of images strikingly specific, as successively transformed by the different actions of the four personified seasons. And the characteristics of the seasons, violent as well as mild, can now by this means be fully emphasised, precisely because they also can now be understood as offering no threat to our sense of harmony which Eve cannot fully contain. For just as the wild landscape could be perceived as harmonious from within the security of the hut, so the seasons can be from within the 'Sylvan Shed', where activities and virtues which themselves promote harmony worship Eve as their tutelary goddess: in the original of line 49 (Collins 1747), these personifications were described as 'regardful of thy quiet rule' – acknowledging themselves as subject to Eve's sway, and as bound to observe her (as it were, monastic) code of discipline and conduct.

By this move, evening becomes more than a time of day: it comes to represent that position, conscientiously sought for by a number of eighteenth-century poets, from which, withdrawn from the world, we can experience as concord whatever, within the world, we experienced as discord. The attainment of this position is of course a means of recovering, by an internal composure of mind, the harmony which was lost at the Fall, when perpetual Spring ceased to reign throughout the year, and the seasons began – a notion which may entitle us to understand Eve, our universal mother, as also redeemed: just as the old Adam is made new, so Eve may now be no longer the 'old' but the 'new Eve' in the harmonious view composed by her namesake.[5] But there was a social as well as a moral Fall recognised by writers of the eighteenth century, by which were introduced, among other things, money, the differentiation of members of society by rank and occupation, and a form of society in which public and private life were divorced; and the 'Ode to Evening' offers us the model of a poetic procedure by which it came to be believed that that breach, also, could be healed.[6]

3

The Public Prospect and the Private View:

The Politics of Taste in Eighteenth-Century Britain

I

I want to offer a comment on some ideas about landscape that are commonly found among writers on art, on literature, and on various other subjects in the second half of the eighteenth and in the early years of the nineteenth centuries in Britain. The main point of my doing this is to show how a correct taste, here especially for landscape and landscape art, was used in this period as a means of legitimating political authority, particularly but not exclusively within the terms of the discourse of civic humanism. [1] If we interrogate writers of the polite culture of this period on the question of what legitimates this claim, one answer we repeatedly discover, though it may take very different forms, is that political authority is rightly exercised by those capable of thinking in general terms; which usually means those capable of producing abstract ideas – 'decomplex' ideas – out of the raw data experience. The inability to do this was usually represented as in part the result of a lack of education, a lack which characterised women and the vulgar; and because women are generally represented in the period as incapable of generalising to any important degree, I shall be very careful in this essay *not* to use a vocabulary purged of sexist reference: when I speak of what men thought, of Man in general, of the spectator as 'he', I am doing so with forethought, and in order to emphasise the point that, in the matter of political authority, legitimated as I have described, women were almost entirely out of the question, and the issue to be determined is which men can pass the test of taste.

This essay developed from a paper given at the conference 'Landscape and the Arts', held at the Humanities Research Centre of the Australian National University at Canberra in July 1984. It is reprinted from *Reading Landscape: Country – City – Capital*, ed. Simon Pugh, Manchester (Manchester University Press) 1990.

To develop the ability to think accurately in abstract terms required more, however, than an appropriate education: one condition in particular was necessary – a man must occupy a place in the social order where he has no need to devote his life to supporting himself and his dependants, or at least (in some versions of the argument) of supporting them by mechanical labour. If he does have such a need, three things will follow. First, he will be obliged to follow one, determinate occupation, and will discover an interest in promoting the interests of that occupation, and of his own success in it; and his concern with what is good for himself, or for one interest-group, will prevent him from arriving at an understanding of what is good for man in general, for human nature, for the public interest. Second, the experience that falls in the way of such a man – especially if he follows, not a liberal profession, but a mechanical art – will be too narrow to serve as the basis of ideas general enough to be represented as true for all mankind, or even for all the members of a state. Third, because mechanical arts are concerned with *things*, with material objects, they will not offer an opportunity for the exercise of a generalising and abstracting rationality: the successful exercise of the mechanical arts requires that material objects be regarded as concrete particulars, and not in terms of the abstract or formal relations among them. The man of independent means, on the other hand, who does not labour to increase them, will be released from private interest, from the occlusions of a narrowed and partial experience of the world, and from an experience of the world as *material*. He will be able to grasp the public interest, and so will be fit to participate in government.

Of this ability, a taste in landscape provides one of various tests. And let me begin my account of that test by saying that it turns on the social and political function of the distinction between panoramic, and ideal landscape, on the one hand, and, on the other, actual portraits of views, and representations of enclosed, occluded landscapes, with no great depth of field. I had better explain that I am using the word 'panoramic', here, simply as a shorthand for the kind of extensive prospect we find typically in a landscape by Claude. But I had better offer some more explanations, because I am aware that I am making a bipartite distinction between a considerable range of kinds of landscapes, some of which – the topographical panorama, the ideal composition of a woodland glade – exhibit characteristics which seem to belong to the different halves of the distinction.

Let me explain the distinction more clearly. It is between landscapes which seek to exhibit substantial, representative forms of nature arranged in a wide extent of land, and views which, even if panoramic, exhibit the accidental forms of nature, and, even if ideal, exhibit their ideal forms within a restricted terrain. That such a distinction is crucial to an understanding of the various kinds of landscape art is, I think, obvious enough; and it is well-known that in eighteenth-century England these different kinds of landscape were often – if not always – assumed to be the production of, and designed for the entertainment of, two different spheres of life, and even of two different classes of people – what and who they were will be considered shortly. It does seem to me however that we continually overlook the importance of the distinction to the eighteenth century; and that it has been possible to do so for a long time is suggested, for example, by a passage from one of Hazlitt's essays on Reynolds, 'On Genius and Originality', published in the *Champion* in 1814. In this essay Hazlitt comments on what he calls Reynolds's 'learned riddle', whether accidents in nature should be introduced in landscape painting. Accidents in nature, as there is probably no need to explain, are *untypical* natural phenomena: sometimes they are regarded as phenomena rare enough to be the result of a complex conjunction of natural causes: storms, rainbows, are accidents. More generally, however, accidents are anything in the prospect of nature which suggests that the prospect is being observed at one particular moment rather than another, and which calls attention to that fact: when the light, for example, strikes objects in such a way as to suggest that it will strike them differently a second later; when the form of a tree is such that it seems to be ruffled by a blast of wind of such or such a particular force, blowing from such or such a direction. Anything, in short, is an accident, which suggests a view of nature as other than abstract, typical, a permanent phenomenon, but particularly untypical effects of light, or untypical forms of objects. The debate about whether accidents in nature should be admitted into landscape was not originated by Reynolds: it was a familiar topic among writers on painting committed to an aesthetic of illusion, as Reynolds was not. For, of course, a landscape full of accidents was likely to deceive our eyes more successfully, but in doing so it would attach us to images of nature less elevating than those represented in entirely ideal landscapes. But, as we shall see, Reynolds's 'learned riddle', posed in his fourth discourse, was about much more than this.

Of that riddle, Hazlitt writes:

> We should never have seen that fine landscape of his [Rubens] in the Louvre, with a rainbow on one side, the whole face of nature refreshed after the shower, and some shepherds under a group of trees piping to their heedless flock, if instead of painting what he saw and what he felt to be fine, he had set himself to solve the learned riddle proposed by Sir Joshua, whether *accidents in nature* should be introduced in landscape, since Claude has rejected them. It is well that genius gets the start of criticism, for if these two great

landscape painters, not being privileged to consult their own taste and inclinations, had been compelled to wait till the rules of criticism had decided the preference between their different styles, instead of having both, we should have had neither. The folly of all such comparisons consists in supposing that we are reduced to a single alternative in our choice of excellence, and the true answer to the question, 'Which do you like best, Rubens's landscapes or Claude's?' is the one which was given on another occasion – both.

(Hazlitt 18: 67)

Hazlitt, characteristically, cuts a knot that Reynolds had attempted to untie; and it seems likely that he does so, not because he is unaware of the importance to eighteenth-century art of the distinction I have referred to, but because he is hostile to the political basis of a division between kinds of landscape, which could also be a division between the kinds of viewer appropriate to each. But either way, Hazlitt suppresses a distinction important to Reynolds, and succeeds in obscuring its importance to us. In this paper I want to re-tie the knot that Hazlitt has cut.

That Hazlitt's response to Reynolds's 'learned riddle' is the result not of a failure to understand the point of the riddle, but of a refusal to accept the assumptions on which it is based, is suggested by the fact that three years later Coleridge, who was not at all antagonistic to the notion that the political republic, and the republic of taste, were constituted on a distinction between two kinds of persons with greater and lesser intellectual capacities, was still able to represent that distinction in terms of a distinction between kinds of landscape. Coleridge describes an allegoric vision, in which a company of men are approached by a woman, tall beyond the stature of mortals, and dressed in white, who announces that her name is Religion.

The numerous part of our company, affrighted by the very sound, and sore from recent impostures or sorceries, hurried onwards and examined no further. A few of us, struck by the manifest opposition of her form and manners to those of the living Idol, whom we had so recently abjured [SUPERSTITION], agreed to follow her, though with cautious circumspection. She led us to an eminence in the midst of the valley, from the top of which we could command the whole plain, and observe the relation of the different parts, of each to the other, and of all to each. She then gave us an optic glass which assisted without contradicting our natural vision, and enabled us to see far beyond the limits of the Valley of Life: though our eye even thus assisted permitted us only to behold a light and a glory, but *what*, we could not descry, save only that it *was*, and that it was most glorious.   (Coleridge 1972 136)

Then 'with the rapid transition of a dream', Coleridge finds himself again with the more numerous party, who have come to 'the base of a lofty and almost perpendicular rock', which shuts out the view; the only 'perforation' in the precipice is 'a vast and dusky cave', at the mouth of which sits the figure of Sensuality.

The distinction between a viewpoint from which a vast and panoramic prospect is visible, and low, sunken situations from which only the nearest objects are visible, only in close-up, is a repeated motif of Coleridge's poems. In 'Reflections on Having Left a Place of Retirement', for example, composed in 1795, the year also of the composition of the first version of the Allegoric Vision, Coleridge compares the low and humble position of his cottage with the view available by climbing from that low dell up the stony mount nearby: 'the whole World', he writes, 'seem'd *imag'd*' in the 'vast circumference' of the horizon: the images in that extensive prospect seem representative and substantial, so that the prospect becomes a microcosm of the world. One theme of 'This Lime-Tree Bower My Prison' (1797) is to consider how objects within the occluded prospect of the bower may be seen, as can the objects in the 'wide landscape' described earlier in the poem, in terms of the relations of things, rather than as things in themselves. In 'Fears in Solitude' (1798), the 'burst of prospect' seen from the hill 'seems like society', in opposition to the 'silent dell' in which Coleridge has considered his fears, in solitude, and in opposition also to his own 'lowly cottage'. There are numerous poems based on the same pattern of opposition, and the meaning of each component – panorama, and occluded view – is complex, and changes from poem to poem. It is possible, however, to abstract and collocate a number of the significances attached to each image: and to notice that, among the meanings attached to the panoramic view, may be the notion of a wider society, and the notion of the ability to grasp objects in the form of their relations to each other; among the meanings attached to the occluded view, from a low viewpoint, are seclusion, of course, and privacy as something opposed to the social in its more extended sense, and also sensuality, which for Coleridge (and also for numerous writers, including Reynolds, before him) was particularly characterised by a tendency to see objects not in terms of their relations, or their common relation to a general, and representative term, but in and for themselves, as objects of consumption and possession.

II

Let me focus first on the opposition between the different landscapes as appealing to two different classes of people, and therefore between the ability to grasp things in terms of their relations – of 'the different parts, of each to the other, and of all to each' – and the inability to do so, which leaves us focusing, myopically, on the objects themselves, on, as Coleridge puts it elsewhere, 'an immense heap of *little* things', the world as perceived by the sensual eye unilluminated by imagination, or the ideal (Coleridge 1956–71 1: 349). For a version of that opposition is of course crucial also to Reynolds's theory of art, and in particular to the doctrine of the central form, which is arrived at by the ability to abstract substance from accident, 'to get above all singular forms, local customs, particularities, and details of every kind' (Reynolds 1975 44). True taste, for Reynolds, is the ability to form and to recognise representative general ideas, by referring all the objects of a class to the essential character by which the class is constituted; the lack of true taste is the inability to perform this operation, so that we take pleasure not in the ideal representation of objects in terms of their generic classes, but in the unpurged, accidental images of objects, minutely delineated. For the Coleridge of 1817, that distinction is grounded, of course, in an idealist philosophy: to grasp them in terms of the idea which is at once the ground of their existence and the end for which they exist. For Reynolds, and for almost all writers in the eighteenth century in England, the distinction is founded on a distinction between those who can, and those who cannot form general ideas, normally by the processes of abstraction; between those who can compose details into a whole, or compose a whole by the elimination of detail, and, on the other hand, the ignorant who, as Reynolds explains, 'cannot comprehend a whole, nor even what it means'.

The critic Thomas Tickell, or it may be Richard Steele, makes the same distinction in the context of pastoral poetry in an unsigned essay of 1713:

Men, who by long study and experience have reduced their ideas to certain classes, and consider the general nature of things abstracted from particulars, express their thoughts after a more concise, lively, surprising, manner. Those who have little experience, or cannot abstract, deliver their sentiments in plain descriptions, by circumstances, and those observations which either strike upon the senses, or are the first motions of the mind.

(*The Guardian* no. 23, 7 April 1713)

For that reason, he argues, the shepherds of pastoral 'are not allowed to make deep reflections', and for that reason too, one of the main pleasures that sophisticated readers take in pastoral is that it exhibits a state of mind which is delightfully simple in itself, at the same time as it promotes the delightful reflection that we are emancipated from its bondage, from the tyranny of external impressions which we cannot control and organise. That is also a reason why pastoral is the lowest of the genres of poetry – because it imitates the motions of the minds of the least rational, the most ignorant, members of society.

Thus, if pastoral or landscape art – however lowly its position in the hierarchy of genres – is to be of value, is to be an object worth the attention of men who *can* abstract, then it must be defended either as Tickell has defended it – so that the pleasure we take in the genre derives from the contrast between the perception of those who are merely in the landscape, and those who are outside it, and observe it – or it must be defended as an art capable of *calling forth* the ability to abstract substance from accident, the general from the particular.

James Harris defends it in this second way. In his *Philological Inquiries*, he considers the cause of the pleasure we derive from natural beauty. 'The vulgar', he notes, 'look no further than to the scenes of culture, because all their views merely terminate in utility'. They are 'merged in sense from their earlier infancy, never once dreaming anything to be worthy of pursuit, but what either pampers their appetite, or fills their purse'; they 'imagine nothing to be real, but what may be touched or tasted'. These dwellers in the cave of sensuality thus 'only remark, that it is fine barley; that it is rich clover; as an ox or an ass, if they could speak, would inform us. But the liberal have nobler views; and though they give to culture its due praise, they can be delighted with natural beauties, where culture was never known'.

But what are the pleasures that the liberal find in natural beauty, which are unknown to the vulgar, the ox and the ass? Harris makes a poor job of explaining what they are – he mostly attempts, simply, to prove that they exist, by adducing those classical authorities who have affirmed their existence. But he *exemplifies* those pleasures with precision; for example, when he writes: 'the great elements of this species of beauty are water, wood, and uneven ground; to which may be added a fourth, that is to say, lawn' (Harris 218, 525–6). That is the pleasure: the enjoyment of the ability to abstract from the labyrinth of nature, from the infinite varieties of accidental and circumstantial appearances, the general classes of natural beauty whose combinations please only when, on analysis, they can be resolved again into their components. It is the same pleasure that William Gilpin experienced when he announced that 'few views, at least few good views, consist of more than a foreground, & two distances': the pleasures, that is, of abstracting the essential from its confusing particulars, and reducing those particulars to order (Gilpin, quoted in Barbier 50).

As Harris makes clear, the pleasures of nature are different, according to whether we are among the company of the liberal, or the vulgar, and it is worth reminding ourselves that in the eighteenth century the word liberal still has its primary meaning: it is the adjective that describes the free man, and the liberal arts are still remembered to be the arts which are worthy of the attention of free men. Free men are opposed to the vulgar or – for the terms are in most contexts virtually indistinguishable – the servile. In the civic humanist theory of art that Harris and Reynolds are heirs to, the word servile most usually occurs as the qualifier of 'imitation': the 'mere' imitation of everyday nature, unabstracted, with all its accidental deformities and details upon its head, is 'servile' imitation, unworthy of the attention of a free man. The imitation of the ideal; of nature, in John Opie's phrase (13), 'as meaning the general principles of things rather than the things themselves'; of the object as freed from the tyranny of sense or need, and represented thus not as a thing, but as idea, and so as incapable of being possessed – this is what makes an art a liberal art. It is such an idea of imitation that is the basis of the hostility evinced by Reynolds, for example, against the notion that it is the job of an artist to deceive the eye, to make us believe that a painted object is really there, could be touched as well as seen.

The kind of landscape that can most fully offer this pleasure is panoramic, and it is so for various reasons, some of which I shall consider in a moment, but for now it will be enough to point out that the panoramic landscape offers a wide range and variety of objects to abstract from: it is like the 'wide experience' which is, according to Tickell, denied to the shepherd, which is not only a more sure basis for accurate generalisation, because it minimises the distorting effect of extreme departures from generic form, but is also capable of offering the most gratifying test of our ability to reduce it to classes and structures. As Fuseli explains, it offers 'characteristic groups' of 'rich congenial objects'. The groups are characteristic, not individual; they are rich, for there is a profusion of them; they are congenial, because organised into reciprocity by the abstracting power of the mind. On the other hand, argues Fuseli, those who imitate the landscape of the Dutch school are worthy of admiration only as they 'learn to give an air of choice to necessity' – by which he means, that imitations of Dutch landscape remain servile imitations so long as the eye is determined in what it represents by necessity, by the mere fact of an object's being there; or is determined by that servile and sensual vassalage to objects as capable of being possessed, which is never far from characterisations of Dutch art as, par excellence, the art of a commercial nation. The more such art appears to rise above the determination of necessity, and to represent landscape in terms of a will free from the tyranny of sense, the more it appears to become free itself, a liberal art (Fuseli 2: 217–18).

By the time Fuseli was appealing to the distinction that I have drawn, it had become so familiar and general that the distinction between the learned and the ignorant, the polite and vulgar, the liberal and the servile, was repeatedly and regularly represented in terms of the ability to apprehend the structure and extent of panoramic landscape. This, for example, is John Flaxman, on the need for what he calls 'a compendious view' in the conduct of intellectual enquiries:

> When we look at any portion of the natural landscape, if the objects are few, a rock, a plain, or a tower, they are understood at once, and without effort; but if they are numerous and complicated, they must be considered attentively, to distinguish woods from mountains, the form and extent of buildings and cities, the winding of rivers, and the expanse of the sea, in order that we may understand the several parts of the view; and it is thus we must conduct our inquiries in art and science: beginning by a search for their natural principles, we must make ourselves acquainted with their relations to, and dependence upon, other branches of knowledge, and we should assure ourselves of their purposes and ends. (Flaxman 215)

A complicated landscape or field of inquiry, in short, needs to be analysed into its several components; it must be understood in terms of its unifying principles and its relation to other possible landscapes or fields. Or take an example from a writer not concerned with the visual arts: this is the rhetorician George Campbell, describing the progress of knowledge:

> in all sciences, we rise from the individual to the species, from the species to the genus, and thence to the most extensive orders and classes [and] arrive . . . at the knowledge of general truths . . . In this progress we are like people, who, from a low and confined bottom, where the view is confined to a few acres, gradually ascend a lofty peak or promontory. The prospect is perpetually enlarging at every moment, and when we reach the summit, the boundless horizon, comprehending all the variety of sea and land, hill and valley, town and country, arable and desert, lies under the eyes at once. (Campbell 1: 5)

Notice how Campbell, like Harris, though his list is longer, is concerned to produce from his eminence an account of all the classes of objects the landscape contains: the knowledge he arrives at is a general knowledge, in that it is all there is – the whole world imaged in the circumference of the horizon – and it is general knowledge, too, in that all the various objects of thought and knowledge are named by singular nouns, and so reduced to their various classes: when we see the sea and land, hill and valley, town and country, arable and desert, we see all there is to see. It will follow, of course, that those who remain imprisoned within their few acres at the bottom of the eminence will have nothing like the same range of objects to examine, and will have no possibility, therefore, of deriving accurate, general classes from them. They will remain, indeed, as objects in the landscape: they will not be observers, but observed.

The point is well exemplified by Aaron Hill, writing to congratulate Pope on his poetry and to apologise for earlier attacks upon him: ''Tis a noble triumph you now exercise, by the Superiority of your Nature; and while I see you looking down upon the Distance of my Frailty, I am forc'd to own a Glory, which I envy you; and am quite asham'd of the poor Figure I am making, in the bottom of the Prospect' (Hill 1). Those who can comprehend the order of society and nature are the observers of a prospect, in which others are merely objects. Some comprehend, others are comprehended; some are fit to survey the extensive panorama, some are confined within one or other of the micro-prospects which, to the comprehensive observer, are parts of a wider landscape, but which, to those confined within them, are all they see.

It is appropriate that Hill should be addressing Pope, who was shortly to be author of a poem, the *Essay on Man*, which attempts to describe the 'scene of man' as a prospect, which can be observed, and comprehended categorically, from some single viewpoint; and it is appropriate too that Pope, at the opening of his poem, should have identified that point of view as the station occupied by the independent landed gentleman:

> Awake, my ST JOHN! leave all meaner things
> To low ambition and the pride of Kings.
> Let us (since Life can little more supply
> Than just to look about us and to die)
> Expatiate free o'er all this scene of Man;
> A mighty maze! but not without a plan . . .
> Together let us beat this ample field,
> Try what the open, what the covert yield;
> The latent tracts, the giddy heights explore

Of all who blindly creep, or sightless soar;
Eye Nature's walks, shoot Folly as it flies,
And catch the Manners living as they rise . . .
(*Essay on Man*, Epistle 1, lines 1–6, 9–14)[2]

In its migration from renaissance Italy to seventeenth- and eighteenth-century Britain, a crucial mutation had occurred in the discourse of civic humanism, a mutation whose origin is identified in the writings of James Harrington, but which was soon eagerly adopted by the range of eighteenth-century spokesmen, including Henry St John Bolingbroke, Thomson, and Pope himself, for the ideals of those groups which we lump together under the title of the country party, and whose writings are, more than those of any other grouping in early and mid-eighteenth-century Britain, concerned with the definition and defence of public virtue. When Florentine republican theory was transplanted to Britain, the ability of the disinterested citizen to grasp the true interests of society had come to be identified as a function of his ownership of landed property.[3]

This was the result of a number of considerations: of the fact that the franchise, the title of citizenship, was attached to a property qualification; of the fact that a substantial landed property produced a sufficient unearned income for its owner to have the time, the leisure, to devote himself to political life; of the fact that he was therefore a member of no profession, and could thus be assumed to favour no particular occupational interest; but, most particularly, of the fact that landed property was fixed property, and therefore its survival was involved (it was believed) in the ability of the state itself to survive the corruptions of accident. The owner of fixed property, even when conscious (according to some theorists) of consulting only his own interests, would also necessarily be consulting the true, the permanent interests of the country in which his family had a permanent stake. Whether, therefore, his independence and his leisure actually enabled him to see the public interest, or whether he was conscious only of consulting his own, made little difference: inasmuch as his own interests were those of the public at large, he was, to all intents and purposes, disinterested in a way that others, more dependent for their income on the fluctuating value of movable property, and thus of property which, like *argent liquide*, circulated instead of remaining rooted on one spot, could not be. It is then as a man of landed property that Bolingbroke (and with him, by association, Pope) can 'expatiate free o'er all this scene of man' – can grasp the 'plan', the design of the wide prospect, which remains simply a maze to those who, situated in one partial position or another, 'latent tract' or 'giddy height', can only 'blindly creep' or 'sightless soar'. And it is thoroughly appropriate that, as Bolingbroke and Pope range freely over the landscape, they do so as sportsmen: they 'beat' the field, and 'catch the Manners' they thus put up. Only the lords of manors, or those possessed of an annual income of £100 or more from a freehold estate, were permitted to shoot game.

III

Let me expand at this point on my introductory remarks on the relation between the ability to generalise, a correct taste in landscape, and the claim to be capable of exercising political authority. In so far as the representation of panoramic prospects serves as an instantiation of the ability of the man of 'liberal mind' to abstract the general from the particular, it was also understood to be an instantiation of his ability to abstract the true interests of humanity, the public interest, from the labyrinth of private interests which were imagined to be represented by mere unorganised detail. It was precisely the ability of the liberal mind of the free citizen to do this which constituted his claim to be a citizen, a free man, or, as he was often described (though the phrase has a range of meanings) a 'public man'. A citizen, a public man in this sense, had long been distinguished in republican political theory by the fact that this ability was a function of his reason; whereas private men, men who were not citizens, who were servile, who were mechanics, had been understood, from Aristotle onwards, to have no ability to understand reason, or to follow anything but their own immediate instincts. That is why Harris can compare them with oxen and asses. And because the civic humanist aesthetic of which such men as Harris, Campbell, Reynolds and Fuseli are the inheritors, is based in the language of republican political theory, their own implied definition of who is properly a citizen of the republic of taste is based on the same distinction. The power to abstract, as metaphorised everywhere in the power to comprehend and organise an extensive prospect, is a testimony of the ability to prefer and to promote an art which itself promotes the public interest, as opposed to ministering to the private appetites and interests of particular men.

The relation between these various concerns is clear, for example, in Reynolds's preface to his 'Ironic Discourse', a work dedicated to pointing out the congruence of the principles of politics and art. According to Reynolds,

A hundred thousand near-sighted men, that see only what is just before them, make no equivalent to one man whose view extends to the whole horizon around him, though we may safely acknowledge at the same time that like the real near-sighted men they see and comprehend as distinctly what is within the focus of their sight as accurately (I will allow sometimes more accurately) than others. Though a man may see his way in the management of his own affairs, within his own little circle, with the greatest acuteness and sagacity, such habits give him no pretensions to set up for a politican. (Reynolds 1962 129)

– or, of course, for a man of taste; for the function of both is to grasp the relation of particular to general which is the same thing as the relation of private to public; and the function of both is to promote, whether in art or politics, the public over the private interest. It was exactly the inability to do this that, in his *Reflections on the Revolution in France*, Burke had claimed to be necessarily a characteristic of the revolutionary assemblies – composed as they were of tailors and carpenters, men accustomed to considering their own interests as in competition with those of others (Burke 1964 46–7). It was exactly this inability that Reynolds, Blake and Fuseli point out in the Dutch and Venetians, the tradesmen, the mechanics of the republic of taste, not its free gentlemen-citizens. The binary by which 'gentlemen' are opposed not only by 'mechanics' but by 'tradesmen', together with the civic notion that it is particularly or exclusively the independent owner of a substantial freehold in land who is capable of exercising political authority, often though not always produces an account of the man of liberal taste as one who is not simply a gentleman, but a landed gentleman. And that connection between the public man, the disinterested citizen, the freeholder, and the man of taste, remains available, though it is increasingly challenged, well into the next century. It is evident in the work of Pope, Thomson, and Richard Wilson, and is more than merely vestigial in the writings of Burke, Wordsworth and Coleridge.

Sometimes, however, by some writers, the ability to comprehend the structure of relations within a panoramic prospect is attributed to a rather wider group of spectators than we have so far encountered, though this may not always involve attributing to them a comprehension of the public interest in its widest sense. *The Wealth of Nations*, for example, throws up the problem that within a complex, commercial society, there may be no viewing-position from which the organisation of society or the public good can possibly be grasped. If the philosopher is as much implicated in the division of labour, is as much defined by the need to truck and barter, and so as much blinded by his own interests as is any other man, then he has as little access as anyone else to that general view which would seem to legitimate a claim to a general social knowledge. The text is reduced to employing a fictitious and disembodied social spectator, the 'philosophic eye', whose viewpoint and whose breadth and depth of vision no individual can be imagined as possessing, unless, as Rameau's nephew puts it, he can 'perch on the epicycle of Mercury' (Diderot 103).[4] But in Adam Smith's earlier philosophical work, *The Theory of Moral Sentiments*, the public interest is conceived of more often in narrower terms, as the propensity to place the interests of another before our own, private interests, and the viewing-position necessary to make that choice is imagined as accessible to everyone. And it is precisely a *viewing-position*, from which the interests of ourselves and of others are visible as if within a landscape. Consider this passage, for example, where Smith seems to be reworking an argument from Berkeley on Passive Obedience:

> In my present situation an immense landscape of lawns, and woods, and distant mountain, seems to do no more than cover the little window which I write by, and to be out of all proportion less than the chamber in which I am sitting. I can form a just comparison between those great objects and the little objects around me, in no other way, than by transporting myself, at least in fancy, to a different situation, from which I can survey both at nearly equal distances, and thereby form some judgment of their real proportions. Habit and experience have taught me to do this easily and so readily, that I am scarce sensible that I do it; and a man must be, in some measure, acquainted with the philosophy of vision, before he can be thoroughly convinced, how little those distant objects would appear to the eye, if the imagination, from a knowledge of their real magnitudes, did not swell and dilate them.
>
> In the same manner, to the selfish and original passions of human nature, the loss or gain of a very small interest of our own, appears to be of vastly more importance, excites a much more passionate joy or sorrow, a much more ardent desire or aversion, than the greatest concern of another with whom we have no particular connection. His interests, as long as they are surveyed from this station, can never restrain us from doing whatever may tend to promote our own, how ruinous soever to him. Before we can make any proper comparison of those opposite interests, we must change our position. We must view them, neither from our own place, nor yet from his, neither with our own eyes nor yet with his, but from the place and with the eyes of a third person, who has no particular connection with either, and who judges impartially between us.
>
> (Smith 1976b 135)[5]

The third person who occupies the position from which the relation of one person's interests and another's can be apprehended is a version of the fictional character whom Smith terms (among other things) the 'impartial spectator', the imagined arbiter among different interests. And he is outside the landscape, and not as we are (in our private capacities), within it, unable to grasp its structure of relations. Unlike most of the other passages I have referred to, this passage seems to suggest that if anyone can attain the viewing-position of this spectator of the moral landscape, we all can. The corollary of that concession, however, is that the extensive prospect cannot be used as the image of a society wider than the one in which most of us make our private determinations on moral questions.

Or consider this record of a spoken observation by Reynolds, on the nature of happiness:

> It is not the man who looks around him from the top of a high mountain at a beautiful prospect on the first moment of opening his eyes, who has the true enjoyment of that noble sight: it is he who ascends the mountain from a miry meadow, or a ploughed field, or a barren waste; and who works his way up to it step by step; – it is he, my lords, who enjoys the beauties that suddenly blaze upon him. They cause an expansion of ideas in harmony with the expansion of the view. He glories in its glory; and the mind opens to conscious exaltation; such as the man who was born and bred upon that commanding height . . . can never know; can have no idea of; – at least, not till he come near some precipice, in a boisterous wind, that hurls him from the top to the bottom, and gives him some taste of what he had possessed, by its loss; and some pleasure in its recovery, by the pain and difficulty of scrambling back to it.[6]

We can read this passage simply as a more than usually eloquent rehearsal of a moral commonplace, that a happiness achieved after pain and effort is a good deal more worth having than a happiness which, because its possessor has never known suffering, is the less grateful to him on that account. But if we read it, as surely it invites us to do, in the context of the assumed connection between an ability to comprehend the order of society, and the ownership of heritable property in land, it becomes an impassioned outburst, the more impassioned because this account of how a 'noble sight' may truly be enjoyed is addressed to a noble company, 'my lords', who claim to enjoy it simply because 'born and bred on that commanding height', from which they seem to observe and *command* the view below. In order to distinguish between the kind of enjoyment that they derive from the prospect, and the kind enjoyed by those who have to toil up to that eminence, Reynolds suggests that to the 'lords' the prospect is not really a metaphor at all: they may presume that the 'expansion of the view' produces a similar 'expansion' of their 'ideas', but it does not; and if to them the prospect has any metaphorical application, it is simply as a figure for the 'eminence' they enjoy as a result of the nature and quantity of their inherited fortunes. The figure achieves its full significance only – as the geography of the passage suggests – for whoever can appropriately be represented as a labourer, who 'works his way up' to the eminence 'from a miry meadow, or a ploughed field, or a barren waste'. The passage suggests that the image of the panoramic landscape could be appropriated from the 'lords' whose political authority it had been used to justify; but it suggests too that a struggle to appropriate the viewing position usually attributed to the landed aristocracy can simply result, whoever comes out on top, the lords or a meritocratic bourgeoisie, in a continuation of the division of society into the observers and the observed, the rulers and the ruled.

IV

Let me now collect up the various characteristics we have so far seen attributed to the two kinds of landscape painting that I distinguished at the start of this essay. On the one hand is the ideal, panoramic prospect, the analogue of the social and the universal, which is surveyed, organised, and understood by disinterested public men: men who regard the objects in painted landscapes always as representative ideas, intended to categorise rather than deceptively to imitate their originals in nature; men therefore who study objects not in and for themselves – not for example the individuals in a society, considered *as* individuals – but in terms of their relations. They are enabled to do this by their ability to abstract, and by their ability to comprehend and classify the totality of human experience.[7]

On the other hand is the occluded landscape, which has so far been treated as representing the 'confined views' of the private man, whose experience is too narrow to permit him to abstract. Such landscapes conceal the general view by concealing the distance: and Fuseli, appropriately, uses an image derived from such landscapes to figure, more generally, the detrimental effect which a profusion of detail has on the 'breadth' of composition he admires: 'the discrepance', he writes, 'of obtruding parts in the works of the infant Florentine, Venetian and German schools distracts our eye like the numberless breakers of a shallow river, or as the brambles and creepers that entangle the paths of a wood, and instead of showing us our road, perplex us only with themselves' (Fuseli 2: 251). The characteristic imagery of occluded landscapes – a cottage, for example, embosomed in trees which permit the distance to appear only as spots or slices of light – is emblematic of a situation in life from which no wider prospect is visible.

On this other hand, also, is topographical landscape, which did not represent objects as classified and comprehended. Topographical landscape seems to become more despised – in the theory, though not in the practice of landscape painting – as the century grows older; not just because of the hostility of the academy, or that hostility taken as something internal to a theory of art disjoined from social and political change. Towards the end of the century it had become increasingly clear that landed property was not as fixed as it had by some been claimed to be earlier in the century; it was involved in an economy of credit, and was not in itself a guarantee of disinterestedness, except perhaps in so far as it permitted its owners the leisure necessary for a career in public life. The hostility to topographical landscape thus comes to be based not only on its un-idealised, un-intellectual character, but on the connection, also, between sensuality as the failure to abstract from the data of sensation, and sensuality as a desire to possess objects which could only be redeemed, as objects worthy of the attention of a free man, by elevating them into representative types which could not be possessed. Thus for James Barry, who describes the property-market in late eighteenth-century Britain as anything but stable, more like 'a game of chance', topographical landscape was simply a portrait of our possessions, or of land as inviting possession; and for Fuseli, such landscapes may 'delight the owner of the acres they enclose', but delight and interest him therefore only in his private capacity (Barry 1775b 207; Fuseli 2: 217).

That last point suggests a distinction between two kinds of landscape I have been considering that is more complex than the one I have largely been making so far, by which the different landscapes appeal to different classes of people, to citizens and to the rest. For they can also be understood as appealing to two different spheres of life of the citizen; the public sphere, where he is enjoined to consult only the public interest, and the private sphere, where he is temporarily released from his obligations as a citizen. This distinction has already been suggested, perhaps, by my remarks on Coleridge's conversation-poems. The distinction made in these terms is not a simple one, and in attempting to understand why it is not, we can approach an understanding of Reynolds's learned riddle, with which Hazlitt expressed such impatience; and we can approach, also, an understanding of Hazlitt's impatience. For if ideal panoramic landscape is constructed as public, in opposition to various different kinds of landscape constructed as private, the fact remains that, within the terms of the doctrine of the hierarchy of genres, landscape-art, of whatever kind, is constructed as private, in opposition to the public art of history painting.

Reynolds, for example, makes it quite clear – as who does not? – that one function (perhaps it is no longer for him the main function) of history paintings in the grand style, is that their subject 'ought to be either some eminent instance of heroick action, or heroick suffering. There must be something either in the action, or in the object, in which men are universally concerned, and which powerfully strikes upon the publick sympathy' (Reynolds 1975 57). We should always remember, when we encounter the term 'public' in civic humanist criticism, that it is never a simple shorthand for the audience, or for everyone. It is the audience, it is everyone, only in their public character: history painting must appeal to whatever concerns us universally; with what concerns us as universal men, as men considered in the light of what is common to all of them, their substantial nature, and not what is of concern to their private and accidental identities. Landscape painting, on the other hand, is, as Reynolds and Barry suggest, concerned with the representation of quietness and repose, with what were understood to be private feelings, and with what were described as private virtues: the only virtues open to be exhibited by those who were not public men, but open to them, also, when in retirement, or for some other reason not acting upon the public stage. It is this function of landscape painting that justifies its existence, but which, in doing so, depresses it to the lower reaches of the hierarchy of genres, as it similarly depresses pastoral poetry below the epic and the tragic. It may be, as Barry points out, that in a society threatened by the forces of corruption, the private virtues are the only secure values left, and that landscape will come to seem preferable even to the subject-matter which history painting exhibits, in an age without public heroes; but in such an age, it is equally true that the public virtues of history painting are more urgently in demand, or should be, and the supremacy of the genre, as the only genre capable of effecting a reform of public life, must be more urgently insisted upon (Reynolds 1975 70; Barry 1809 2: 405).

It is at the interface of these two classifications of ideal panoramic landscape that Reynolds's learned riddle is engendered. According to one system of classification, the representation of such landscapes is an instantiation of the political capability of the public man, perhaps especially of value in an age in which the sphere of action of such a man was steadily being confined, as I have argued elsewhere, to the *comprehension* of the social order, rather than its reformation; to the vindication of social structure as ordained by providence, or by the market, rather than to the creation of a social order other than that created by commerce, by the forces of private interest (Barrell 1983, 17–50). On the other hand, according to the system of classification of the hierarchy of genres, landscape art is the instantiation of private virtues, often as a muted criticism of the values of that parody of a truly public, civic life which is the actuality of affairs in courts and cities.

How then should landscape be represented? If as a public genre, it is essential that it should eliminate accident, and should exhibit ideas, as George Campbell puts it (2: 104), 'not in their private, but as it were, in their representative capacity'. If on the other hand it is a private genre, it seems that the representation of accident is appropriate to it; and that Reynolds, for all his seeming decision in his fourth discourse in favour of Claude's landscape, purged of accident, over the accidental forms of Rubens, is nevertheless impressed by the argument from the privacy of the genre, is clear by the terms in which he poses his riddle. He does not ask, as Hazlitt suggests, simply whether the landscape painter should 'introduce' the accidents of nature. His terms are far more specific than that. He asks whether 'landscape painting has a *right* to *aspire so far* as to reject what the painters call Accidents of Nature' (Reynolds 1975 70; my emphasis). His meaning is that an artist who, like Claude, does not so reject them, may be aspiring above his station, and presuming to give to a private genre the universal and public status of history painting. To answer, no, it shouldn't thus 'aspire', is to deny the power of images of panoramic landscape to instantiate the intellectual abilities and talents of public men, of the disinterested citizens of the republic of taste and of the political republic alike. To answer, yes it should, risks threatening the public status of history painting, by encroaching upon it, and by suggesting, perhaps too openly, that public virtue is now indeed rather a matter of seeing than of doing. The riddle could not be solved, and though in his fourth discourse Reynolds appears to decide, as Hazlitt suggests, in favour of Claude, in his later discourses he shows considerable approval of the representation of the accidental forms of nature by the happy accidents of technique. This is a concession he makes only to landscape painters, and only to them on the understanding that they work in a private genre, one addressed to our privacy, in which we may therefore take pleasure in accidental images unidealised into generic form.

V

We can sum up the problem which generates Reynolds's 'learned riddle' in some such way as this: for Reynolds, though history painting is still unchallengeably at the top of the hierarchy of genres, its position there is no longer easily justifiable in terms of a *rhetorical* aesthetic, and an aesthetic of illusion, by which it deceives us into a sympathy with its actors which can move us to desire to perform the acts of public virtue which they perform. Reynolds justifies its pre-eminence, instead, as a genre which casts the spectator in the role, less of potential agent than of observer, the observer of a common humanity represented by general forms. As far as landscape painting is concerned then, as long as it is considered as a private genre – as occluded landscapes always, but as ideal landscapes only sometimes are – it is still imagined to be governed by a rhetorical aesthetic: it moves us to delight in, and to wish for, tranquillity and repose; and, as such, it can be enjoyed by all, for it is a law constitutive of a rhetorical aesthetic that *all* can feel the effects of art, even if all cannot determine the principles on which those effects are produced.

But when ideal panoramic landscape is treated as a public genre – as I hope I have shown it continually but not invariably was, in Britain in the period I have been considering – it was not accorded that status by means of a rhetorical, but of what may be called a philosophical aesthetic: the best landscape painters, and those best equipped to appreciate them, are those few who can successfully reduce concrete particulars to abstract categories, the signs of which are less natural and more arbitrary than those employed in occluded landscapes, and are absolutely not intended to deceive the eye. If landscape can appeal to its audience in this way, however, and no longer simply rhetorically, then there are good reasons why it should be treated, as for rather different reasons Ruskin would treat it, as a genre as important, and as public, as history painting; for it is now the aim of both to enable the exercise of that broad and comprehensive vision and that ability to abstract representative from actual nature that are now more clearly the qualifications for citizenship than a disposition to perform acts of public virtue. In short, it is by Reynolds's philosophical aesthetic that landscape has a claim to be regarded as a genre with a public function, which it does not have in terms of a rhetorical aesthetic.

Why then should Hazlitt, who is unlikely to have been unaware of the implications of the riddle, choose to ignore them? One reason is that he clearly considers it one of his tasks as a writer to abolish the distinctions between the public and the private – in politics, as a distinction between those who can and those who cannot participate in government; in painting, as a distinction between one kind of picture that appeals to us as citizens, another than appeals to us as private individuals. But still his impatience with the distinction is a political impatience, in so far as it is related in particular to a distaste for the habit of addressing the politer part of that audience as 'the public', whether they acted as a public or simply as the acquisitive purchasers of pictures as private property. Anything that perpetuated this flattery, and the political division on which it was based, was an object of his attack; and he was especially hostile to the notional connection between the ownership of landed property and the claim to political disinterestedness.

For these reasons, I cannot help admiring Hazlitt for treating Reynolds's 'learned riddle' as a knot to be cut; but nor can I help regretting that he could do so, as it seems to me, only by denying the connection between art and politics, or rather between art and the public sphere, which had given such explanatory power to the writings of Reynolds, Barry, Blake and Fuseli, and had insisted on the interdependency of the republic of taste, and the political republic, which Hazlitt was determined to dissolve.[8]

4

The Dangerous Goddess:

Masculinity, Prestige and the Aesthetic in Early Eighteenth-Century Britain

I

The criticism of the visual arts in early eighteenth-century Britain was largely framed in the terms of the republican discourse we have come to describe as civic humanism.[1] Its founding texts are a pair of essays written around 1710 by Shaftesbury: an account of his design for the painting of *The Choice of Hercules* by Paolo de Matthaeis, and a brief letter on the function of the fine arts; and in addition to these, he wrote an extensive draft of a major treatise on painting which he did not complete.[2] According to Shaftesbury, the primary function of the fine arts was moral and rhetorical: their task was to persuade the citizen to wish to perform acts of public virtue in defence of the political republic. If, and only if, they were successful in this task, were they to aspire to perform the subsidiary but much-valued function, of presenting the civic spectator with images of an ideal beauty by which he might be polished as well as politicised. The fine arts, then, are charged first to produce a citizen with the rough integrity of a Cato, and then to polish him until he shines like Cicero. The danger, of course, is that it may be imagined that this order of priorities could be reversed, and that the beautiful forms displayed by painting and sculpture will be valued more highly than the 'Virtue' and 'laudable Ambition' they should inspire (Turnbull 128). An art whose first priority is to make Cato fit for the salon may make Cicero unfit for the senate.

It is clear enough, I imagine, that this theory of the fine arts may be regarded in terms of an attempt to legitimate the power of what is conceived of by the discourse of civic humanism as a ruling class.[3] If the primary object of the fine arts is to promote the public performance

This essay was originally written as a paper to be delivered at the conference 'Discursive Strategies and the Economy of Prestige', University of Minnesota, April 1988. It is reprinted from the special issue of *Cultural Critique* (no. 12, Spring 1989) devoted to the proceedings of that conference.

of acts of public virtue, then they must be thought of as addressing themselves only to those who are imagined to be capable of performing such acts. The qualifications for citizenship in the republic of taste become the same as the qualifications for citizenship in the political republic, and of these the most important is to be a man of independent means, for the best guarantee of political independence is economic independence. It may be, though this is disputed, that those who fail to meet this qualification, and who are thus not acknowledged as citizens and have no opportunity either to exercise public virtue or to understand its nature, are still able to appreciate beautiful forms, but if they are, this is only to say that they are capable of abusing the fine arts, not of using them. For according to George Turnbull, the Scottish critic who was Shaftesbury's most dedicated disciple, if the fine arts display 'merely corporeal Beauty' to the exclusion of 'the Beauties and Excellencies of Virtue, and the Turpitude of Vice', they will 'effeminate the Mind and promote Luxury', and luxury is the prime agent and symptom of corruption, whether in the individual or in the state as a whole; and it follows from this that to display works of art to those incapable of understanding what virtue is, is simply to reinforce their ineligibility as citizens by reinforcing their taste for luxury (Turnbull 81, 84, 129).

Thus the civic discourse on the fine arts, in the writings of Shaftesbury and Turnbull, seeks to identify those whom it wishes to represent as true citizens – as members of a ruling class, capable of ruling as well as of being ruled – by claiming that only they are capable of profiting by the moral lessons that works of art must teach. More than this, it announces that only the true citizen is capable of being polished, and not corrupted, by the more purely aesthetic characteristics of works of art. Those who are not citizens are excluded as firmly from participation in the republic of taste as they are from the political republic, and they include two groups in particular: the vulgar, and women. The terms of this act of exclusion therefore disclose – as Turnbull has already suggested they do – a politics of gender in the civic discourse, as well as a politics of class.

The discourse of civic humanism was the most authoritative fantasy of masculinity in early eighteenth-century Britain; it was this discourse, above all, which represented public virtue as 'manly' virtue, and which described the corruption of the citizen or the state as 'effeminacy'. It represented civic freedom not only as an emancipation from servility and dependence, but as an emancipation from desire. The ownership of an independent landed estate was curiously but still widely accepted as offering a *prima facie* guarantee that a man was emancipated from the desire for material possessions, but it was no certain test, and it gave no particular guarantee that he was also proof against the promptings of sexual desire. It was thus important to invent narratives of a civic emancipation from sexuality, and for two related reasons. First, because 'manly' virtue, or 'virile virtue' as Shaftesbury termed it, was effeminated as much by submission to 'female charms' as by the rage to acquire and spend; and second, because the vocabulary of the civic discourse, which could describe acquisitive and especially commercial activity in the same terms as it described sexual indulgence – the attractions of both could be termed 'luxury', their effects on men could both be described as 'effeminacy' – enabled emancipation from sexual desire to stand as a mark of emancipation from material desire, and vice-versa (Shaftesbury 1914 161).

To enable the citizen to triumph over his own sexuality was thus a primary object of civic education, and was to be a primary objective of the fine arts. *The Choice of Hercules* is a case in point (Figure 11). Hercules is represented as choosing whether to accompany Virtue along her steep and rugged pathway, or to linger with Pleasure in the flowery vale.[4] His attitude – turning away from Pleasure to attend to the arguments of Virtue – indicates that he is on the point of

11. Simon Gribelin, after Paolo de Matthaeis, *The Judgment of Hercules*, from the Earl of Shaftesbury, *Characteristicks*, 4th edition, 1727. 7.5 × 9.3 cm

making the right choice, the choice that legitimates the claim to exercise political power. But which way will the spectator turn? If the choice of virtue the citizen is obliged to make is to be represented as an act of heroic self-denial, then Pleasure must be made as alluring as possible; and if the fine arts are to be allowed to polish as well as to politicise, this function will – it is universally agreed – be achieved more surely by the exhibition of beautiful forms whose perfection is not too much obscured by drapery. Thus the evident danger of a work like this is not only that the desire of the spectator will be rather inflamed than cooled, but that he will try to claim an aesthetic sanction for preferring the figure of Pleasure to that of Virtue.

Shaftesbury acknowledges that 'effeminacy' may indeed be 'an evil consequent' of the exhibition of nudity, and of the demand that art should exhibit the naked body if it is to make the citizen polite as well as virtuous. But, he argues, the fine arts do not necessarily have this effect, 'if the magistrate provides, without totally banishing, or prohibiting' (Shaftesbury 1914 104). In the absence of a public official charged with the policing of the fine arts, it falls to the critic to perform that function; and one task of the civic discourse on the fine arts is therefore to produce a theory of art which prescribes not only how images of the naked body are to be produced, but how they are to be consumed, if their didactic and aesthetic functions are to be compatible. And the hardest case the critic-as-magistrate had to confront, was the case of Venus, the goddess whose beauty offered at once the most dangerous threat to manly virtue, and the most perfect polishing agent the fine arts had been able to conceive. Images of Venus, therefore, were thought to be as unstable, as untrustworthy, as the character attributed to the goddess herself; but, like Pleasure, she cannot be left unrepresented, because not to represent her allure is to be incapable of representing her repudiation, one of the most awesome acts of self-denial the civic hero can aspire to.

How then should images of Venus be produced, and how should they be consumed? This essay will examine the attempt made by the civic discourse to find an answer to that question, and the question will turn out to be quite as unstable as Venus herself is claimed to be. Seen from one point of view, it is a question about the value of images of female bodies whose perfection does not seem to fit them for any particularly civic form of action, but only for pleasure. Seen from another, it is a question about whether manly virtue, as defined by the discourse of civic humanism, is not inevitably compromised by the male sexuality it is enjoined to repress. From a third point of view, it is a question which represents Venus as a metonymy for the fine arts themselves, and it asks whether an interest in art is not always, and unavoidably, an unmanly and effeminate interest. It is a question, too, about the feminisation of commerce in the civic discourse, and its consequent difficulty in seeing commerce except as a symptom or agent of corruption. And it is a question, finally, about the viability of the civic discourse itself; about whether it is possible to hold on to an ideal of *virtus* in a society which aspires to be not only civic, but civilised. All these questions will turn out to be implicated in the issue of prestige: the prestige attached to the ability to speak the civic discourse on the fine arts, or rather, the different kinds of prestige attached to it, for these varied according to the position from which the discourse was spoken.

II

Venus, by that account, can mean nothing but trouble for the civic discourse on the fine arts; and indeed, as we shall shortly see, the instability attributed to her could disclose a corresponding instability in the discourse, so profound as to overturn what Shaftesbury announced as the founding doctrine of civic criticism, 'the absolute opposition of pleasure to virtue' (Shaftesbury 1914 9). But that is not to say that all eighteenth-century critics who consider the problem of Venus seem much embarrassed by it. A number of writers of the generation after Shaftesbury, when they attempt to describe, for example, the Venus de' Medici in the Tribuna at the Uffizi (Figure 12), acknowledge the danger she represents to the integrity of the citizen, but seem rather complacent about it, and are even willing to let on that the pleasure they take in the statue is a sexual pleasure. And they allow this to be disclosed, at the same time as they seem confident that they remain firmly within the orbit of a discourse which claims to prohibit the enjoyment they evince.

We can understand this shift, I believe, in terms of a developing difficulty in the decades after the death of Shaftesbury in conceiving of the republic of taste and the political republic as fundamentally the same constituency. The civic discourse continued, through the middle decades of the century, to provide the only available terms of criticism for the higher genres of the visual arts in Britain, because only in those terms could the claim of painting to be a liberal profession, and not a mechanical and a mercenary trade, be defended. But in those decades, and until the founding of the Royal Academy in 1768 and the attempt then made by Sir Joshua Reynolds to put the relation between the political and the aesthetic on a new footing (Barrell 1986 69–162), the civic discourse on the fine arts begins to develop a relative autonomy from the institution it had been developed to define. In Shaftesbury's and Turnbull's writings on art, that discourse had been deployed to empower the institution of aristocracy, and to legitimate it, in the years after the Glorious Revolution, as a republican and a patrician ruling class. It could define the function for the higher genres of art only in terms of their use in educating those who were, or were destined or were qualified to be, members of the visible institutions of government, the Houses of Parliament, or, in the terms of patrician republicanism, the 'senate'. But by the very terms of the civic account of history, this concern with defining the moral qualities of the aristocratic republican hero was almost bound to be attenuated by the mid-century, as Britain became an increasingly commercial society, which offered fewer and fewer occasions for civilian heroism, and which saw little value in an abstinence defined in stoic rather than in Christian terms; and this attenuation was further promoted by the related emergence of the institution of literary criticism, with its own developing autonomy from the institutions of government, and concerned to define the value of literature and the arts for a middle-class audience.[5] Thus there emerged, in the decades after the death of Shaftesbury, a generation of non-aristocratic writers on art (Jonathan Richardson senior and junior, James Thomson, Joseph Spence, Edward Wright) who represent themselves as fully capable of understanding and of defining the function of the visual arts in terms of the discourse of civic humanism, but who write as if the fine arts could be *enjoyed* independently of the possibility of exercising political power, though their value could be *described* only in terms of the effective identity of the political and the aesthetic.

It is this that I have in mind when I speak of the development of a civic discourse on the fine arts which enjoys a relative autonomy from the institution which had produced it; and it is here, particularly, that the appreciation of the fine arts engages with the question of *prestige*. As long as the possibility of appreciating the higher genres of the art was thought of as available only to the aristocracy, it was certainly imagined that an informed concern with painting and sculpture conferred status on the noble or gentle connoisseur; it confirmed his standing as a patrician in the fullest sense of the word, as someone not only born to exercise power, but fit to exercise it. As a result, a form of prestige became attached to the ability to articulate the civic discourse, and that ability could remain to some extent a source of prestige when the discourse came to be spoken by, and addressed to, those with no claim to be regarded as patricians. The kind of prestige it conferred certainly changed: to lay claim to an understanding of the visual arts was now no longer to announce

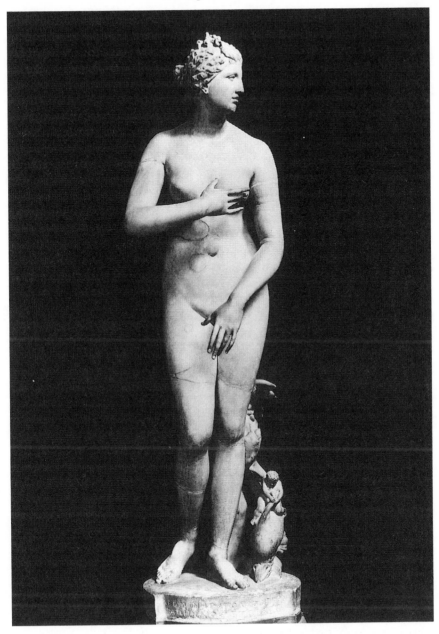

12. *Venus de' Medici*, artist and date unknown. Height 1.53 m. Florence, Uffizi (Tribuna)

oneself as a true patrician, but as someone who shared something of importance with those who were – something less material than an independent fortune, and less accidental than high birth, but something which was arguably no less valuable for being so.

The developing autonomy of the civic discourse on the visual arts, and the different nature of the prestige it conferred on those who could articulate it, may not at first sight seem to have brought about any very radical change in the discourse itself. Most of what such writers as Thomson or Spence have to say about the function of the visual arts can be read as a repetition or an endorsement of what Shaftesbury had said, and in this paper I shall often be able to draw on their writings in my attempt to illustrate and to amplify the critical and political principles of Shaftesbury. But when such writers consider the representation of the naked female body, and of Venus in particular, this uniformity disappears. All those questions which, I have argued, were entailed in the question of how Venus was to be represented become more apparent, but seem to be suddenly less urgent, when put in the scale with the pleasure which (it is almost openly acknowledged) is to be had from gazing at her nakedness; and in the excited descriptions offered by Thomson, Spence and Wright, of the Venus de' Medici, it seems almost to be implied that the safety of citizen and state alike may be well lost for love.

One way of describing this development would be to see it in terms of the different nature of the prestige which attaches to the civic discourse on the visual arts, as it develops a more attenuated relation to the institutions and the exercise of political power. If the connection between taste and public virtue became a matter of less urgent concern among the followers of Shaftesbury, it also became less important that male sexuality be constituted within the discourse only in order that it might be renounced. And this was not simply a matter, I want to suggest, of a weakening of the old institutional constraints on civic criticism. For the very weakening of the connection between taste and public virtue was necessarily a weakening of the foundation on which the prestige of civic criticism was based. It led inevitably to a tentative valorisation of the aesthetic for its own sake – as connoisseurship, and as a special receptivity to aesthetic form – and as a result the ability to appreciate the visual arts in aesthetic terms began to emerge as a new basis of authority and prestige in the criticism of the visual arts. The discursive strategies by which the aesthetic could begin to be separated from the political are described at the end of this paper. What I want to emphasise here is, first, that within the terms of civic criticism, such a separation was more or less illegitimate, and could neither be argued for nor fully accomplished so long as criticism of the visual arts remained within the orbit of the civic discourse; and, second, that it was nevertheless only by taking advantage of that incipient separation that the sexuality silenced in the writings of Shaftesbury and Turnbull became able to speak itself, and to put in question that ethic of manly abstinence which was so crucial a constituent of the discourse of civic humanism.

Thus, when Thomson and Spence and Wright seem to take a light-hearted and a playful attitude to the threat Venus poses to public virtue, they are producing an account of the aesthetic, and a representation of masculinity, very different from what Shaftesbury had offered: masculinity, in particular, now becomes a matter of virility rather than of abstinence; of the ability to enjoy the pleasures of sexuality rather than to resist them. It is the emergence of this new kind of concern for the aesthetic, and this new representation of what it is to be manly, which establishes the relative autonomy of the civic discourse on the visual arts from the institution of aristocracy; and it is the implicit, the covert, the hesitant form of their emergence which announces that autonomy as relative only. The emergence of a new relation between the political and the aesthetic turns therefore on a representation of woman, and, through that, on masculinity itself.

I shall begin the narrative that follows in the middle of things, with an analysis of a passage by Thomson in which the invocation of Venus disrupts, in a most dramatic way, the connection of taste and virtue; and I shall go on to attempt to demonstrate how Shaftesbury in particular had imagined that the connection could be protected from the threat that Venus posed. In the final sections, I shall attempt a fuller account of how that connection is both affirmed and put in question in the writings of his successors, and of how the civic discourse on the visual arts found a way to accommodate, under the cover of the aesthetic, an account of masculinity as virility which it had earlier been obliged to prohibit.

III

In the second book of his poem *Liberty* (1735–6), Thomson attributes the rise of the fine arts to the liberty enjoyed by the republics of classical Greece. The art of sculpture, in particular, was the result of those civic and public virtues which can develop only in free states, and without which, he tells us, the world would never have seen

> *Jove's* awful Brow, *Apollo's* Air divine,
> The fierce atrocious Frown of sinew'd *Mars*,
> Or the sly Graces of the *Cyprian Queen*.
> (Thomson 1986, *Liberty*, II, lines 304–6)

Why Venus, of all the heathen deities, and why this image of Venus, not merely graceful but sly, should be imagined as an appropriate creation of the civic artist, seems to stand in need of some explanation. And when, fifty or so lines later, the poem does offer something like an explanation, it becomes only too clear how sly, capricious and unstable Venus can be, and how much trouble she can cause the civic discourse on the fine arts. Thomson is describing the function those arts performed in the Greek republics.

> To Public Virtue thus the *smiling Arts*,
> Unblemish'd Handmaids, serv'd; the *Graces* they
> To dress this fairest *Venus*.
> > (*Liberty*, II, lines 365–7)

The *'smiling Arts'* were still *'Unblemish'd* Handmaids', of course, because they had not yet prostituted themselves to tyranny and luxury. They were, indeed, *'Graces'*, who combined in their efforts to dress 'this fairest Venus', who is now none other than 'Public Virtue' herself. The official argument seems to be that public virtue, though beautiful, can be a brusque, a raw, a naked affair unless clothed by the fine arts: like Shaftesbury, Thomson believes that a degree of politeness can be good for the polity; a *'Venustum'* – the word is cognate with 'Venus' – a 'decorum', can develop in the citizen a pleasing urbanity of demeanour, and allow him to combine, as William Pitt was said to do by his friend James Hammond, 'A Roman's virtue with a courtier's ease' (Shaftesbury 1727 1: 138; Hammond 39: 333). His virtues will not be corrupted by the luxury of dress, so long as that dress is transparent enough not to conceal his civic character, but only to adorn it. But if that is what Thomson has in mind, he has said something very different, and Venus has evidently exceeded the place assigned to her in and by the civic discourse. Instead of Public Virtue being clothed by Venus, she *becomes* Venus, and it is Venus's body, and Virtue's only in so far as she *is* Venus, that is clothed by the Graces.

This metamorphosis strikes at the heart of civic discourse on the fine arts, because civic iconography defined Virtue, more specifically Public Virtue, as at all points the opposite of Venus. Essential to the accurate representation of Venus, argues Joseph Spence, is her 'indolent character', and 'it is for this reason', he argues, 'that Venus is so often opposed to Minerva, and Virtus; the two deities which presided over an active and stirring life', the *vita activa* to which civic virtue was dedicated (Spence 1755 74). Virtue 'is generally represented,' he tells us, as a military lady. She is sometimes in a coat of mail, or a short succinct vest; with her legs and arms bare, as the Roman soldiers used to be. She has a manly face, and air; and generally grasps a sword, or spear, in her hand. Her dress shows her character, or readiness for action; and her look, a firmness and resolution, not to be conquered by any difficulties or dangers, that may meet her in the way.   (Spence 1755 140)

Spence goes on to remark that Virtue is generally opposed to Voluptas, to Pleasure, as she is in accounts and representations of the Choice of Hercules; and he further identifies Venus as the goddess of Pleasure (Spence 1755 141, 143). In Shaftesbury's account of *The Choice of Hercules*, he too attributes to Virtue a manliness, expressed in her clothes, which should be those of an Amazon or of Minerva; in her identifying emblem, the 'Imperial or Magisterial Sword', and in the firmness of her posture. 'As for the *Shape, Countenance,* or Person of VIRTUE,' he continues, 'that which is usually given to PALLAS may fitly serve as a Model for this Dame; as on the other side, that which is given to VENUS may serve in the same manner for her Rival,' who should be distinguished from Virtue by a 'Softness', an '*Effeminacy*', and a 'supine Air and Character of Ease and Indolence' (Shaftesbury 1727 3: 363–4, 370–1).

Thus when, in *Liberty*, Public Virtue is transformed, by the fine arts, into Venus, she is transformed into her polar opposite, into the other against which her essential character has been defined: in being softened by the 'smiling arts', Virtue is softened up, and feminised. The failure of Thomson's text to deliver up the official civic doctrine, and its transformation of that doctrine into its opposite, can be precisely glossed by Spence's remark that the Romans were 'of so military a turn,' that 'they generally gave Fortitude the name of Virtus, or Virtue, by way of excellence: just as the same nation, now they are so debased and effeminated, call the love the softer arts, Vertù.' A similar point is made by Gilbert West, who notes also that the 'ciceroni', the guides who introduce tourists in modern Rome to the 'gay refinements' which mock the memory of the austere Roman republic, are named after the most eloquent defender of that republic (Spence 1755 139).[6]

Thomson's substitution of Venus for Public Virtue suggests that his poem, whose entire subject is supposed to be civic freedom, has also been appropriated by a debased and effeminate discourse on the fine arts, associated with the corruption of post-reformation and post-republican Italy, and the appropriation speaks of a difficulty often apparent in civic discourse, a fear that the 'smiling arts' may indeed be the 'softening arts', the product not of virtue but of luxury, of exactly that which most threatens corruption to the state, and moral detumescence to the citizen. That fear is already present in the justification Shaftesbury borrows from Ovid for the representation of beautiful forms: *'emollit mores'* (Shaftesbury 1914 104).[7] There is a positive and a pejorative sense in the verb 'emollire', to soften: it can mean to make mild or gentle, or to enervate, to render effeminate; and the same ambiguity troubles Spence's account of Venus, who, he says, 'polishes savages, and softens all the world'. George Lyttelton, Thomson's patron, was described, once again by James Hammond, as being 'Firm as man's sense, and soft as woman's love'; we would only have to change that 'and' to 'but' to get a sense of how thin is the film of polish which separates courtliness from effeminacy (Spence 1755 75; Hammond 39: 332).

This fear – by the end of the essay it will begin to look more like a desire – is often managed by making a strict distinction between the intellectual pleasures the fine arts are supposed to offer, and the pleasures of luxury which are the pleasures of sense. 'Every-one pursues a GRACE, and courts a VENUS of one kind or another,' claims Shaftesbury, and this is a legitimate and a civic pursuit, provided that this 'VENUS' is a *'moral GRACE'*, a *'Beauty'*, a *'Decorum'*, of the *'inward kind'*, a Venus neutered into a *'Venustum'* (Shaftesbury 1727 1: 138, 137).[8] But to pursue Venus in 'an inferior Order of Things', in the mere outward appearance of the human frame, or even in inanimate objects, is another form of effeminacy; it is a characteristic, he argues, of the debasement of the fine arts into objects of luxury, that they cater to 'the whole fantastick Tribe of wanton, gay, and fond Desires', and encourage 'Effeminacy and Cowardice' to such a degree as to ensure that 'the more eagerly we grasp at *Life*, the more impotent we are in the Enjoyment of it' (Shaftesbury 1727 1: 139, 314).[9] The terms on which the beautiful forms represented by painting and sculpture could be defended as appealing only to the intellect were complicated, at least before Sir Joshua Reynolds put the argument on a new footing, and I shall consider them soon. But earlier in the century, among civic humanist critics, there *does* exist some sort of agreement that, as Shaftesbury argued, if 'ugly' forms 'barbarise' the mind, 'beauteous forms' may 'polish' it, so long as there is no question of 'libidinous representation in plastic art', and flesh is never 'painted as flesh' (Shaftesbury 1914 104, 171, 114). The difficulty of this theory, as we shall see, is the difficulty of imagining a painting in which the representation of flesh, however unlibidinous its execution, could not be *seen* as flesh by the spectator.

IV

The embarrassing identification that Thomson has made, between Venus and Public Virtue, is the result, I have suggested, of a discursive slippage, of a kind which the instability of Venus's character both reflects, and is only too likely to produce. Shaftesbury's demand is that the gentleman-citizen should cultivate a courtly lightness of touch, a *Venustum*; and the danger, for Shaftesbury, in that demand – clearly evident in civic reactions to Chesterfield's later version of it – is that the *Venustum* will represent itself not simply as the dress but as the badge of virtue. The demand rests on the possibility of distinguishing between virtue and vertù, between manly politeness and luxurious effeminacy. We have seen that Venus can appear as the agent of both, and one way in which this duality can be sorted out is by appealing to a further distinction, the traditional one between a 'heavenly' and an 'earthly' Venus, between Venus Caelestis or Urania, and Venus Pandemos, who, according to Lemprière's entry on the goddess in his classical dictionary, 'favoured the propensities of the vulgar and was fond of sensual pleasures'. In so far as Venus can slide from one to the other side of the division between the polite and the effeminate, she must herself be divided in two.

But this traditional distinction has itself a long history of instability: Venus is the last deity to entrust with two functions of opposite moral tendency, since it is essential to Earthly Venus that she is deceitful, and can easily conterfeit her heavenly manifestation. Civic humanist theory of the fine arts attempted to confirm the distinction by consigning each Venus to her appropriate discursive site: it defines a public and a private sphere of activity, each with its appropriate aesthetic. The arts have a public function, where they are imagined to operate rhetorically, to persuade us to wish to perform acts of public virtue, and it is here that the Earthly Venus belongs, only ever as the goddess whose designs upon him the civic hero must frustrate. But the arts have also a private function, where they operate in terms of a philosophical aesthetic, appropriate to the contemplative, not the active life, and where the citizen believes he can acquire a polish from inspecting the body of Heavenly Venus, so long as he can regard its form as an object of intellectual, not of sensual delight. The policing of the fine arts that Shaftesbury has called for can of course be a matter of *public* policy only, for he consistently asserts that the freedom of private speculation should be unconstrained; and this seems to amount, in Shaftesbury's writings, to a belief that public images of Venus must always be images of Earthly Venus, and must be enclosed within narratives which leave us in no doubt as to her bad character; images of Heavenly Venus are permitted to be enjoyed, it seems, disjoined from narrative, but only within what is imagined to be a private sphere of the arts.

Thus, as far as painting is concerned, and epic history painting as the most public of all genres, Venus will always be an enemy of the public. We have already seen how, in *The Choice of Hercules*, the hero was required to choose between Virtue conceived of as public virtue, directed towards 'the deliverance of Mankind from Tyranny and Oppression', and Pleasure whose body is modelled on the body of Venus (Shaftesbury 1727 3: 351). Elsewhere, Shaftesbury considers another possible design from the story of Hercules, where the hero has been seduced by Omphale, and exchanges his club and arrows for a distaff and spindle. The story, explains Shaftesbury, is 'a case of the weakness of human nature, or the virile virtue in opposition to the female charms or those of love'. What kind of a 'machine', what kind of allegorical commentary would such a painting require? Cupids, decides Shaftesbury, insulting the fallen hero, and enjoying their triumph; and a laughing Venus (Shaftesbury 1914 161).[10]

As far as the public art of history painting is concerned, Shaftesbury is everywhere concerned to point out the dangers of a philosophical aesthetic, if it invites us to take pleasure in mere symmetry of form, in mere beauty, disjoined from purposive action. 'Symmetry', he argues, 'is separate and abstract from the moral part and manners' in painting; 'the moral part ... lies but little in the forms ... but is expressed in the air, feature, attitude, action, motion'; 'Characters which in painting are mere forms are not moral' (Shaftesbury 1914 98). As soon as Venus finds her way into a history painting, she must be shifted therefore from formal to moral, from the body as symmetry to the body as moral tale. The requirement that she *do* something, that she participate in a narrative, will, or should, immediately betray the kind of moral character she has, and should persuade us, in terms of a rhetorical aesthetic, not to surrender to her blandishments.

But if Shaftesbury insists on this narrativisation, his contrary insistence elsewhere that the examination of beautiful forms can have a civilising and a polishing effect has suggested that it might somewhere be possible to represent a very different image of Venus, whereby her body could be enjoyed as pure form, precisely because that enjoyment was not conceived of as bodily; where the perfect unity and proportion of her form, contained by no narrative, could be understood as the means by which the civic character can also become civilised and polite. Such images, as we have seen, would need to be imagined as occupying a private sphere of the arts, where a contemplative and a philosophical aesthetic could be allowed to replace the active and rhetorical aesthetic of public art. The problem for Shaftesbury is that Venus cannot appear as a visual image in this sphere: there is, for him, no imaginable private sector in the visual arts. The terms public and private define, for him, not two different kinds of painting, but the difference between the visual arts and the arts of language. In the literary arts, he suggests, the beauty of form is a legitimate source of moral interest; in the visual arts, it can be so only when it is connected with moral action. Heavenly Venus, the object of the philosophical aesthetic, can be *named*, but she must not be *shown*.

Shaftesbury does not explain why this should be so, but the reason no doubt lies partly in the intrinsic differences between the literary and the visual arts, and partly in the differences between the consumers of each. The literary arts, which make use of arbitrary signs, can offer only mediated representations; because they address the intellect, not the eye, they do not have the same power to inflame as does the visual image, and those most easily inflamed, the vulgar, are largely illiterate and so unable to enjoy them. The 'natural' signs employed by the visual arts, however, and the immediate representations they offer, are capable of being enjoyed by all, and what all will enjoy is precisely their immediacy. It is in vain for Heavenly Venus to invite us to look beyond the perfection of her body to the perfection of the spirit, for what lies beyond a natural sign is a natural referent, and that referent can only be, like the sign itself, a thing, something that has mass and extension – a body. Venus visualised will always be Venus vulgarised, Venus Pandemos, everybody's Venus.

Had this distinction between the literary and the visual arts been more fully articulated, it would no doubt have obliged Shaftesbury to acknowledge a further distinction between public and private, operating within the literary arts themselves. It is in what he describes as 'mere . . . Pieces of Wit and Literature', in the private genre of the letter, the soliloquy, the miscellany, that he himself pursues his contemplations of symmetry and *Venustum* (Shaftesbury 1727 1: 357). It is perfectly clear, on the other hand, that he regards epic poetry as a public genre, in which the permission granted to the literary arts in general to represent forms which are merely beautiful is overridden by a more urgent imperative to provide lessons and examples of civic heroism (see especially Shaftesbury 1727 1: 317–18). In epic, according to the civic humanist critic of poetry, Thomas Blackwell, Venus is the goddess of '*Effeminacy*', or she should, at least, be represented as such. Thus for Blackwell it is an inevitable but nevertheless an 'unlucky' aspect of the *Aeneid* that its hero is the son of Venus, and that she should therefore be 'the chief Divinity who guides the *holy, wise*, and *brave Eneas*'. 'She might well tutor *Paris*,' he writes, 'and favour all the *Trojans* who had their Seraglio's even then', for – as this mention of seraglios suggests – in the *Iliad*, or at least in a civic account of it, the Trojans are defeated as much by their own oriental, and therefore 'effeminate' manners, as by the manly virtue of the Greeks. But in Virgil's epic the Trojans must appear as the originators of that very virtue in the Romans, and 'it was hard,' Blackwell argues, to make Venus appear 'in a *virtuous Cause*', when it was so out of character for her to do so. It was no less hard to allow her to appear in her usual character, which was not to encourage but to destroy civic virtue. Accordingly, Venus was obliged to appear as 'a *mere Person*', with no distinctive characteristics other than her divine power. She exhibits the kind of concern a mother might feel for her son, but not the kind of zeal we might expect from the tutelary goddess of a 'pious hero' (Blackwell 215, 217, 312). Thomson's failure to distinguish between Venus and Public Virtue is thus analagous to Virgil's inability adequately to characterise Venus: it is the result of a failure to remember that in the public genre of what he described as an 'Epic performance',[11] Venus should always be Earthly Venus, in whatever guise she appears.

It remains true, however, that it is by virtue of the different *nature* of the different arts, disjoined from the particular functions attributed to their various genres, that Heavenly Venus remains an appropriate object for representation only in writing. It is imagined to be of the nature of the visual arts that they invite us to prefer the sensual to the intellectual, and so transform Heavenly into Earthly Venus, and it is this belief that generates the strange paradox, that a theory of the visual arts which acknowledges, and claims to condemn, the inescapable sensuality of beautiful images of the naked female body, should find itself obliged to permit only such images of Venus as call attention to her sensuality. Thus a civic theory of painting can licence the image of what threatens to enervate and undermine the polity, while it denies the possibility that painting could represent an image of Venus which would claim to offer no such threat, and would offer itself, indeed, as the means by which society proceeds from barbarism to civilisation. And it follows from this that if the citizen can indeed be polished without being made effeminate by the supreme image of female beauty, it can only be by images of Earthly Venus, whose body, however, he must be taught at once to admire as form, and to resist as agent. The magistrate who is charged to police, but not totally to banish or forbid, the representation of beautiful forms, can perform that task only by ordaining that visual representations of Venus should be earthly – should be indolent, sensual, and capricious – and by ordaining also that they should be held within, and judged in terms of, an unambiguous structure of narrative.

V

It is narrative, then, that does the police, and licenses the presence of Earthly Venus among the subjects proper to be painted, in a civic society which wishes to become also a civilised society. But where does this leave sculpture – or, more particularly, free-standing sculptures of Venus, which are not apparently contained, as relief-sculptures, and as sculptured groups such as the Laocoon and the Niobe evidently are, within a narrative structure? Some such statues were positioned within a narrative by their attributes, whether original or acquired during restoration: one of the statues of Venus in the Tribuna of the Uffizi had been given a new hand at the end of the seventeenth century, and an apple to hold in it, to indicate in what contest she had been victorious. And thus she acquired also a name, the 'Venus Victrix', which, however erroneously conceived, served to attach her to a narrative (Richardson 57; Haskell and Penny 332).[12] The name of the most favoured statue of Venus, however, the Venus de' Medici, spoke of her provenance, not of her character or actions; the dolphin which, mounted by a Cupid, supported her on her base, seems not to have been thought to identify her as the Venus of any particular story.[13] It was perhaps this absence of a narrative context, as much as the 'Fleshy Softness' regularly attributed to and admired in her body, which is responsible for the extraordinary fascination the Venus de' Medici exerted over eighteenth-century visitors to Florence, and which blinded them to the other Venuses in the same room. 'When I had spent ten hours in this Gallery', writes the younger Richardson, '. . . 'twas yet impossible to keep my Eyes off of this three Minutes whilst I was in the Room' (Richardson 56).[14]

The same lack of a narrative context must certainly have been responsible for the regularity with which the Venus de' Medici was regarded as an unstable mixture of characteristics themselves unstable – 'melting', 'dissembled', 'slippery' – and so as an image of Earthly Venus, easily distinguishable from the 'Celestial Venus' which was also housed in the Tribuna. The Celestial Venus was known also as the 'Venus Pudica', because she was holding her drapery so as to make sure that her sexual parts were concealed. By contrast the Venus de' Medici, it seems to have been fairly generally felt, was making only a token attempt to cover her nakedness – was directing attention to what she failed to conceal.[15] Much of Spence's dialogue is imagined as taking place in a temple in the garden of Polymetis 'set apart . . . for the great celestial deities', which houses a copy of the Venus de' Medici. 'It would have been more proper,' acknowledges Polymetis,

to have had a figure of the Venus Coelestis in it: but, to confess
the truth to you, I am so much in love with the Venus of Medici,
that I rather chose to commit this impropriety, than to prefer any
other figure to hers. The thing perhaps is not quite so reasonable,
as it should be; but when did lovers act with reason?

(Spence 1755 68)

The Venus de' Medici, by this account, seems to pose a threat to the
civic discourse, but she does not do so simply by virtue of the
viciousness attributed to her character. For though Venus has always
the potential power to conquer and effeminate, and to reduce the free
and manly citizen to the sensual condition of the vulgar, it is a power
that she has no power to do, so long as she can be trapped in some
network of narrative, and so long as that narrative produces a third
party, someone other than the spectator himself, who is faced with
the choice of conquering or being conquered. It is the fact that
sculpture in general, and the Venus de' Medici in general, resists
being put into narrative that makes her so much more dangerous than
any historical painting of Venus could be. And the appropriately civic
response, therefore, is somehow to overcome sculpture's resistance to
narrative.

One way in which this could be done was by composing epigrams
or inscriptions, to be placed (or to be imagined as placed) beneath the
statue, and with the intention of policing the meanings it could
generate. A case in point is the inscription composed by Shenstone
to accompany the copy of the Venus de' Medici in his garden at the
Leasowes. This Venus, Shenstone's 'sober' verses make clear, is *not*
the goddess whose 'amorous leer prevail'd/To bribe the Phrygian boy'
(Paris). Nor is she the 'bold', 'pert', and 'gay' Venus who is worshipped
at Paphos. Her pose, half-revealing and half-concealing her nakedness,
is an emblem of good taste, of taste as absolutely opposed to the
luxurious, effeminate, and meretricious display which may be taken
to characterise the goddess in some of her other manifestations
(Shenstone 2: 318–20).[16] The tourist and connoisseur Edward Wright
composed an epigram on the Venus de' Medici, which specifically
acknowledges, again by reminding us of the fate which befell Paris,
that the statue has the power to make the spectator forget his civic
duty:

> Thus *Venus* stood, and who could blame the Boy,
> For giving Sentence, tho' it ruin'd *Troy*?
> Were they t'appeal, and you to judge the Prize,
> Must not *Troy* fall, were *Troy* again to rise?

(Wright 2: 409)

And having made this acknowledgement, the poem can exhort the spectator to turn away from the image, as Hercules turned away from pleasure; and so the epigram ends, appropriately, with an admonition:

> Be gone, lest you these naked Beauties view
> So long, you make *Pygmalion's* Story true.

Whoever speaks this admonition hopes to represent himself as not, himself, in danger of being seduced by Venus. It is someone else, it is 'you', who is at risk. The truly civic spectator is thus constructed as one who has learned to resist the threat offered to his virtue by Venus's 'Fleshy Softness'; and that lesson safely learned, he can announce himself as one who, like Shenstone, can be safely trusted to admire, and to acquire a polish from, the naked stone.

Another way of narrativising sculpture, and sculptures of Venus in particular, was to arrange them in pairs. So different, for Spence's Polymetis, is the Venus de' Medici from Celestial Venus, that he describes the image he so adores as a representation of the 'Vitious' Venus, as the Venus who was brought to 'public shame . . . by her amours with Mars', and was 'caught in the net made by Vulcan'. And 'on account,' he explains, 'of this old story,' he positions his own copy of the statue alongside a statue of Mars, and reproduces the narrative effect of the group sculpture of the two divinities also in the Uffizi (Spence 1755 75–6).[17] By this means it is intended that the Venus should be no longer a danger to the civic spectator, but should become, like the story of Hercules and Omphale, a rhetorical exemplum of the danger posed by sensuality to military virtue. In the garden of the great civic palace at Stowe of Viscount Cobham, a copy of the Venus de' Medici was placed in the Rotondo, a structure similar to, and acting, within the garden, as a pendant to, the Temple of Ancient Virtue, so that the goddess is located in a version of the narrative of the Choice of Hercules; and perhaps to make the right choice clear beyond question, the statue was gilded, and thus invited the association of effeminacy and luxury.[18] The practice of pairing copies of antique statues is neither a uniquely British nor a uniquely civic habit; my point is that whatever function it may have served elsewhere, within the terms of the civic discourse on the fine arts it often seems designed to stabilise and so to legitimate the slippery goddess, who, contemplated by herself, would rupture that discourse, and threaten the fantasy of virtuous masculinity it was designed to protect.

VI

Softness, sensuality, indolence, luxury, duplicity, effeminacy – Venus, and the Venus de' Medici in particular – was scribbled over with all the pejorative terms of the discourse of civic humanism. The official civic doctrine, which we came upon most clearly in Shaftesbury's account of Hercules and Omphale, is that the virility of the civic hero is not confirmed but wasted by his sexuality. But as I have suggested, the changing circumstances in which the civic discourse on the visual arts came to be articulated seem to have made it neither necessary nor desirable to end the matter just there, without finding any space for that meaning of virility whereby it denotes male sexuality rather than a manly and therefore asexual virtue. When critics and connoisseurs of the middle decades of the century offer actually to describe the Venus de' Medici, they seem willing to let on that the pleasure they take in her body is a sexual at least as much as an aesthetic pleasure, and they seem somehow to believe that they can allow this to be implied, without forfeiting their civic character.

To attempt to account for this, I need to expand on the account I have so far offered of the opposition that operates in the civic discourse between the private and the public. For the public sphere is involved not in one but in two binary relationships with the private. In the binary I have so far considered, the public is constructed as the *opposite* of a private sphere which is openly theorised by the discourse of civic humanism, and which defines what the citizen *should* do in his private capacity. In the second binary, there is another version of the private, constructed as the *contrary* of the public. This second version of the private is rarely acknowledged and only occasionally visible, for the good reason that it is best left unacknowledged; and it defines what the citizen *may* do in private, so long as he is not thereby disabled from maintaining his public character and performing his public function; and so long as he is not, of course, he may indulge any vice he chooses. 'Publick Virtue' writes John Dennis (2: 113), 'makes Compensation for all Faults but Crimes'.

By this account of the private, there is no question of the enjoyment of images of Venus being pure, spiritual, and aesthetic. Indeed, in this private capacity, the citizen may enjoy exactly those images of Earthly Venus which in public are occasions for moral condemnation; and he may enjoy them for exactly what, in public, he reproves – their sensuality. In the garden at Rousham, the Venus de' Medici appeared at the end of a view which was punctuated, at left and right, by statues of Pan and a Faun, and on the garden-front of the house – the private front – she is placed in the company of some entirely uncivic deities, Bacchus among them.[19] In the house at Stourhead, she is paired with the narcissistic and exhibitionist Callipygian Venus. In the White Hall at Hagley, the home of George Lyttelton, a copy of the same Venus is paired with the Dancing Faun, also from the Tribuna, as she is also in the entrance hall of the early eighteenth-century house at Towneley in Lancashire (Haskell and Penny 326)[20] These groupings can hardly be read as intending to warn the spectator that sexual indulgence effeminates and brutalises. They seem instead to convert the spaces they inhabit into private spaces, in the terms of this second binary I have been describing; and they seem to say that sexual pleasure does not necessarily effeminate, if it can be sealed within a leakproof private container.

But the container was far from leakproof, and it was always likely that these different notions of the private would invoke and seep into each other, the more so as the civic discourse on the visual arts developed a relative autonomy from the institutions of aristocracy and of aristocratic government, and it became less urgent for it to attempt at every point to define the value of art in terms of its public function, its tendency to promote public virtue. And as the criticism of art became detached from the aristocratic public sphere, so necessarily the notion of the private as the opposite of the public diminished in importance, and the second version of the private, which was altogether more serviceable as an account of the space inhabited by those who enjoyed no opportunity to participate in public life, became, if not more visible, at least closer to the surface of the civic discourse. Because this second version of the private was defined as the contrary of the civic notion of the public sphere, it always offered the possibility of inverting the stoical sexual morality of the public sphere; and because it was, nevertheless, defined in terms of the civic discourse, it was relatively insulated from the protestant code of morality by which middle-class life is more usually imagined to have been regulated. This did not mean, of course, that Thomson or Wright or Spence could now openly, and without qualification, avow that their interest in representations of the female nude was a sensual interest. But it does suggest that the claim made by the civic discourse, that it is possible to subtract the sensual from the aesthetic, or to detach the aesthetic from the sensual, and so to enjoy Venus's body on aesthetic terms while remaining unmoved by her sensuality, may have come to serve some new purposes. It can be understood as providing a justification for the category of the aesthetic as to a degree independent of the political, and as an attempt, also, and a far from whole-hearted one, to mop up the sensual, which, by virtue of that very independence, threatened to become explicit enough to contaminate the aesthetic.

In the process, of course, the mop itself gets saturated. What we have been observing could be redescribed as an attempt to distinguish the aesthetic gaze from the scopophiliac stare, one which seems always to issue in the sensualisation of that gaze, as an unacknowledged sexuality finds eager expression in a concern for the aesthetic, a concern which itself seems to exceed the space it can legitimately occupy by virtue of a prior renunciation of the sexual. The critic who, before he begins to describe the Venus de' Medici, makes a display of his civic credentials, announces himself as one whose aesthetic interest in Venus's body is made possible by virtue of his emancipation from her sexual potency. He is then free to gaze, and gaze, and gaze again; and if he can get close enough to the original, he evinces the innocence of his pleasure by getting out his calipers and footrule. 'Every detail of the goddess's anatomy,' write Haskell and Penny (325), 'was specially examined.' 'The Head,' noted the Richardsons (55), 'is something too little for the Body, especially for the Hips and Thighs; the Fingers excessively long, and taper, and no Match for the Knuckles, except for the little Finger of the Right-hand'. 'One might very well insist,' writes Spence,

> on the beauty of the breasts . . . They are small, distinct, and delicate to the highest degree; with an idea of softness, . . . And yet with all that softness, they have a firmness too; . . . From her breasts, her shape begins to diminish gradually down to her waist; . . . Her legs are neat and slender; the small of them is finely rounded; and her very feet are little, white, and pretty.　　　(Spence 1755 66–7)

There is more of this kind of thing, by other writers, and it is what passes itself off as an announcement that the threat posed by Venus's sensuality has been safely neutralised by narrative, and is now being seen in aesthetic terms – in terms of the degree of the sculptor's skill, and the pure harmony of proportion. But if that is what these descriptions tell us, as it were, in their official capacity, they seem to take a positive and a playful pleasure in telling us much more besides. In particular there is the repeated refusal of the aesthetic gaze to remain, not merely aesthetic, but a gaze at all: the sense of sight only too eagerly invokes the sense of touch.

This is clear enough in the passage just quoted from Spence; and the Richardsons' careful analysis of the various parts of Venus's body gives way to the observation that the statue 'has . . . such a Fleshy Softness, one would think it would yield to the touch' (Richardson 56). For Thomson, who wrote a lengthy and excited paragraph on the statue, the power of the goddess to displace the visual with the tactile is another aspect of her sly character, her instability, but within the terms of what represents itself as an aesthetic account of the statue, this is apparently something to be enjoyed rather than repudiated. He writes:

> The *Queen of Love* arose, as from the Deep
> She sprung in all the melting Pomp of Charms.
> Bashful she bends, her well-taught Look aside
> Turns in enchanting guise, where dubious mix
> Vain conscious Beauty, a dissembled Sense
> Of modest Shame, and slippery Looks of Love.
> The Gazer grows enamour'd, and the Stone,
> As if exulting in it's Conquest, smiles.
> So turn'd each Limb, so swell'd with softening Art,
> That the deluded Eye the Marble doubts.
> (*Liberty*, IV, lines 175–84)

'Melting', 'dubious', 'dissembled', 'slippery' – Venus is anarchic and unstable; her swelling body so exceeds the medium in which she is represented and should be confined, that she seems not a woman turned to stone but a stone turning into a woman.[21] But if Thomson evinces no urgent concern to stabilise the statue by containing it within a narrative of repudiation, that is, I suggest, because the passage itself is part of a narrative poem dedicated to recording the triumphs of civic liberty, and thus Thomson's public virtue is already sufficiently on display. With a similar display of his civic character, Edward Wright commands that we should 'Strictly examine every part'; his own examination, however, is less than wholly strict, and by the end of the very first line he is already anxious to touch:

> So just, so fine, so soft each Part,
> Her beauties fire the lab'ring Heart.
> The gentle Risings of the Skin
> Seem push'd by Muscles mov'd within:
> The swelling Breasts, with Graces fill'd,
> Seem easy, to the Touch, to yield;
> Made lovelier yet by a Modesty,
> Forbidding us in vain to see.

– and there follows a lacuna in the poem, which suggests that the sequel was too indecent to be printed (Wright 2: 407–8).

What I have called this eager invocation of touch by sight suggests that, after Shaftesbury, the civic discourse found a way to have its cake and eat it too. And it could do so especially in relation to the Venus de' Medici, by taking advantage not only of the uneasy separations of the political from the aesthetic and the aesthetic from the erotic, but of the fact that the statue belonged to no narrative. As we have seen, this absence of a containing narrative could be exploited so as to encourage the critic and connoisseur to provide one for himself, but he did not always provide the kind of story by which Shaftesbury had imagined the body of Venus could be stabilised and made available as a polishing agent. This other kind of narrative could represent itself as the story of an aesthetic response, and so, like the eager descriptions of the various parts of Venus's body, it could pass itself off as of a piece with the aesthetic discourse which the spectator earns the right to speak by resisting the sensuality of Venus; and, like those descriptions, it gives willing utterance to the very sensuality that the aesthetic discourse claims to have displaced.

The standard version of this narrative is recorded by Spence: 'At your first approaching her . . . you see aversion or denial in her look; move on but a step or two farther, and she has compliance in it: and one step more to the right . . . turns it into a little insidious and insulting smile; such as any lady has, when she plainly tells you by her face, that she has made a sure conquest of you.' Spence himself ridicules this account of the Venus: these are 'imaginary beauties,' he claims. 'I have paid, perhaps', he writes, 'a hundred visits to the Venus of Medici in person; and have often considered her, in this very view.' But 'I could never find out the malicious sort of smile, which your antiquarians talk so much of' (Spence 1755 68). But it is a narrative that he records as being common among 'men of taste', at a time when to claim that identity it was necessary to lay claim also to a civic concern for the moral effects of art.

The narrative is as unstable as is the statue itself in Thomson's description: to some, the expression of Venus seemed to change as they approached nearer to her, to others as they moved around her.[22] But, as in Thomson's account of the reaction of the spectator, it always ends in conquest: not in a conquest, by the civic spectator, over his lustful and effeminating passions, such as Hercules achieved when he chose Virtue in preference to Pleasure, but a conquest by Venus over the civic spectator, as Hercules was conquered and effeminated by Omphale, while Venus looked on and laughed. Even Spence is clear enough that the statue had conquered his reason: it was for that reason that he felt obliged to couple Venus with Mars, and it was by doing so, of course, that he was able to continue to indulge the fantasy of coupling with her himself.

Among these writers, then, of the generation after Shaftesbury, the civic discourse appears to have found a way of embracing exactly what it was developed to denounce. The sexuality which is constituted in that discourse, and repressed at the public level of content, of narrative, returns at the private level of aesthetic form and of aesthetic response.

It is because, I have suggested, the aesthetic discourse is understood as situated within a private sphere, that it is available to be appropriated by the sexuality that speaks through it. And the return of sexuality is enthusiastically welcomed, in a private celebration of sexual licence, the prior and necessary condition of which is a public renunciation of sexuality. The prestige of a male ruling-class, it is claimed by the civic discourse on the fine arts, has to be earned by that act of renunciation; but the prestige of the middle-class critic and connoisseur comes to be earned in a more complicated fashion. It is won by a public *display* of renunciation, which by granting a legitimacy to an interest in the aesthetic, gives a license to exactly what it appears to have renounced.[23]

5

Visualising the Division of Labour:

William Pyne's *Microcosm*

I

Since the late eighteenth century the idea of the division of labour has been a crucial tool in the attempt to isolate and define a notion of cultural modernity; but it has always been a double-edged tool. We are most familiar nowadays with the idea as it was used by Marx, and so with the notion that the narrative it recounts is a bad narrative – a story of alienation, from the unity of the productive process, from the social totality, from the self. But in the late eighteenth century, the idea of the division of labour functioned as a fully articulated discourse, offering a comprehensive account of human history, which could be appealed to by aestheticians, linguists, literary critics and speculative historians. It was predominantly associated, however, with the institution of political economy: with the celebration of economic expansion and industrial improvement, and with the attempt to vindicate the structure of modern commercial societies as, precisely, a structure, as something which, despite its arguably chaotic appearance, was available to be known, to be comprehended. And for political economists, of course, it was a discourse which had, for the most part, a good story to tell. It posited a primal, pre-social moment of undifferentiated occupational unity, when each person performed all the tasks necessary to his or her survival. The coming together of men and women in communities, however, enabled and produced a differentiation of occupations. As population increases and communities become larger, an ever-greater degree of occupational specialisation

This essay was originally written as a paper to be delivered at the conference 'Materialism and Criticism' at the University of Colorado at Denver, March–April 1988. This version of the essay was produced for inclusion in a volume of the proceedings of that conference which is yet to appear. A rather different version of the essay, delivered at the annual conference of the Social History Society at York in January 1988 was published in Arthur Marwick (ed.), *The Arts, Literature, and Society*, London (Routledge) 1990.

is required and encouraged, and the products, whether of manual or of intellectual labour, become increasingly refined by being the products of progressively more specialised labour.[1]

As elaborated in writings on economics, the discourse of the division of labour acknowledges that specialisation can be understood as a threat to social cohesion, for diverse occupations can also be seen as competing interests – to put it briefly, it is in the interests of each occupational group to sell its own product as dear as possible, and to acquire the products of other groups as cheaply as possible. The field of intellectual production is also acknowledged to be an arena of specialisation and conflict, in which the various discourses of a culture can be understood as so many 'faculty languages', or occupational idiolects, which severally attempt to interpret the world in terms of the different occupational interests they represent and articulate. But whereas, in other fields of enquiry, the discourse of the division of labour could be used to suggest that this atomisation of occupations, interests and discourses might lead in time to the corruption of the body politic, in political economy it enabled a new conception of social cohesion, as something which is itself predicated upon occupational division. When each of us produces only one thing, or has only one service to offer, we are obliged to depend on each other for every other service and product that we need. Those apparently in competition with each other are in fact dependent on each other; apparent economic conflict is the basis of actual social coherence. This mutual interdependence, by which 'the structure of the body politic', as the statistician Patrick Colquhoun described it, comes to be defined in economic terms, in terms of the structure of employment, and of the market, thus becomes a guarantee of the unity, and so of the health of society, and not a symptom of its corruption (Colquhoun ix).

The problem in this account, however, was that of defining the place from which that social coherence could be perceived, for the discourse of the division of labour seemed to deny the very possibility of the social knowledge it sought to invent. It represented every individual within a modern, commercial society, as performing a specialised task, and so it represented every subject-position as partial, as defined and constrained by the specialisation necessary to compete successfully in the market. What people could know was no more than a function of what they did: in Adam Smith's famous example, the philosopher and the street-porter were both creatures defined by the propensity to truck and barter, and the relations between them were governed by an unspoken agreement – the porter would carry the philosopher's burdens on his back, if the philosopher spared the porter the burden of philosophising. The porter's knowledge of the world was no more than the knowledge of what was good for porters; and all the philosopher knew, was what was it was in the interests of philosophy to call knowledge. Everyone, therefore, has an occupational interest which must occlude the perception of occupational difference in the recuperated form of social coherence: that, after all, is why the mechanism that ensures that everyone, in acting for themselves, acts also for the common good, was described by Smith as an 'invisible hand' (Smith 1976a 1: 28–9, 456).

In short, the very invention of this account of social organisation and social knowledge required also the invention of a knowing subject who, within the terms of the discourse, could not conceivably exist within any developed, commercial society. This problem is sometimes managed by delegating the task of comprehension to an abstract viewing-position, borrowed from the discourses of natural science, 'the philosophic eye'. It would probably take, we might reflect, such a disembodied observer to see an invisible hand at work; and the phrase has the additional advantage of maintaining the pretence that the discourse is articulated by no one in particular, that it represents no interest, that it is not, finally, a discourse at all.

But the problem is more usually managed by making a simple division, which is never clearly articulated, between manual labour and intellectual labour, and thus between those whose labour is visible, who can be seen to do things, and those whose function Smith describes as 'not to do any thing, but to observe every thing' (1976a 1: 21). By this distinction, the diversity of manual labour is used as a synecdoche to represent all forms of doing, all occupational diversity. Society becomes divided between the observers and the observed, and the occupational identities of the observers are ignored. In his early draft of *The Wealth of Nations*, Smith had written that

> Philosophy or speculation, . . . naturally becomes, like every other employment, the sole occupation of a particular class of citizens. Like every trade it is subdivided into many different branches, and we have mechanical, chymical, astronomical, physical, metaphysical, moral, political, commercial, and critical philosophers.
>
> (Smith 1978 570)

In the published version, this passage is considerably revised: the varieties of philosophy are no longer listed, and 'trade' is replaced by 'employment', with the effect that philosophy becomes less plural, and less directly comparable with manual trades (Smith 1776a 1: 21–2). More generally in the *Wealth of Nations*, though the philosopher is formally acknowledged, in the opening chapters, as a specialist participating in the market economy, he is quickly accredited with an impartiality, an integral subjectivity (manifested in the pronoun 'we'), and a disinterestedness, which enable him to perceive the real history of society as the real and unchanging coherence of continuously subdivided activities and interests; and he is imagined as articulating that perception in terms which, because they cannot be identified as the terms of any specific occupation, elude the constraints of specific discourses as entirely as they elude determination by an economy of exchange. Knowledge becomes a disinterested knowledge of what the public is, and of what is good for the public, and it becomes the property of a particular *social*, and not simply of a particular occupational, class. Ignorance too becomes the property of a particular class, the class which is the object of knowledge, and so the object of the discourse.

II

I want to look further at the problem of authority in the discourse of the division of labour, by offering a reading of an early nineteenth-century text, the *Microcosm*, a text which consists mainly of hundreds of vignettes of figures engaged in agriculture and in manufacturing and distributive trades. These vignettes were drawn and etched by the watercolourist W.H. Pyne and aquatinted by John Hill; an introduction, and what the title-page calls 'explanations of the plates', in the form of brief prose essays, were provided by someone called C. Gray. The first complete edition of the *Microcosm* was published in two volumes in 1806 and 1808; the plates had earlier begun to be issued in monthly parts, in 1803.

The text has an alternative title which gives a fuller account of what its authors supposed to be their intentions: *A Picturesque Delineation of the Arts, Agriculture, Manufactures, &c. of Great Britain, in a Series of above a Thousand Groups of Small Figures for the Embellishment of Landscape*, and so on. These alternative titles disclose that the book has two separate objects, which the introduction to the first volume tries to represent as easily compatible. The *Microcosm*, it claims,

> presents the student and the amateur with picturesque represen-
> tations of the scenery of active life in Great Britain. And, by means
> of this, it, at the same time, places before them actual delineations
> of the various sorts of instruments and machines used by her in
> agriculture, in manufacture, trade, and amusement.[2]

Now evidently what is imagined to be at stake in this 'double object' is an opposition between 'picturesque representations' and 'actual delineations', where the actual is conceived of as extra-textual, a real which can be directly reproduced by one kind of drawing but not by another. But as we shall see, the competition between the two is played out as a competition between discourses inside the text itself, discourses which must, I want to suggest, be incompatible.

One of these discourses is that of the division of labour itself; and its presence within the introduction is signalled by the claim that the *Microcosm* will represent the *variety* of occupations which together compose the economic structure of Britain. Thus the *Microcosm*, the introduction argues,

> is devoted to the domestic, rural, and commercial scenery of Great Britain, and may be considered as a monument, in the rustic style, raised to her glory. While it assists the students of both sexes in drawing, and teaches them to look at nature with their own eyes, it sets before them, in pleasing points of view, the various modes in which her capital is invested, and by which her industry is employed: in short, the various ways by which she has risen to her present high situation, as one of the first among nations.

This acknowledgement of the variety, of occupations, of labour, of employment, in a modern commercial society, is a defining feature of the discourse of the division of labour. But the acknowledgement is always predicated on the ability of the discourse to produce some general truth about that variety, such as will describe its *unity*, when it is examined by the eye of the economic philosopher. Thus Smith, for example, after examining 'all the variety of labour' that goes into the production of a labourer's tools and woollen coat, continues:

> Were we to examine, in the same manner, all the different parts of his dress and household furniture, the coarse linen shirt which he wears next his skin, the shoes which cover his feet, the bed he lies on, and all the different parts which compose it, the kitchen-grate at which he prepares his victuals, the coals which he makes use of for that purpose, dug from the bowels of the earth, and brought to him perhaps by a long sea and a long land carriage, all the other utensils of his kitchen, all the furniture of his table, the knives and forks, the earthen or pewter plates upon which he serves up and divides his victuals, the different hands employed in preparing his bread and his beer, the glass window, which lets in the heat and the light, and keeps out the wind and the rain, with all the knowledge and art requisite for preparing that beautiful and happy invention, without which these northern parts of the world would scarce have afforded a very comfortable habitation, together with the tools of all the different workmen employed in producing these

different conveniences; if we examine, I say, all these things, and
consider what a variety of labour is employed about each of them,
we shall be sensible that without the assistance and co-operation
of many thousands, the very meanest person in a civilized country
could not be provided, even according to, what we very falsely
imagine, the easy and simple manner in which he is commonly
accommodated.   (Smith 1976a 1: 23)

The strategy and structure of this extraordinary sentence (which are
closely matched in some sentences by Mandeville (359–60) on the same
topic of the 'variety' of employment) have the effect of instantiating
precisely the transcendent form of knowledge which is taken to
characterise the subject of the discourse of the division of labour. It
begins with a proliferation of examples of the 'variety of labour', and
the sheer number of these examples, the random order in which they
are mentioned, the listing of general categories and particular objects
confusedly together ('the furniture of his table', the knives, forks, and
plates), the multiplication of binary terms (sea and land, heat and light
and so on), and the tendency of some items to prompt reflections
which delay the conclusion of the list (the glass windows, for example),
have the effect of producing a consciousness which seems to be
constituted by, and dispersed among, the numberless consumable
articles that demand attention in a modern commercial society. The
next sentence will contrast the vast number of such articles available
to the European labourer with the frugal accommodation of 'the African
king'.

   But the conditional form of the sentence is available to rescue this
dispersed consciousness, and acts (so long as we do not lose sight of
it) as a promise, whose fulfilment becomes the more urgent the more
it is deferred, that order will finally emerge, and that some general
truth will be produced from all these confusing particulars. The
conditional form is eventually reactivated, at 'if we examine, I say',
announcing the imminent fulfilment of the syntactical contract; more
to the point, the parenthetic 'I say' (Mandeville uses precisely the
same expression, at precisely the same rhetorical moment in a similar
sentence[3]), can be read as a guarantee – a claim at least – that
one consciousness, the philosopher's, has never been bewildered:
throughout this long recital, he has had his eye on the enunciation of
a general truth, though the reader may have been blind to it, and a
transcendent truth, because it will be produced by a transcendent
subject.

   The acknowledgement of *variety*, in occupations and employments,
is therefore always predicated, in the optimistic version of the discourse
of the division of labour, on the possession of a position of knowledge

beyond discourse, beyond occupation and interest; and so on the possession of a knowledge of the effective *unity* of apparently divided labours (the 'co-operation of many thousands'). It is this which enables the concern for variety in the first place, and it is this which accounts for and justifies the concern of the *Microcosm* to represent the various modes in which capital is invested and labour is employed, and 'the various sorts of instruments and machines' used in British agriculture, manufacture, and trade.

In offering to present an image of the unity of apparently divided labour, the *Microcosm* does not offer its reader an ascent to the elevated viewing-position from which the knowledge of that unity is originated. Its pedagogic address to 'young people' offers that vision of unity in the more restricted, the more marketable and the more easily consumable form of 'useful knowledge' – as a 'useful knowledge', for example, 'of the practical part of various arts and manufactures'. The educational movement of which this phrase was the watchword sought to represent as true knowledge only what it was 'useful' to know, and its notion of usefulness was tailored to fit a subject more easily identifiable as an intelligent artisan or mechanic than as a member of the polite, more liberally educated classes (see Hans 152–60; Hudson 29–35; Kelly 78–9). This subject was imagined to be impatient with all knowledge which was not empirically derived, and which had no practical application; and it is to young people destined to become just such subjects, to whom the useful and the practical were one and the same, that the introduction addresses itself.[4]

It was as a branch of 'useful knowledge' that the teaching of political economy was legitimated in the early nineteenth century, for example in Bentham's plans for chrestomathic education, and in the Mechanics' Institutes (see J. Harrison 79–84); and it was their occupational identity as mechanics, of course, which meant that those who attended such institutes could be thought of as acquiring only the conclusions which political economy arrived at, and not the principles by which those conclusions had been reached. I take it that the *Microcosm* is offering a knowledge of the 'variety of labour' on the same terms. It is predicated on the assumption that the knowledge necessary to produce the book, and the knowledge it seeks to impart, are very different: the authors are able to *initiate* a knowledge of how the body politic is organised; the young people who read it, will be able to do no more than *recognise* that organisation when it is presented to them, and to understand, perhaps, where they belong within it. Thus 'useful knowledge', when it takes in political economy and the division of labour, becomes a hybrid or transitional form of knowledge - neither one of the variety of functions to be observed, nor at the point where observation originates.

III

But the *Microcosm*, as we have seen, has a 'double object': it seeks
also to offer 'picturesque representations' – it wishes to please as well
as to instruct, and it is looking for a market among those whose
interest is in art as a polite accomplishment, as well as among those
concerned to acquire 'useful knowledge', or concerned that their
children should acquire it. And in order to describe this second aim,
the introduction engages a discourse which, like that of the division
of labour, had come to be fully articulated only in the final decades
of the eighteenth century. This discourse of the Picturesque, as
originally developed by William Gilpin, and subsequently by Richard
Payne Knight and Uvedale Price, can be understood as giving definition
to the aesthetic concerns of the connoisseur and the amateur,
gentleman-artist. In doing so, it represents itself as thoroughly hostile
to the values inscribed within political economy; but, except in the
later writings of Knight (see Funnell 82–92), it seeks also to privilege
the concerns of the gentleman-amateur over those of the professional
artist, especially the professional artist in landscape and *genre* (I use
the word 'professional' to mean simply the opposite of amateur, rather
than to describe artists who thought of themselves as engaged in a
learned profession, as opposed to a manual trade). For the discourse
of the Picturesque reinscribed the traditional distinction between the
intellectual and the mechanical aspects of painting, in terms which
suggested that modern painters, if left to themselves, and unguided
by the gentleman connoisseur, would become preoccupied with matters
of execution at the expense of a concern for correctness of taste.

A sign of these distinctions, between gentleman and economist and
between amateur and professional, is the concern everywhere evinced
within the discourse of the Picturesque with the visible appearances
of objects, to the entire exclusion of a consideration of their use or
function. This concern is often expressed in connection with a disdain
for manual labour: the discourse represents itself as capable of being
articulated only by a subject who is sufficiently remote from the need
to regard the material base of economic life to be able still to consider
an interest in the useful as a mean interest, as an interest in the
mechanic at the expense of the liberal arts. Here for example is Gilpin,
on the objects worthy to be represented in a picturesque landscape.
'We hardly admit the cottage, and as to the appendages of husbandry,
and every idea of cultivation, we wish them totally to disappear'.[5] Or
here he is again, on the 'vulgarity of . . . employment' which, he says,
'the picturesque eye, in quest of scenes of grandeur, and beauty, looks
at with disgust' (Gilpin 1792 2: 44–5).[6] And here he announces a
primitive version of the Group Areas Act: 'in grand scenes, even the

peasant cannot be admitted, if he be employed in the low occupations of his profession: the spade, the scythe, and the rake are all excluded' (Gilpin 1792 2: 43–4). And here, finally, he is more generous, acknowledging what was implicit in the previous quotation, and allowing the peasant entrance into picturesque scenery, if he leaves his tools behind:

> In a moral view, the industrious mechanic is a more pleasing object, than the loitering peasant. But in a picturesque light, it is otherwise. The arts of industry are rejected; and even idleness, if I may so speak, adds dignity to a character. Thus the lazy cowherd resting on his pole; or the peasant lolling on a rock, may be allowed in the grandest scenes; while the laborious mechanic, with his implements of labour, would be repulsed.   (Gilpin 1792 2: 44)

The object of the Picturesque, in that last quotation, is represented as being seen 'in a picturesque light', rather than in a 'moral' light; and in the same way the subject of the discourse is sometimes identified as the 'eye of taste', or the 'picturesque' eye. The phrase has the effect of acknowledging that this subject is a partial subject only, one among the various discursive identities available to the inhabitants of the polite world – an acknowledgement essential to the legitimation of the discourse, precisely because, especially in its lofty disdain for manual labour, for industriousness, it defines itself in contradistinction from the moral as well as from the economic.

The fact, however, that this disdain for labour can also be read as the gentlemanly disdain of the amateur, enables the Picturesque to lay claim to that transcendent viewing-position which had through the eighteenth century been regarded as the perquisite of the gentleman; a transcendence (as I have argued elsewhere; see Barrell 1983 'Introduction') similar to that claimed by the political economist in that it represents itself as disinterested, but distinct from it also, in that it is characterised by a tendency to overlook, rather than to comprehend, the details of trades and occupational identities. In an essay on his own sketches, for example, Gilpin had described a picture of the Colosseum, 'adorned with a woman hanging linen to dry under its walls. Contrasts of this kind,' he commented,

> may suit the moralist, the historian, or the poet, who may take occasion to descant on the instability of human affairs. But the *eye*, which has nothing to do with *moral sentiments*, and is conversant only with *picturesque forms*, is disgusted by such unnatural union.
> (Gilpin 1808 165)

Gilpin represents the Picturesque here as if it were a *faculty*, of pure unmediated vision: it is the 'eye', unqualified by any adjective, disjoined from any specific occupational and discursive identity, entirely disinterested. He considers three occupational identities, moralist, historian, and poet, and the vision of each of them is shown to be mediated by their specific interests, with the result that each is imagined to approve of a picture which, for Gilpin, depicts an 'unnatural' union of forms and sentiments. As opposed to these, the 'eye' – not even, now, the 'picturesque' eye, or the 'eye of taste' – is pleased only by what is *natural*: the natural is located in picturesque forms devoid of ethical, political, or sentimental meanings. If they are not devoid of such meanings, he argues, they are 'disgusting' – they appeal only to a partial, or to a perverted, taste.

That this claim to a transcendent vision could serve to distinguish the amateur student of picturesque forms from the professional artist in landscape and *genre* will be clear enough, if we consider the rural subject-pictures produced in the 1790s by such artists as George Morland, James Ward and Francis Wheatley, which are everywhere concerned with just such meanings as Gilpin rejects. But if we consider the art of painting in terms of its institutional history in the late eighteenth and early nineteenth centuries, it will be apparent that artists who painted for a living found no great difficulty in accommodating, within their own self-image, the opinions of the gentleman-connoisseur on matters of taste, however much they resented the claim of the connoisseurs to dictate to them on such matters (see Owen and Brown, chapters 9 and 10). For the master-narrative of that institutional history is the continual concern to represent painting as, precisely, a profession, a liberal profession, and not a mechanical or a manual trade, and thus to claim for the painter at least as much gentlemanly status as the practitioners of other professions laid claim to. The disdain for mere execution, for the manual aspects of painting, expressed by the picturesque connoisseur, could certainly be understood as a negation of this claim; but it could be used, also, to validate it. For to establish painting as a liberal profession, it was not sufficient simply to establish visible institutions, such as the Royal Academy, and to substitute professional training in the place of apprenticeships. It was also necessary to appropriate such discourses as presupposed a liberal, a gentlemanly subject to articulate them.

Painters of history were justified, by the long tradition of amateur criticism, to mobilise a version of the discourse of civic humanism to represent their aims and status (see 221, n.1). There was also a tradition of heroic landscape-painting in oils, continued in the nineteenth-century especially by Turner, which could arguably be defined and defended in civic terms. Essential to the civic theory of painting was the claim that the painter of heroic subjects, at least, was an inventor and not a mere maker of objects, and thus the practitioner of a liberal art. But this discourse was not easily available to painters in the lower genres of landscape and *genre*, unable to depict heroic actions or the ideal forms of humanity; and it was especially unavailable to artists in watercolour (Pyne himself was primarily an artist in watercolour, and was to become an active propagandist of the medium).[7] The restricted size of landscapes in watercolour, and the traditional use of the medium to produce images for the purpose of conveying factual information rather than moral instruction, required that the professional aspirations of landscape artists in watercolour should be defined in other terms. What was taken to characterise the art of watercolour, especially in the newly popular technique of painting in watercolour, as opposed to colouring in or washing over a previously drawn image, was the spontaneous facility necessary to a medium in which mistakes could not easily be corrected. For artists in watercolour, therefore, the disdain for labour and the concern for pure aesthetic values of the Picturesque were a valuable resource, in the early decades of the nineteenth century, in the representation of their professional and gentlemanly aspirations.

It was doubly necessary to represent painting in watercolour as a liberal, a polite activity, for what was at stake was not simply the status of the artist as practitioner, but the economic viability of watercolour-painting as an occupation. Professional artists in watercolour made their livings not simply by selling their works; equally, if not more important to most of them, were the fees they received for teaching their art, and this required them to represent it as an accomplishment suitable to the sons and daughters of the politer part of the middle class, or of those aspiring to politeness (see Clarke, chapter 5); and for this purpose too the discourse of the Picturesque, with its connotations of amateur status and gentility, could be a valuable resource. It became, therefore, the primary discourse employed in the numerous instructional manuals produced by watercolour artists in the early decades of the nineteenth century (Clarke, chapter 5), and the *Microcosm*, as its full title indicates, offers itself as just such a manual. The offer is repeated in the claim that the book 'presents the student and the amateur with picturesque representations'. The 'amateur' is the polite connoisseur of the Picturesque; and the 'student', I take it, is not here conceived of as one studying to enter the profession: the students of art referred to later in the introduction may be 'of both sexes' (this at a time when women were excluded from an institutional education in the fine arts), and are apparently studying art as an accomplishment and a pastime.

It is this pedagogic concern which announces that the discourse of the Picturesque is articulated, in the *Microcosm*, not by an amateur such as Gilpin, but by a polite professional, such as Pyne wishes to be considered. And in the terms of the discourse of the division of labour, the appropriation of the Picturesque by such men as Pyne must identify the Picturesque as a discourse which has forfeited its claim to be a disinterested, transcendent form of knowledge. It has come to be used to market a specific service, to define a specific interest, and to claim a specific status for the practitioners of a particular occupation.

On the one hand, then, the *Microcosm* intends to represent the 'variety of employment', packaged as useful knowledge, and this intention is announced within the terms of the discourse of the division of labour. On the other, the *Microcosm* offers the pleasures of the picturesque, and that intention is inscribed within the discourse of what, within a commercial publication such as this, must be understood as a specific occupational interest, a defining characteristic of which is a disdain for the 'vulgarity of employment', the very occupations the book is committed to representing. Thus, at a time when the importance of drawing was being increasingly emphasised as a useful part of mechanical education, the *Microcosm* is anxious to stress the accuracy of its illustration; and at a time when drawing was also becoming pre-eminent among the polite accomplishments, it is equally concerned to stress how well it combines the 'agreeable' with the 'useful'.

There is no necessary incompatibility between these two intentions and concerns at the level of social practice: we need not even think of the *Microcosm* as addressing itself to two different markets, for it is not hard to imagine the existence of large numbers of parents among the upwardly mobile or upwardly aspiring middle classes who would have been anxious to encourage their children in both practical and liberal pursuits. Nor, in the first decade of the nineteenth century, was the distinction between technical and what we may call 'aesthetic' drawing as rigid as it soon became. The problem faced by the introduction is a discursive problem: it is a problem of how to describe two social practices which may not have been experienced as incompatible, in the terms of two discourses which are quite evidently so. The problem is to make these two discourses act in concert, and not in conflict and contradiction; and the introduction seeks to manage the problem by treating this discursive opposition as if it can be seen as a matter of due balance between equal concerns, and as if the pleasure offered by the picturesque could be additional to, a supplement to, an 'actual' account of the variety and coherence of economic activities.

It attempts at one point to describe this balance by conceiving of the illustrations themselves as divided into two discursive units, whereby the machines carry the responsibility for the usefulness of the book, and the figures are left free to give pleasure – a resolution hardly compatible with the unwillingness of the Picturesque to represent manual labour. This solution is probably borrowed from the convention established in the late eighteenth century for the illustrative plates of encyclopaedias of arts and sciences, whereby one half of a plate would be devoted to a bustling *atelier*-scene in which a number of artisans pursued their divided labours with the tools and machine-parts delineated in the other half. But the basic strategy of the introduction remains to announce, simply, that the book does *this*, and that it does *this* too; it does so much of the one, and the same amount of the other. It is as if each discourse has a similar kind of status and authority, when what is at stake is precisely the negation, by the division of labour, of any claim that a merely occupational discourse might have to articulate an objective form of social knowledge, and when one defining characteristic of the Picturesque is such as to cast doubt upon the value of the very knowledge that it is the object of the division of labour to impart.

But if the introduction can handle this discursive opposition only by offering to re-cast that opposition as balance, the book itself constructs a set of relations between the discourses of the Picturesque and of the division of labour in which their opposition is apparent if it is not acknowledged, and in which each can be read as attempting to appropriate the other. In the next two sections of this paper, I want to examine how this discursive conflict is played out in the *Microcosm*.

IV

I want to begin by concentrating on one half of the 'double object' of the *Microcosm*, the attempt to represent the various divided labours of commercial Britain, and to grasp that occupational variety in the form of economic and social unity. From the point of view of the discourse of the division of labour, the Picturesque as it has so far been characterised seems to be entirely disabled from assisting in that attempt, by virtue of its reluctance to represent manual labour, and by virtue also of the fact that, in the view of the economic philosopher, it must be identified, by that very reluctance, as an occupational, and so as an interested discourse. The profession of the artist, or more specifically of the landscape and *genre* artist in watercolour, is evidently in these terms one of the divided labours that the philosophic eye must attempt to comprehend in its vision of the social totality, rather than a situation from which a view of that totality can be advanced.

But equally evidently, if the illustrations to the *Microcosm* instantiate a visual discourse of the Picturesque, they must embody a version of that discourse very different from the Picturesque of Gilpin, or of the artist whose claim to be a member of a liberal profession depends upon his lofty disdain for the mechanical. To depict, as this book does, picturesque groups of workers, is one thing; but to depict picturesque groups of workers actually *working*, as well as sitting idly around (see *Woodmen*, (Figure 13), is immediately to compromise that gentlemanly disdain for manual labour, and to that degree also to compromise the occupational specificity of the Picturesque. To the philosophic eye, we could say, picturesque drawing, once it has overcome that disdain, ceases to instantiate a discourse at all, in that it no longer instantiates a claim to define its own proper objects of attention, and its own hierarchy of values, and to generate its own specific kind of social knowledge. In the *Microcosm*, we could say, picturesque drawing has become a victim of the process by which, as social knowledge was increasingly defined in the late eighteenth and early nineteenth centuries as economic knowledge, the arts were increasingly denied a cognitive function. And so it has become, rather, a rhetoric, a style, and one which, I shall suggest, can usefully be appropriated by the discourse of the division of labour to give a visible form to its account of social organisation.

13. W.H. Pyne and John Hill, *Woodmen*, plate 98 of Pyne's *Microcosm*, 1806/1808. Approx. 23 × 29 cm

14. After William Gilpin, *A Few Landscape Groups*, from Gilpin's *Three Essays*, 3rd edition, 1808. 22 × 13.8 cm (page-size)

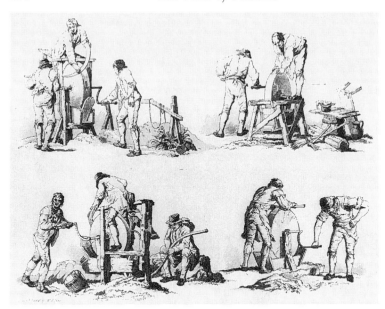

15. W.H. Pyne and John Hill, *Grinders*, plate 14 of Pyne's *Microcosm*, 1806/1808. Approx. 23 × 29 cm

Considered as a style, rather than as the instantiation of a mode of knowledge, there were characteristics of picturesque drawing which made it particularly appropriate to the representation of the unity of a commercial and manufacturing economy. The Picturesque, as I argued earlier, is concerned only with visible appearances, to the exclusion of the moral and the sentimental. The picturesque eye is a Polaroid lens, which eliminates all sentimental and moral reflection. It is thus also absolutely hostile to narrative; and when it depicts figures it attempts to do so in such a way as raises no question about their thoughts or feelings or their interactions with other figures. Picturesque drawing – Figure 14 is an example by Gilpin himself – seeks to represent figures as, precisely, figures, no more than that. It employs, for example, none of the conventional signs, physiognomic or pathognomic, by which, in other contemporary visual discourses, the stereotypes of individuality are encoded. Accordingly, the working figures in the *Microcosm* – Figure 15, *Grinders*, is a case in point – are distinguished by the attitudes they adopt and the movements they perform; by their physical relations to the various objects they work with and work on, by their occupations, rather than by their thoughts or feelings about those occupations. They are what they do: identity becomes largely a matter of what movements they make, and of which implements they apply to which raw materials.

The non-narrative neutrality which characterises picturesque delineations of the human figure is reinforced by a characteristic method of drawing. The picturesque line is often hardly a *line* at all: it is discontinuous, spiky, concerned to represent texture at the expense of outline. Texture is communicated in the *Microcosm* both by Hill's aquatinting, and by Pyne's etched lines, which are broken as if to represent the building-up of an image out of rapid, successive scratches of the pen as it stumbles over the textured surface of hand-made paper. The line seems to call attention to its own discontinuity, and so to the spontaneous movement of the masterly hand which produced it; but the notion of the 'natural' in this sketching from nature represents 'mastery' not in terms of the individuality of the artist's manner, but of the 'accuracy' with which it registers the visual appearances of objects supposed to be humble and informal. It is expressive of a neutrality, not an idiosyncrasy of vision; it instantiates a conception of 'accuracy' which governs indifferently the representation of both people and things, in such a way as assimilates each to the other by suggesting that both are capable of being observed with the same kind of neutral aesthetic attention. The neutrality of picturesque vision can thus be read as the sign of a disinterested, not a partial observation. In short, the picturesque as style, applied to the representation of manual labour, becomes an ideal visual vehicle for the representation of an account of the various occupations by which the British economy is constituted, one which can reinforce the claim that the knowledge and understanding of that variety proceeds from no occupational interest or identity at all.

Each plate in the *Microcosm* consists of two or three, but more usually four or more small vignettes of individual figures, groups of figures or, occasionally, implements of trade. For the most part each plate is devoted to a particular mechanical trade or occupation. And in each plate, there is evidence of Pyne's concern to pattern the various individual vignettes into a well-designed page. When two groups are illustrated on the same horizontal axis, they will be carefully balanced or contrasted, as in Figures 16 and 17, *Market-Groups* and *Dairy*. Where the page is arranged vertically, as in Figure 18, *Sheepshearing*, it is usually organised into three tiers, with the largest vignettes at the bottom and the smallest at the top; sometimes a vignette may artfully invade the space of the tier above it, as in the same plate of sheep-shearing.

More or less the same principles of organisation inform the plates which are arranged horizontally, except that a good number of these are divided into four vignettes of about equal size, the composition of one answering that of the other on the same tier, as in Figures 19 and 15, *Mills* and *Grinders*. This careful patterning of separate vignettes on the same page clearly announces the genre Pyne thought of himself

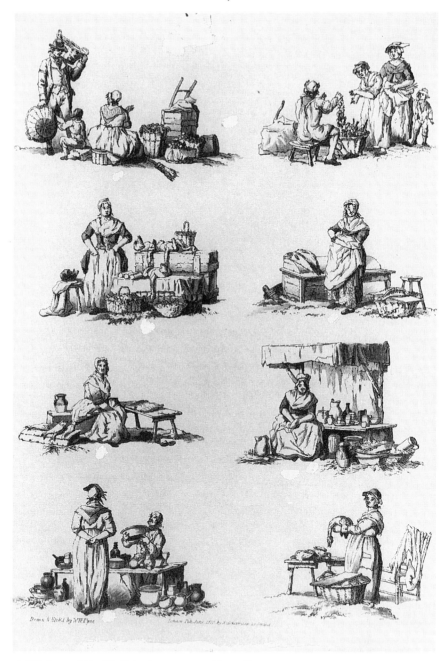

16. W.H. Pyne and John Hill, *Market Groups*, plate 71 of Pyne's *Microcosm*, 1806/1808. Approx. 23 × 29 cm

17. W.H. Pyne and John Hill, *Dairy*, plate 51 of Pyne's *Microcosm*, 1806/1808. Approx. 23 × 29 cm

18. W.H. Pyne and John Hill, *Sheep-Shearing &c*, plate 45 of Pyne's *Microcosm*, 1806/1808. Approx. 23 × 29 cm

19. W.H. Pyne and John Hill, *Mills*, plate 65 of Pyne's *Microcosm*, 1806/1808. Approx. 23 × 29 cm

as working within. In the 1790s George Morland in particular, but other artists as well, had taken to publishing volumes of etchings which purported to be of reproductions of their private notebooks or sketchbooks. These volumes sometimes devote a single sheet to the reproduction of a single finished drawing, but as often a number of separate studies are grouped together on the same plate, with a careful attention to the balance of each composite sheet – though never, so far as I have observed, with quite as meticulous an attention as Pyne's.[8] This style of presentation, which became very common in nineteenth-century drawing manuals (see Spelman, no date, and Bicknell and Munro 1987), seems to have been governed by a specific aesthetic. Ten of Morland's published sketchbooks have the title *Sketches from Nature*, just as Pyne's vignettes are said on his title-page to be 'accurately drawn from nature'. The notion involved here is that sketches and drawings from nature are, precisely, accurate, because, unlike finished oil-paintings, they instantiate, once again, a vision unmediated by fancy or sentiment.

But this specifically picturesque concern with the patterning of vignettes is useful to the aim of the *Microcosm* for more reasons than the fact that the vignette-sketch can be taken to represent a vision of objects disjoined from narrative, or from a concern with anything other than supposedly neutral visual appearances. For the patterned page, when it no longer depicts, as in Morland's sketch books, a random collocation of figures and objects, but a deliberate sequence of actions, could of course also be used to propose a new form of narrative structure, different from the sentimental narratives that inform contemporary rustic *genre*-painting, and of particular use to the representation of the *division* of labour, when the point of doing so is to make a claim for the *coherence* of divided labour, or for the ability to understand it *as* coherent. Each vignette can be used to represent the various stages of a divided productive process. In the depiction of this process, the separate figures and groups may appear as preoccupied with their own particular tasks, and so as unaware of themselves as participating in this new form of narrative; and in this light, the *Microcosm* can be seen as a depiction of a fiction of alienated labour, labour in which the other various stages of production are conceived of as incomprehensible to those whose task is confined to just one of those stages.

The contrast with the bustling *atelier*-scenes of collective work in the plates of late eighteenth-century encyclopaedias could hardly be more marked. That contrast is to be understood in discursive rather than in material terms. It is not that the work of artisans is being differently performed in 1800; it is being conceived differently, by those who do not perform it, as a collection of individual and separate operations.[9] By conceiving of manual and artisanal labour in this way, those who do not perform it – the readers of the *Microcosm* – can establish their superiority over, and distance from, those who do, by the claim that they (and only they; that is the fiction) can construct the narrative that links each operation to the others.

That task is made easier in the *Microcosm* by the prose essays that accompany the plates (for the sequence of actions the plates illustrate cannot always be read from left to right and top to bottom – Figure 20, of potters and leather-dressers, is a case in point). The meticulous patterning of the plates positively invites us to understand these different stages of production as together composing not just a coherent story, with a beginning, a middle and an end, but a unity. To understand *how* the different stages of a productive process cohere into unity, it seems, what is necessary is to take up a position outside that process – it is from there that its unity can be observed, from the place, so to speak, of the philosophic eye; and of the picturesque eye too, now that the Picturesque has been reduced to a style, and employed in the attempt to give a visible shape to the otherwise invisible structure of the division of labour.

V

So much, then, by way of justifying my contention that in the *Microcosm* the discursive conflict I identified results in an appropriation of the Picturesque by the discourse of the division of labour: an appropriation, I have argued, which has the effect of divesting the Picturesque of its character as an occupational idiolect, the discursive articulation of an occupational interest. I want now to represent another result of that conflict, in which the Picturesque, instead, can be understood as resisting the totalising and appropriating efforts of the discourse of the division of labour, and as advancing its own competing version of social knowledge.

The point can be made by examining what occupations the *Microcosm* does and does not illustrate. In 1815, Patrick Colquhoun published a table which attempted to 'ESTIMATE THE NEW PROPERTY ARISING ANNUALLY IN GREAT BRITAIN AND IRELAND, Arising from the Use of Capital combined with Human Labour and Machinery . . . as derived from *Agriculture, Mines and Minerals, Manufactures, Inland Trade, Foreign Commerce and Shipping, Coasting Trade Fisheries, and Foreign Income* in his *A Treatise on the Wealth, Power, and Resources of the British Empire* (Colquhoun: 89–96). Colquhoun's estimates are for the year 1812, a few years after the publication of the collected edition of the *Microcosm*. His text is probably the most comprehensive attempt, contemporary with the *Microcosm*, to understand the economic structure of Britain in terms of the discourse of the division of labour. When I tried to divide the occupations illustrated by Pyne into Colquhoun's categories, I was struck by two things in particular. To begin with, I had somehow gained the impression that a far greater proportion of plates than was in fact the case were devoted to representations of agricultural employments. I had assumed, that is, and wrongly, that the claim made by the Picturesque, to a special privileged perception of 'the natural', and the stated object on the title-page, that the vignettes would be used for the embellishment of landscape, would have tended to privilege agricultural over manufacturing employments as suitable subjects for representation. The hostility of the Picturesque to images of manufacturing industry is far greater than its hostility to images of industrious agricultural workers,[10] as Gilpin's distinction between the 'laborious mechanic' and the 'loitering peasant' has already suggested to us, for his implication is that we associate the mechanic with industry, but that we can more easily associate the peasant with a sauntering disinclination to labour. But in fact, only about 19 of Pyne's plates represent agricultural employments, while some 29 depict what Colquhoun classified as manufactures, and some 22 depict subjects of inland distributive trades. Another three illustrate

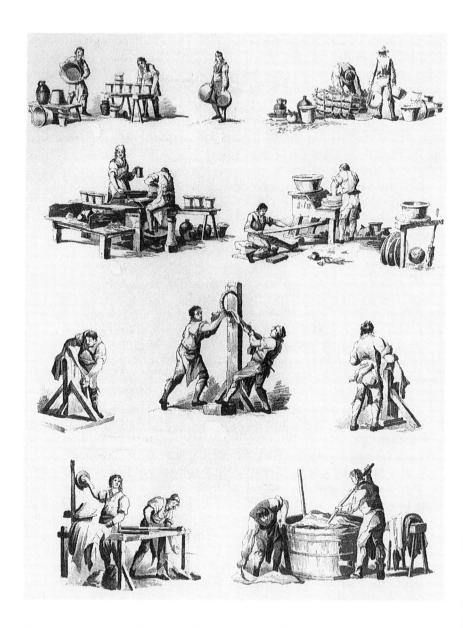

20. W.H. Pyne and John Hill, *Pottery* and *Leather-Dressing*, plate 10 of Pyne's *Microcosm*, 1806/1808. Approx. 23 × 29 cm

trades associated with mines and minerals, and about four each represent coastal trade and fisheries – the figures are approximate because not all the plates can be easily classified.

Secondly, however, I was struck by the fact that of what were, according to Colquhoun, by some way the four most productive manufacturing industries, Pyne chooses to illustrate only the leather industry, which appears in two plates. Thus apart from one plate of sheep-shearing, the *Microcosm* makes no acknowledgement at all of the textile trades in Britain and Ireland, cotton, woollen and linen manufactures, to the increasing mechanisation of which Colquhoun among others attributed Britain's economic miracle (Colquhoun 68). Of exportable manufactures, 'by far the most extensive', according to Colquhoun, were '*cotton, woollen, leather, linen, fabricated metals, glass,* and *porcelain*', in which he includes all ceramic manufactures (Colquhoun 68). Of these seven, Pyne illustrates only three; and of the sixteen most productive manufacturing industries, according to Colquhoun's estimates, only eight are depicted by Pyne.

These two things are of course related. At the point at which woollen and linen production become manufacturing industries, they move, for the most part, indoors, and are lost to the landscape and the rustic *genre* artist. My impression that there was a bias towards images of agricultural employments was the result not only of the bias of my own interest in landscape, but of the fact that, of Pyne's 121 plates, only about ten or eleven illustrate occupations that are carried on wholly or partly indoors.[11] Three of these are plates of cottage interiors and domestic work, a favourite theme of rural subject-painters, and in the case of none of the others is the interior location suggested except by the absence of the usual landscape motifs. What purports, then, to be a 'microcosm', a comprehensive and a disinterested delineation of the 'various modes' in which Britain's 'capital is invested', and 'her industry is employed', turns out to be a thoroughly partial view from the vantage-point of a particular occupation, that of the artist in landscape and *genre*.

Thus employments are divided and distinguished by Pyne according to the different possibilities they offer for the embellishment of landscape, and the potential of figures to embellish is so much more important a qualification for their inclusion in the *Microcosm* than their ability to contribute to Britain's wealth, that in disregard of his own stated purposes, and in deference to an imperative enunciated by Gilpin, Pyne devotes a number of plates to labour conceived of as so unproductive that it is not recognised as labour at all. In his poem 'On Landscape Painting', Gilpin had advised the artist not only to exclude, as usual, the 'low arts of husbandry' from 'rocky', 'wild', and 'awful' scenes, but to invite in their place 'gypsey-tribes' and 'banditti fierce', who would be as appropriately 'wild as those scenes themselves' (Gilpin 1808: 165). And accordingly, Pyne introduces two plates of gipsies, who, for all their 'sloth and idleness', as Gray describes it, 'certainly afford us some very picturesque groups' (Pyne 1806: 17).[12] There is a further plate devoted to smugglers, partly on the grounds that 'the scenery . . . in which they are generally found, has much of the grand and the wild', and partly because they can stand as home-grown substitutes for the 'banditti' who provide the conventional *staffage* of landscape-painting in the style of Salvator Rosa (Pyne 1808 25).

But in case there are some for whom only the real thing will do, Pyne also provides (Figure 21) four vignettes of banditti in the genuine Calabrian style, wearing armour, lounging on rocks and under trees, and contributing only in the most unimaginably indirect way to the economic progress of Britain. By plates like these, but also by the nearly exclusive concentration on outdoor employments, social knowledge is defined as knowledge useful to the landscape artist. And in this connection, it is worth noticing that when the book was republished in 1845, by which time a clearer division had been produced between technical and decorative drawing, its title was changed. 'Microcosm' was dropped, the main title became *Picturesque Groups for the Embellishment of Landscape*, and reference to whatever useful application the book still aspired to was relegated to the small print of the title-page.

In this process of resistance to the totalising aspirations of the discourse of the division of labour, that discourse is itself revealed as an occupational, an interested discourse, with its own specialised account of what knowledge is. For the whole point is that gipsies, smugglers, banditti (or armed robbers, for that is how they are treated in the accompanying prose-essay) were indeed *participants* in the economic structure of early nineteenth-century Britain. They performed a variety of labour, which was, however, ignored in accounts of the division of labour, not because it was illegal, but because it was invisible to the philosophic eye. And it was so, because economic philosophy conceived of society as structured like a market, in which each person exchanged the goods and services they had to offer, for the goods and services they needed or desired. Gipsies, who were almost universally regarded as thieves, robbers, and smugglers, were all excluded from the visible market; the goods they had to exchange had not been acquired by anything that a political economist could understand as labour, or could recognise as an act of exchange.

The absence of such occupations from the economic and social totality envisaged by the discourse of the division of labour reveals, as I say, that this discourse offers a restricted and an interested account

21. W.H. Pyne and John Hill, *Banditti*, plate 60 of Pyne's *Microcosm*, 1806/1808. Approx. 23 × 29 cm

of what social knowledge is. It could be argued that the presence of such occupations in the *Microcosm* and the absence of images of large-scale manufacturing industry, reveals the occupational bias of the Picturesque. But it could equally be argued that the Picturesque, by virtue of its ability to notice and to represent the activities of criminals and of others who are invisible within the commercial market, and by virtue too of its ability to represent leisure as well as industry – the *Microcosm* includes plates of archery, cricket, hunting, skittles and so on – produces an account of the variety of social activities no less expansive, though certainly less methodised, than that revealed to the economic philosopher.

I have not been able to compress my account of the plates sufficiently to allow me to discuss the accompanying essays at any length, so I can only give the most general idea of what interests me about them. It is, that they seem unable to produce an account of the various occupations they describe which can represent them as other than divided, and as divided beyond the point of being comprehensible in terms of their participation in what might be, however invisibly, a coherent form of social organisation.

We have seen how the possibility of envisaging a coherent society depended, for the discourse of the division of labour, upon the production of a unified and a disinterested subject to articulate that discourse. The visual discourse of the Picturesque, deployed through the plates, could produce the illusion of such a subject, by bestowing the same kind of alienated attention on all the objects illustrated. There is no equivalent coherence in the essays, because there seems to be no similarly coherent discourse available to govern the representation of all the various occupations they describe. Their incoherence arises partly from the fact that many of those occupations present themselves to the writer far more thoroughly inscribed within their own individual discursive histories: the shepherd within the Pastoral, the ploughman within the Georgic, the haymaker within the Comic, the soldier within a language of popular patriotism, and so on. It arises also from that hospitality to discursive variety which characterises the essay-genre in the eighteenth and early nineteenth centuries. Thus some employ-ments are discussed in terms of their history, and some in terms of the supposed moral condition of their practitioners; of others, Gray simply observes that there is nothing much to say about them. Interwoven with all these discourses is the discourse of the division of labour, which attempts to establish a unified subject, with a stable viewing-position and with a coherent grasp of each occupation in particular, and of the structure of the body politic in general. But it is unable ever to silence those other discourses for any length of time, and becomes just one of a hubbub of voices, which together produce the representation of a society irretrievably atomised and dispersed.

VI

In his notes to the contributors to this conference, David Simpson has asked us what 'materialism' can mean for criticism in the humanities. 'What can it most easily explain, and what problems arise?' He has invited us to consider these questions in the context of what he calls 'the intrinsically disintegrated condition of materialist criticism', divided, as he sees it, between one view which announces that 'efforts towards integration are unjustifiably totalitarian'; and another which 'sees in this retreat from totality merely a sophisticated version of the dominant ideology'. My own paper seems probably to belong within the first version of materialism, whose task – to quote from Simpson's notes one last time – 'must . . . consist in the detailed and patient reconstruction of the precise occasions of each item under inspection', what he also describes as 'the specific details of empirical practices'. I am happy enough with that as an account of what my paper has tried to do, but only if that 'reconstruction of precise occasions' is not predicated on the assumption that we can somehow reconstruct a real history from the traces of the past. The past is available to us only in the form of representations, and it was, equally to the point, available to the past only in the same form. To attempt to reconstruct the precise occasions of history is to attempt to reconstruct them in the only form in which they are or were available to be known, as representations articulated within the different discourses which combine and compete to represent the 'real'.

The problems of constructing a totalising materialist account of the history or the culture of a society have been reiterated often enough to require no lengthy rehearsal here. Materialism announces that human subjects are not coherent and independent entities, but are the incoherent products of a history which it defines as a material history. It conceives of subjects as constrained by the discourses they articulate and by the ideology inscribed within those discourses: a totalising account, on the other hand, which makes a claim to be true, to be a quasi-scientific description of what is really the case, must presuppose an integral and a transcendent subject, undetermined by discourse and ideology. And yet if materialism does not attempt to produce such accounts, it deprives itself of the possibility of constructing the narratives of change and conflict which seem to constitute its *raison d'être*; it is reduced, at best, to the analysis of isolated and arbitrary moments, which can be connected within larger narratives only with an equal arbitrariness.

It is with this problem of authority, the problem involved in defining the place from which the real processes of history can be perceived, that my paper has been concerned, with whatever degree of indirection. What interests me about the *Microcosm* is the competition played out within it between the discourse of the division of labour and the discourse of the Picturesque, a competition in which the first attempts to arrogate to itself the privilege of being the totalising discourse, which includes and can account for the other forms of discursive representation within the text, and in which the Picturesque responds by elaborating a field of knowledge no less expansive, and which in turn localises and particularises the claim to generality, to totality, of the discourse of the division of labour. The totalising discourse is thus revealed as the discourse of a subject which defines its own partiality even as it denies it; it operates as a form of oppression, in that it defines what knowledge is, in accordance with its own exclusive interests; and in doing so, it calls up a resistance to itself, in the form of a competing discourse, which can articulate the interests it excludes.

I am not offering this conclusion as a means of endorsing one side of the division in materialist criticism that Simpson has located, but rather as a contribution to the archaeology of that division. In recent debates, the question of the loss of the possibility of totalisation has been described in terms of the transition from the modern to the postmodern. What I have been trying to show is that that issue has always been present in the competition among the various discourses of capitalism to claim the totality for themselves.

6

Imaginary Treason, Imaginary Law

The State Trials of 1794

I

In 1794, two men were found guilty of high treason in Edinburgh, David Downie and the former government spy and possible *agent provocateur* Robert Watt. Later in the same year in London, three men were found *not* guilty of high treason: the radical political activist Thomas Hardy, of the London Corresponding Society; John Horne Tooke, the philosopher of language and long-time member of the Society for Constitutional Information; and John Thelwall, lecturer, pamphleteer and poet. Among those originally indicted in London, but later discharged, was the novelist and dramatist Thomas Holcroft. The acquittals have generally been regarded both as the greatest triumph of the revolutionary or reform movement in Britain in the 1790s, and as the point at which that movement went into decline, under the pressure of new laws defining seditious and treasonable practices, and of the need of the accused, during the trials, to insist that their aims were limited and entirely constitutional.

This essay is the start of what I expect to become a larger attempt to study the political arguments of the 1790s by focusing on the treason trials, and by seeing them as the occasion of a dramatised and staged conflict between the various discourses in which politics was debated in that decade, a conflict in which the stake was the ownership of the institution of Law itself. The legal process, it argues, operates by attempting to silence – to rule out of court – all discourses other than the discourses of law itself. But in these trials the defence refused that form of exclusion and was able to mobilise and exploit a wide range of discourses whose very profusion made it impossible for the court to fix the meaning of the law on its own terms. This tactic was used

This essay, previously unpublished, is developed from a paper originally delivered at the conference 'The French Revolution and British Culture' at the University of Leicester, July 1989. It was delivered again, in revised form, as the first annual Enlightenment Lecture at the University of Essex, May 1990.

under cover of a demand that the law should be clarified and codified so as to be utterly univocal, utterly free of implication or inference.

Recent literary theory has set up something of a hierarchy between mobility and fixity in the operations of discourse, privileging mobility as part of a general critique of the *logos* or of sexual imperatives or norms. The privileging of that discursive mobility, however, has often been criticised for failing to demonstrate the historical specificity and effectivity of the notion of the fundamental instability of language. This essay relates more than obliquely to those theoretical interests, in so far as it shows, through a detailed case history, how this mobility of language was exploited in a specific historical situation and with very specific historical effects. It also suggests that we may need to be wary of assuming an easy opposition between mobility and fixity, and of attributing a 'progressive' character to whatever unfixes, loosens, undermines the authority of the logos, and of a 'reactionary' character to whatever valorises the fixity of language, may need to be rethought. 'Political positions are not simply identifiable as progressive or reactionary,' writes Homi Bhabha (8), 'prior to the act of *critique engagée*, or outside the terms and conditions of its discursive and textual address. It is in this sense that the historical moment of political action must necessarily be thought as part of the history of the form of writing'. In these trials, in what is precisely a political 'action' at law, the fixed and the fluid both appear for the defence: the Enlightenment (and especially the Benthamite) fantasy of a legal code so clearly and fully articulated that it would hardly need interpretation – that fantasy of the Enlightenment *logos* is lined up on the same side of the court with an attitude to the language of law so playful and anarchic that at times the court threatens to float away on a stream of polysemy. But it is because the defence believes so firmly in the authority of the logos that it is able to mock the pretended stability of the language of law, and to reveal its actual instability.

The treason trials, I want to suggest, were political trials in more senses than one; they were about, among other things, the politics of the law, and it was obviously inevitable that in show trials of such importance the nature and function of the law itself should have been put in question. The question is different, of course, in London and in Edinburgh. The English statute which defined High Treason had been adopted into Scottish law early in 1708, following the Act of Union, and in the trials in Edinburgh the English authorities who had interpreted the statute and extended it by construction were admitted as authorities by the judges, despite the protest of Robert Hamilton, the counsel for Watt, that the Scots had adopted the statute only, not 'the whole of the law of England', opinions, precedents, and interpretations (ST 23W: 1331–2).[1] That issue, obviously enough, is absent from the London trials, and it is those trials I shall be mainly concerned with, referring to the earlier Scottish trials only when it is convenient and not misleading to do so.

It was all the more inevitable that in London the trials put the nature and function of the law itself in question, in that the discourse by which it had always been asserted that the Common Law was the perfection of reason was the same discourse – I call it the discourse of custom, or the customary discourse – by which Burke had so recently and so influentially argued for the perfection of the whole constitution. Even before the revolution, the claims of the customary discourse as it had been employed by Blackstone in his eulogy of the Common Law had been thoroughly questioned by Bentham in his *Fragment on Goverment* (1776) and *Principles of Morals and Legislation* (1789); in 1793 it had been questioned too in Godwin's *Political Justice*, and Godwin was directly influential on the arguments deployed by the defence in the London trials. On many issues to do with the question of law, Bentham and Godwin were miles apart, of course, even opposites: Godwin looked forward to a society in which anything other than natural law would have ceased to exist; Bentham, who ridiculed the concept of natural law, looked forward to a system of laws perfectly drafted and methodised.[2] But they developed these positions in relation to a critique of the English legal system, in particular, which raised the very same questions which were to be raised in the treason trials. What, in England, is meant by a law? Does the law in England enable us to predict whether an action we perform is lawful or not? If not, isn't the dispensation of justice in England entirely arbitrary? And considered 'as a System of General Rules,' isn't the English Common Law, as Bentham described it, 'a thing merely imaginary'? (Bentham 1977 119).

II

But there were also some much more specific reasons why these questions became so central to the treason trials, which have to do with the nature of the law of High Treason itself, about which I will need to say something fairly brief. And to help keep it brief, I will drop from now on the adjective 'high' before treason. The adjective was used to distinguish those treasons which were offences against the sovereign from what was called 'petty treason', an aggravated degree of murder which involved the violation of some private or domestic allegiance – when a servant killed his or her master, a wife her husband, or an ecclesiastical person his superior, this was petty treason until 1828.

The law of treason consisted in the first place of a statute of the reign of Edward III. This was generally agreed to be a 'declaratory' statute, which is to say it was concerned not to define treason as it were *de novo*, but simply to declare, as Blackstone puts it, 'what the common law is and ever hath been' (1 Comm. 86) on the question of treason, so as to remove disputes about the matter.[3] The statute defined a series of specific treasons; the one which especially concerns us – the treason with which Watt and Downie, and Hardy and Horne Tooke and Thelwall were charged – is the first. It is treason, says the statute, *when a man doth compass or imagine the death of our lord the king.*

In the interpretative literature which by 1794 had come to surround the statute of treasons, the meaning of those verbs, 'compass or imagine', had received very little attention – surprisingly little, in view of the fact that the meanings attributed to them in the statute were meanings they had retained in no other context. Sir Matthew Hale, whose chapters on treason in his *History of the Pleas of the Crown* had probably become the most authoritative commentary on the statute, remarks of the two verbs that 'they refer to the purpose or design of the mind or will' (Hale 1: 107). More illuminatingly, Blackstone explains that the verbs are 'synonymous terms', but regards the first as the one in need of a gloss: 'the word *compass* signifying the purpose or design of the mind or will, and not, as in common speech, the carrying such design to effect' (4 Comm. 78). In 1766 Daines Barrington had suggested, with 'great deference' to the venerable wording of the statute, that 'the word imagine is not sufficiently explicit, and is likewise too figurative to be made use of in describing this the most capital of all criminal offences' (221–2). But no legal authority, so far as I am aware, had commented on what had become the strangeness of the use of 'imagine' in this purposive sense, to mean 'to intend', though as we shall see the unfamiliarity of that meaning will continually be pointed out by the defence in the trials and by radical writers commenting on those trials. 'The statute,' comments Robert Cullen, who defended David Downie,

> was written in the French language, and the words are "compaser, ou ymaginer la mort nostre seigneur le roy." It is perhaps singular, as has been well remarked by an ingenious writer, that the life of every British subject prosecuted by the crown for high treason should continue to depend upon the critical construction of two obsolete French words. (ST 24D: 123)[4]

The treason of compassing or imagining the king's death is, as

Thomas Erskine puts it in his defence of Hardy, a 'complete. . . anomaly' in English law, for the crime is 'wholly seated', as he puts it, 'in unconsummated intention' (ST 24H: 896). Until 1800, indeed, the law took the will so completely for the deed that 'a man cannot be indicted,' as Erskine pointed out, 'for killing the king'; there was no punishment in English law for killing the king, only for intending his death, and in that case punishment was to be exacted independently of whether or not the king died as a result of the intention, and independently even of whether any attempt was made upon his life. At the trial of the regicides, the man who did the actual beheading of Charles I was accused only of compassing or imagining his death, and the fact that he did, actually, put the king to death was judicially cognisable only in so far as it was an act which manifested his prior, treasonous intention to do what he then did (Foster 194; ST 24H: 896). But because compassing or imagining is an 'internal act' (Hale 1: 107), is 'secret in the heart' (Coke 14), and can be known only to God, an intention to kill the king becomes itself judicially cognisable only when it is manifested by some such open or – in the words of the statute – 'overt act'. That act need not be a direct attempt on the king's life. To buy a weapon with the intention of killing an ordinary subject is neither murder nor attempted murder; but to buy a weapon with the intention of killing the king is every bit as much evidence of treason as a successful or unsuccessful attempt on his life would be (see Smith 1978 294–5).[5]

But just because the crime of treason was itself an 'internal', a 'secret' act, and because it was a crime of such enormity, the statute insisted that clarity of proof was essential. As Coke explained,

> It is to be observed that the word in the act . . . is *provablement:* *i.e.,* Upon direct and manifest proof, not upon conjectural presumptions, or inferences, or strains of wit, but upon good and sufficient proof. And herein the adverb *provably* hath a great force, and signifieth a direct plain proof, which words the Lords and Commons in Parliament did use, for that the offence of treason was so heinous, and was so heavily and severely punished, as none other the like, and therefore the offender must be PROVABLY attainted, which words are as forcible as upon direct and manifest proof. Note, the word is not *probably* . . . but the word is *provably* be attainted.
>
> (Coke: 12)

The defence in all the 1794 treason trials made much of the word 'provably' in the statute, and in two cases quoted Coke's opinion at length (ST 23W: 1333; 24D: 134; 24H: 891; 25T: 274): it was one of several passages from commentaries directed against 'constructive' treasons (see also below, 138–9), and helped limit the authority of the constructions of the commentators themselves.

There is one other feature of the statute that I want to call attention to, because it has always been of great importance in the history of trials for treason, and it became of quite crucial importance to the trials of 1794. At the end of the list of seven specific treasons defined by the statute, the statute continues:

> Because other like cases of treason may happen in time to come, which cannot be thought of nor declared at present, it is accorded, that if any other case supposed to be treason, which is not above specified, doth happen before any judge; the judge shall tarry without going to judgment of the treason, till the cause be shewed and declared before the king and his parliament, whether it ought to be judged treason, or other felony.

This appears to be an explicit prohibition, in relation to this particular act of parliament, of the process by which statutes, once they are construed by Common Law theory as acts declarative of ancient common law, come to be interpreted and applied according to traditional Common Law categories (see Postema 17) and come to be treated, effectively, as a part of the Common Law, or (as Bentham put it) as 'another branch of customary law, which striking its roots into the substance of the statute law, infected it with its own characteristic obscurity, uncertainty and confusion' (Bentham 1970 240). All the authorities from Coke onwards interpret this clause as a prohibition, therefore, of constructive, judge-made treasons, treasons invented by claiming that such and such an overt act in the instant case was analogous with such and such an overt act in a precedent case; though this does not prevent them giving approval to judicial decisions which do indeed appear to make constructive treasons. It is partly because they are armed with this clause of the statute that those who acted for the defendants in the 1794 trials were able to argue not only against constructive treasons as such, but against the whole process by which statute law, which expressed the intentions of the legislature, could be treated as if it was a declaration of the Common Law, and could then be interpreted not by judges only but by those who interpreted their interpretations.

III

So much for the statute; but according to the critics of the common law, the law of treason was by no means wholly comprised in the simple statute. Though philosophers of jurisprudence might insist that judicial opinions and precedents were evidence of law, rather than law itself, they seem often to have been treated by the courts as just that; and so was an influential series of works by commentators who had come to be regarded as authorities – on extraordinarily arbitrary or haphazard grounds, according to Bentham (Bentham 1970 186–92, and 1977 207–15). The writings on treason of Sir Edward Coke, Sir Matthew Hale, Serjeant William Hawkins, and Sir Michael Foster were in 1794 treated by the courts as to all intents and purposes as much a part of the law of treason as the statute itself, and the history of the interventions of these authorities had done much to develop the law in relation in particular to the specific treason of imagining the king's death.[6] Especially at issue was the doctrine concerning the overt acts in which a treasonous imagining was manifested. Originally, the effort seems to have been to define what sort of acts could be *alleged*, in an indictment for treason, as overt acts which manifested an intention to kill the king. In particular, there was an attempt to define acts performed in pursuit of the intention to depose the king, imprison him, or to usurp his authority if not his throne, as overt acts which could be offered as evidence of intending his death, on the grounds that the death of the king must be one of the probable or natural consequences of such acts. But as Hamilton points out, in his defence of Robert Watt, the commentators from Hale onwards were quick to depart from what Hamilton saw as 'the plain and unequivocal construction put upon the statute by Sir Edward Coke' (ST 23W: 1334); and once defined, these overt acts came to be treated as if they themselves constituted the treason, and as if all that was necessary to secure a conviction for treason was to establish that the accused had performed such-and-such an overt act, not that s/he had formed such-and-such an intention.

In 1762, when Foster's discourse on treason was published, the argument that the overt acts were themselves part of the treason became fully explicit. 'Overt-Acts,' argued Foster, 'undoubtedly do discover the Man's Intentions: but I conceive they are not to be considered merely as Evidence, but as the *Means made use of to Effectuate the Purposes of the Heart*' (Foster 203).[7] Foster's argument is that the overt acts are not merely evidence, they are also proof of the intention, for the performance of them presupposes the intention; it is hardly surprising that Sir John Scott, the Attorney-General (later to be Lord Chancellor Eldon), made this doctrine crucial to his prosecution of Hardy (ST 24H: 253–5). The effect was to turn matter of fact into matter of law; and to offer it as a presumption of law that the performance of a specific action was proof of a treasonous intention, whether or not the defendant was conscious of intending anything of the sort (ST 24H: 1361; 25T: 725).

By 1794 it was therefore possible, as Erskine points out in his defence of Horne Tooke, to ground a prosecution for treason on the argument that, in point of *law*, a defendant intended the king's death, when it was acknowledged, even by the prosecution, that in point of *fact* s/he intended no such thing (ST 25T: 36, 267). The attempt was to argue, as Erskine also points out, that the intention of an act could be gathered from its probable or possible consequences (ST 24H: 878–81, 1190; 25T: 27, 266–7). It was possible to argue, for example, that to organise in order to argue for a reform of parliament was an act which could be interpreted as an attempt to overawe the king so as to oblige him to act in a certain way; that this was to endanger his authority; that the probable consequence of this would be that the king would be deposed; and that the probable consequence of his deposition would be his death (ST 24H: 264–5, 901, 904), even though the defendant was conscious of no design even to depose him, or even if, intending to depose him, the defendant had made elaborate plans for conveying him to a place of safety (ST 24H: 259).

It was repeatedly argued, for example, in the trials of 1794, in Edinburgh as well as in London, that though on the authority of Coke the crime of imagining the king's death could apply only to the natural body of the king (e.g. ST 23W: 1331–4; 24D: 127, 130, and see Kantorowicz 15), and not to his political body or his royal majesty or authority, it was nevertheless the case that to endanger the authority of the king was an overt act proving the intention to kill his natural body (ST 24H: 243–7, 264–5, 1183). For the king, so the argument went, was bound by his Coronation Oath to resist any challenge to his authority, even to the point of risking his life; any challenge to his authority, therefore, may be treasonous, because it may result in his death (ST 23W: 1389; ST 24H: 244–5). And all this could be argued by prosecutors and by judges in spite of the clause against constructive treasons in the statute, and even – so they could claim – in the very spirit of that clause (ST 24H: 251–2; 25T: 501). Indeed Sir John Scott, leading the prosecution of Hardy, goes so far as to claim that such arguments must be within the spirit of the statute, partly on the grounds that they are advanced by such authorities as Hale and Foster, who were perfectly well aware that the statute prohibited constructive treasons, and would 'have suffered death', so Scott assures the court, rather than countenance a constructive treason (ST 24H: 253).

In answer to such arguments, Cullen in Edinburgh, and Erskine and his fellow-counsel for the defence Vicary Gibbs in London, repeatedly make the point that overt acts were never in themselves treasonous, and could only ever be adduced as *evidence* of treason, to be weighed by the jury. To represent intentions as matters of law, they argue, and not as matters of fact, is to attempt to ensure that cases of treason are decided by the judge, not by the jury, and is often to deprive the defendant of any possible defence (ST 24D: 133; 24H: 880–1, 894–5, 898–9; 25T: 273, 454).[8] If a defendant denies performing the act which is specified as the overt act in the indictment, the jury has the job of deciding whether or not the act has been performed, but must accept direction from the judge on the question of what intention is manifested in the act. If the defendant acknowledges performing the act, the jury has no function at all except to pronounce the guilty verdict. Indeed, in his charge to the Grand Jury which examined the indictments before the London treason trials, Lord Chief Justice Eyre went so far as to claim that the hardest part of their task had effectively been done for them, by earlier judicial decisions, and by Hale and Foster, who on the authority of adjudged cases had to a large extent decided what overt acts were to be taken as manifestations of treasonous imaginings (ST 24H: 202).

The debate initiated by the defence in the London trials can be seen as a continuation by other means of the argument about the question of intent, and the function of the jury, in cases of seditious libel, which had apparently ended with the passing of Fox's Libel Act of 1792 (seconded by Erskine) but which had hardly been resolved thereby. Before 1792 the official doctrine on these issues – strongly resisted throughout most of the century – was that the questions of whether a publication was seditious, and of whether it had been published with the intention of 'scandalising' the government, were matters of law, to be determined by the judge. The only matters of fact, and so the only issues to be decided by the jury, were whether or not the publication did indeed mean (in a narrow sense) what the prosecution said it did, and whether or not the accused had indeed published the alleged libel. This doctrine was strongly reaffirmed in the second half of the century, in particular by Lord Chief Justice Mansfield in the cases of seditious libel arising out of the publications of Junius in 1770, of Horne Tooke in 1777 and of Sir William Jones in 1783–4 (see Junius 1: 94–9, 305–16, 471–3; ST 20 803–923, 651–802, and ST 21: 847–1044).

The opponents of what came to be regarded as Mansfield's doctrine (Green 328) advanced one of two arguments. They could argue that the intention of the accused in cases of seditious libel was as much a matter of fact as in other criminal cases, and that the jury should not be obliged to pronounce a general verdict of guilty without being permitted to consider the whole matter at issue. More radically, they could concede that the question of intention was indeed matter of law, and then, by pointing out that in all other criminal cases the jury had the right to come to a decision on the intention of the accused, they could argue that this established the right of the jury to find law as well as to find fact. To the argument that the jury would be ignorant of the law, it could be retorted that it was obviously contradictory to hold that while a defendant must always be presumed to know the law he was accused of having broken, the jury is always supposed ignorant of it.

The Act of 1792 did not, according to Thomas Green, 'explicitly convert the questions of intent or seditiousness into questions of fact.' But it did establish that the jury had the right to 'give a general verdict of guilty or not guilty upon the whole matter put in issue', and was not 'required or directed . . . to find the defendant or defendants guilty, merely of the proof of the publication . . . and of the sense ascribed to the same' (Green 330).[9] It remained open, of course, to judges in libel cases, as in all cases heard before a jury, to advise them of the law in such a way as to suggest, as Eyre had done, that it was very much more settled, and beyond controversy, than in fact it was.[10] For this reason, and no doubt also because the reform of the libel law had been so strongly resisted by Mansfield, Erskine made an early opportunity, in his speech for Thomas Hardy, to point out that in the trial of Lord George Gordon for treason, following the Gordon Riots, the great Mansfield himself had insisted that it was the task of the jury to decide what Gordon's intentions had been (see ST21: 647).

And it is the claim by judge and prosecution that the reports of adjudged cases and the writings of earlier Crown Lawyers have made the cases so clear which led Erskine and Gibbs, in the trials of Hardy and Horne Tooke, to ask where the law against treason was to be found: in the statute, or in the commentaries upon it. In the case of Horne Tooke especially, with the innocence of Hardy already established, they warm to the task of attacking the authorities to whom Eyre so willingly deferred. 'If there are any decisions,' insists Gibbs,

> which state it as a conclusion of law, to be drawn by the court, not an inference of fact for the jury, that a conspiracy to depose the king involves in it a compassing his death, the Court will have to decide between the authority of those decisions and the statute itself; for I think it impossible to support those decisions by the statute.   (ST 25T: 455)

Gibb's point here, of course, is that if the authorities and precedents are in conflict with the statute, they are in conflict with the expressed will of the sovereign power, and *must* be disregarded. The same point is made by Erskine. 'I admit,' he argues, in a characteristically elaborate sentence which seems worth quoting in full, that a statute, like the common law, must receive a judicial interpretation; and that, wherever the letter of an Act of Parliament is ambiguous, the constructions which have been first put on it, if rational, ought to continue to be the rule. But where a statute is expressed in such plain, unambiguous terms, that but one grammatical or rational construction can be put on it; when the first departure from that only construction does not appear to have taken its rise from any supposed ambiguity of its expression in the minds of those who first departed from it – which is the general history of constructive departures from written laws – but comes down tainted with the most degraded profligacy of judges notoriously devoted to arbitrary and corrupt governments; when the very writers and judges whose writings and decisions first supported such original misconstructions, honestly admit them to be misconstructions, and lament and reprobate their introduction; when the same lamentation and reprobation of them is handed down from commentator to commentator, and from court to court, through the whole series of constructive judgements; and lastly, when Parliament itself, in different ages, as the evil becomes intolerable, has swept them all away; when, to avoid the introduction of new difficulties, it has cautiously left the old letter of the statute standing to speak for itself, without any other commentary than the destruction of every one that ever had been made upon it, and the reversal of every judgment which ever had departed from its letter, concluding with the positive prohibition, in all future time, of the one and of the other; – in such a case, I do maintain, and, as an English lawyer, feel myself bound for the public safety to declare, *in opposition to whatever authorities may be found to the contrary* [my emphasis], that if the statute of Edward the Third can be departed from by construction, or can be judged otherwise THAN IF IT HAD BEEN PASSED YESTERDAY, there is, properly speaking, no such thing as written law in England. (ST 25T: 268–9)

By written law, of course, Erskine means statute law, as opposed to the unwritten, common law of England, and it is precisely the process I referred to earlier, by which statutes made by the sovereign power could be assimilated to the common, the customary law, that he is objecting to here. The rule of action in cases of treason, he insists,

depends upon a WRITTEN UNALTERABLE record, enacted by the legislature of the kingdom for the protection of the subject's life, and which the judges upon the bench have no right to transgress or alter a letter of, because other judges may have done so before them. As far as the law stands upon tradition, it is made by the

> precedents of judges, and there is no other evidence of its existence;
> but a statute is ever present to speak for itself, in all courts, and in
> all ages.   (ST 25T: 268)

There are two things in particular that interest me in this account
of the higher authority of statute of common law, and of the impropriety
of treating statutes as if they were a part of the common law. One is
the reverence expressed by Erskine for the acts of an unreformed
parliament, in a case which is all about the legality of the means by
which a reform of parliament could be achieved.[11] The second is that
for all Erskine's acknowledgement that any statute must be interpreted,
he still indulges the Benthamite fantasy that the language of legislation
is, or could be, a perfectly unambiguous and transparent language.
On the one hand, the language of the statute of treasons is unambiguous
because it is written, and therefore unalterable, while the judge-made
common law is spoken, and survives only in the imprecisely
remembered reports of the oral pronouncements of judges. On the
other hand, just because the statute is written, it 'is ever *present* to
speak for itself': it has all the unambiguous authority which accrues
to what is spoken in the present, as against the musty judgments of
common law, which, though once delivered orally, are now able only
to be read, and survive in the form of words that occasion dictated,
not in a codified form approved by sovereign power. By this two-way
and contradictory binary, statute law has all the authority of writing
and all the authority of speech, and the Common Law has no authority
at all. The argument is strikingly similar to Bentham's, in his
unpublished (until 1945) treatise 'Of Laws in General': 'Written law
. . . is the law of those who can both speak and write: . . . customary
law, of those who neither know how to write, not how to speak.
Written law is the law for civilized nations: . . . customary law, for
brutes' (Bentham 1970 153).

Which brings me back to the first part of my opening argument,
that in the London treason trials in particular, it was the very institution
of the law that was in question, and that it came to be put in question
not just because of the enormous political importance of the trials as
such, but partly also because treason was not an offence at common
law but was defined by statute. The task of defending Hardy, Tooke
and Thelwall was a task which involved mounting a defence of statute
law against a Common Law tradition which represented statutes as
an inferior, clumsy kind of law, of value only as 'through continual
use, judicial exposition, and interpretation' they became 'part of the
structure of Common Law' (Postema 24). This defence projected Erskine
and Gibbs into a position much closer than they may at other times
have wished to occupy, to the position developed by Bentham in his

unpublished 'Comment' on Blackstone's *Commentaries*, written in the 1770s, and in his *Introduction to the Principles of Morals and Legislation*, published in 1789.[12] Both works were a relentless attack on the Common Law as described and eulogised by Blackstone. And among Bentham's objections to Common Law – I will have more to say about them later – were that customary laws were not the expression of the commands or the will of any specific legislator, and were not expressed in any agreed and unambiguous form of words. A customary law is 'a fictitious composition, which has no known person for its author, [and] no known assemblage of words for its substance'; it is a body of ideas with no single and authoritative set of words to express it (Bentham 1948 123).[13] Statute law, or 'real' law as he sometimes described it, had a fixed and therefore perfectible expression, and because it was the expression of the intention of a known body of legislators, it was possible to interpret statute law by reference to those intentions, which in the case of the Common Law was impossible; of a particular common-law maxim, he remarks that 'the name of its father' is nowhere to be found (Bentham 1948 137), which generates the paradox that the whole of the Common Law is illegitimate (and see Bentham 1977 408n.). Bentham's programme for reform had as its main demand the wholesale legitimation of the Common Law by converting it into a code of statute law, drafted with complete clarity, and open to be altered only by the legislature itself; and it is the most thoroughgoing example of the Enlightenment ideal, or fantasy, of a complete, and entirely unambiguous, legal code (see Bentham 1970 156–83).[14]

The interference in common law by legislation was denounced by Blackstone as 'innovation' (1 Comm. 70), as argument comparable, says Bentham, with those of 'doating politicians, who, when out of humour with a particular innovation without being able to tell why, set themselves to declaim against *all* innovation, because it is innovation' (Bentham 1977 410n.). Unsurprisingly, therefore, when the defence in the London trials represents the history of the statute of treasons as a history in which 'the commentary has conspired against the text', as Coleridge (1971 288) was to put it, the prosecution and the Lord Chief Justice describe their arguments as 'innovation'. When Gibbs attempted to deny that an attempt to subvert the constitution could be represented, as a matter of law, as an act of imagining the king's death, the Solicitor General Sir John Mitford, prosecuting in London alongside Scott, replied that he

> should have been astonished to hear this doubted, if in the present age I could be astonished at any thing; but it is the temper of the times to hold out to the world that every thing which has been

revered for ages, is now no longer to be revered; that the reason of
man is become more powerful than it was in former times; and
upon every subject new lights are to break in upon his mind; he
is to be a new creature, no longer to be governed by the wisdom
of former times, but to proceed entirely upon the theory of his own
conceptions.   (ST 24H: 1184)

This hoary collection of clichés, the usual terms in which enlightenment
is denounced by the discourse of custom, is so familiar that it is easy
to overlook the fact that what Mitford worships as something 'revered
for ages' is nothing but a judge-made constructive treason. Of Erskine's
denunciation of constructive treason, Sir John Scott simply says 'we live
in an age of innovation', as if that remark in itself were sufficient to
discredit the point (ST 25T: 502); and of Erskine's suggestion that the
judges may declare the common law but have no business interpreting
an unambiguous statute, Eyre comments (with evident disbelief) that it
is the first time anyone has ever attempted to run such an argument.
All three, the two prosecutors and the judge, clearly see that what is
threatened by the arguments of the defence is the institution of the
English legal system itself. Whatever is threatened by the activities of
the defendants, the monarchy, the constitution, the unreformed House
of Commons, it is the law itself which is threatened by the defence. 'It
was observed' by the Attorney General, says the Lord Chief Justice, that
'this is an age of innovation; it is necessary we should keep to our
principles, and that we should rally round the law' (ST 25T: 726). Perhaps
such anxious tones were not heard again from the bench of judges until
Lord Mackay made his recent attempt to eliminate double manning
in court, and to allow solicitors rights of advocacy.[15]

IV

I remarked earlier that the questioning of the nature of English law that
was provoked by the trials was facilitated also by the fact that the specific
treason invoked in the five trials of 1794 was the treason of 'compassing
and imagining the death of the king'. In fact, the words 'imagine',
'imagining', 'imagination', have an extraordinary history in this sequence
of trials. The main point I want to make in the rest of this essay is that
the presence in the statute of such radically ambiguous words, at a time
when ideas of the imagination and the value put on its operations were
so many and so different, produces a situation in which the defence and
the defendants in all these trials find themselves endorsing, in effect,
Bentham's accusation against the Common Law system, that it is an
entirely 'imaginary' system (see above, 121), and I want to ask what that

accusation might have meant. But in order to do that I will need to give some idea of what I have called that extraordinary history.

Now it goes without saying that all those professionally involved in these trials would have known that the meaning ascribed by legal authorities to the verb 'to imagine' as it is used in the statute was 'to intend'; and that what those authorities intended when they talked of 'imaginings' and 'imaginations' was 'intentions'. But such antique terms of law, apparently preserved on the grounds of their precision, are inevitably imprecise by reason of their very antiquity. They readily lend themselves to figurative usages, because they are continually open to being borrowed by other discourses in which their meanings are more familiar. Daines Barrington's objection to the word 'imagine' in the statute was precisely that it was insufficiently 'explicit' – it had too many of those 'implications and inferences' which made room for artful constructions; it was too 'figurative' a term to be used in a written law, which should mean what it says, and no more (see above, 122). It is hardly surprising, therefore, that in these trials the meaning of the word was not effectively constrained or limited by its consensual legal meaning, and that 'imagine' and its cognate terms were incapable of staying as close to their faculty meanings as a nice legal mind might have wished. Indeed, the prosecution has an interest in exploiting the word to attribute to the defendants a dark and Gothic character: they speak of 'the wicked imaginations' in the heart of the traitor, the 'wild', the 'desperate imagination' of the supposed revolutionary (ST 24D: 133; ST 24H: 209, 271). And whether deliberately or not, they gloss the word 'imagine' as it is used in the statute in such a way as to suggest that even to imagine the king's death in the weak sense, of picturing it to oneself, by an association of ideas however involuntary, is to be a traitor. In his prosecution of Watt, for example, Anstruther defines a traitor as 'he who intends, he into whose imagination it enters, he who conceives the design of destroying the sovereign', for 'the crime,' he argues, with cheerful ambiguity, 'is in the imagination of the person' (ST 23W: 1190–1), where the word 'in' means 'consists in', or is 'located in', according to which meaning of imagination you find yourself adopting.

But it is in the London trials that the word takes off entirely, circulating among a range of meanings of 'imagination', in what I'll call for brevity's sake ordinary language, and in at least four specialised discourses, the law, sensational literature, philosophical radicalism – where the imagination had a particularly pejorative connotation – and aesthetic enquiry, if I can use that term to cover that extensive study of the powers and pleasures of the imagination, where its nature and its creative functions were being defined, as well as its 'diseases' and 'disorders'.[16] Precisely because the legal process attempts to suppress as far as possible all discourses except that of the law itself, the ambiguities in the word, and the discursive slippages that occur whenever such a polyvalent word is required to function as a term of art, became in all these trials especially salient. The prosecution in London, as in Scotland, seems to have been able to accommodate a fairly narrow range of the various uses of the 'imagination', and of course it will usually be in the interests of the prosecution to attempt to limit the interdiscursive play of the language of law, and especially where that language is palpably antique. For the discourse of law gathers much of its authority from antique terms, much of its claim to be a univocal discourse which deals with universals and is pitched high above the contingencies which produce the ceaseless changes of meaning and the uncontrollable ambiguities characteristic of other discourses. But the defence in these trials, the defendants and their supporters, had no similar concern for the authority of the discourse of law, and as they included such intellectuals as Horne Tooke, Thomas Holcroft, Thelwall, Erskine and Godwin, they were confident in their invocation of a wide range of discourses in which the word had some specific meaning, and were able and eager to exploit every shift and slippage.

In a letter to the *Morning Post* in 1796 Bentham complains that Lord Grenville's Treasonable Practices Bill still retained the obsolete language of 'imagining' of the statute of Edward III. And he made the obvious point that we all have a strong personal interest in seeing this word changed, for if it is treason to imagine, to figure to oneself, to contain the picture of the king's death in one's mind, then everyone is a traitor, and certainly everyone in the court – 'judges, jury, counsel, audience, all who contribute to, or are present at, the trial of a traitor ... will be traitors' (Bentham 1843 10: 320–2). Bentham's letter is only the clearest statement of a point that had never been absent from the minds of the defence, and which they exploit to suggest, if never quite to enunciate, that to imagine the death of the king is a kind of contagion, that the true traitors must be those in whom the contagion originated, and that it originated in the ministry, and in the prosecution, not in the minds of the defendants. The continual subtext of the defence, and the text itself of various radical writings ancillary to the trials themselves, is that it is the prosecution, and not the defendants, who have imagined, or who first imagined, the king's death, and who are now imagining the death of the defendants. The point is the most extreme version of a point that Fox had been making in the House of Commons for the past two years: that the republican conspiracies and imminent insurrections which the government used to justify the repression of political societies were conspiracies and insurrections it had itself invented or imagined. These trials however, and the wording of the law of treasons, now enabled that accusation to take off as never before. 'If there have been treason, who are the traitors?' demanded Holcroft, when the trials were finally abandoned (Holcroft 1795b 44).[17]

The prosecution was set up for this line of attack by the Lord Chief Justice himself, in his Charge to the Grand Jury before the London trials. Eyre freely acknowledged that the claim of the prosecution, that an association like the London Corresponding Society, working for a reform of parliament, had somehow committed the crime of High Treason, might seem to the Grand Jury somewhat unlikely. But the process by which the members of the society might have become traitors, might have imagined the death of the king, was in fact, he assured them, 'very simple'. 'Let us,' he suggested to the jury, 'imagine to ourselves this case ...' – and so on (ST 24H: 206). Armed with the wording of the statute and this treasonous invitation from the Lord Chief Justice, Godwin took hold of the word and wrung it practically dry. Eyre's charge, he commented in his *Cursory Strictures*, is the most extraordinary instance in the history of English law, of 'wild conjecture', 'premature presumption', 'licentious imaginations', 'dreams full of sanguinary and tremendous prophecy'. Every paragraph now presents us with a new treason, real or imaginary, pretendedly direct, or avowedly constructive', with the intent 'to bewilder the imaginations ... of the Grand Jury and the Nation'. 'The Chief Justice' enumerates varieties of treason ... 'which are all the mere creatures of his own imagination' (Godwin 1794 11, 19, 21).

The same accusation, that it is the prosecution, not the defence, which has imagined the death of the king, is made by two of the accused. In a letter transcribed into his prison journal, responding to the second report of the House of Commons Committee of Secrecy (see Goodwin 333–6), Horne Tooke wrote that he had been been unable to form 'even a conjecture concerning what sort of treasonable practices I could be suspected. But now, having read 'that Report of Horror', he understands 'what sort of a picture their lordships have drawn of me in their imagination, and ... have exhibited of me to the world' (Tooke 1: opposite page 117). In the speech Thelwall was prevented by Erskine from delivering at his trial, he claimed that the treasonous conspiracy was all in the mind of Adair, the counsel for the prosecution:

> I avow myself a "sans culotte:" a phrase which Mr. Serjeant Adair has thought fit to define in terms the most gross and monstrous that the imagination even of an assassin could have suggested. ... that I ever conspired, or connived at any conspiracy for purposes of violence, plunder, or insurrection, is a calumny so black and infamous as could have entered the imagination of none but the most practiced assassin.   (Thelwall 1795 84, 91)

'How,' demands Holcroft, in an open letter to the Attorney General after the trial, 'could you so impose upon your understanding as to imagine [my peaceful exhortations] treasonable?' (Holcroft 1795a 91).

The point was summed up, after the trials, by Coleridge, in his remark that 'three successive verdicts of impartial juries' have 'proved, that a conspiracy against the constitution has existed only in the foul imagination of the accusers' (Coleridge 1971 61). But it was a point made also throughout the trials themselves. The imagination of the prosecution, Erskine argues, has raised up at best an entertainment from the Arabian Nights,[18] at worst a nightmare of 'chimeras', 'hydras', in an effort to 'taint' the 'imaginations' of the jury (ST 25T: 292; 24H: 925, 943, 930), and the closeness – in the context of a trial for high treason – of the words 'taint' and 'attaint' is enough to suggest that the prosecution is trying to involve the imagination of the jury in its own treasonous imaginings. By putting these everyday meanings of 'imagination' into circulation, the defence can play them off against the legal meaning, and both Erskine and Holcroft insist that only as an absurd point of law, never as a matter of fact, can a defendant be regarded as guilty of imagining what never entered his imagination (ST 24: 899; Holcroft 1795a 23).

The accusation, that the treasonous imaginings are all in the mind of the prosecution, takes two forms in the trials and in the ancillary writings, according to which discourse the word imagination finds itself attached to at one time or another. On the one hand the defence exploits the developing notions of the creative or productive imagination, which, as defined for example by Akenside or Alexander Gerard or Abraham Tucker, has the power of associating a vast range of ideas into a unitary design, of inventing, as it were intuitively, probable designs and structures by which apparently disparate ideas might be combined, or of projecting a complete design on the basis of an incomplete set of data or sequence of ideas.[19] On the other hand, the defence is able to exploit the pejorative meanings of the imagination as the demonised, untrustworthy faculty it had become to philosophical radicalism, as that which usurps the place of the sound reasoning and solid judgment without which no judge, counsel or jury can properly discharge their duties.

As we shall see, it is the second of these ways of exploiting the ambiguity of the term 'imagination' which was to challenge and to threaten the institution of the Common Law itself in the course of these trials. But that challenge was certainly more effective in relation to the suggestion that the productive imagination of the prosecution was only too productive, was entirely out of control. Late eighteenth-century theories of the imagination as a creative, as a synthesising, as a completing power, always observed a limit point, where aesthetics was happy to pass the concept of imagination over to medicine. The imagination might seem to operate as if its choices were purely instinctive – Gerard compared it with a dog on the scent, bounding from idea to idea, resisting the rival attractions of other trails, infallibly leading the man of genius, at least, 'into those tracks where the proper ideas lurk' (Gerard 47). But just because the imagination appears to have an instinct if not a mind of its own, the inventions, the structures, the designs it produces need always to be guided by the reason or judgement, or checked out afterwards against the findings of those less mercurial powers. An imagination which, usually under the overwhelming power of the passions, operated independently of such constraints, became 'disordered', and produced elaborate structures of ideas associated on accidental rather than on substantive grounds. Worse still, it might then be doomed endlessly to repeat itself, focusing interminably and obsessively on one single design, one sequence of associations, unable to conceive of any other pattern into which they could be arranged. These diseases of the imagination, these different kinds of obsessive behaviour, were varieties of madness, the seriousness of which depended on the seriousness of the occasions when the imagination slipped its lead.[20]

It's an extraordinary moment, then, in the trial of Horne Tooke, and a moment which could have been produced only in the extraordinarily light-headed, almost flippant mood of the defence in that trial, when Erskine suddenly suggests to the Solicitor General that he is mad. He does so, of course, in terms which are as circumspect as could be imagined, and they may recall Imlac's account in *Rasselas* of the 'maladies of the mind' consequent on the 'dangerous prevalence of the imagination' (Johnson 1759 2: 116–22). Indeed, Erskine manages to make the suggestion sound almost like a compliment – but his meaning is perfectly clear. He announces that the construction put by the Solicitor General on the indictment is one which he 'cannot possibly reconcile with any one principle or precedent in English law.' But, he continues,

I am persuaded that he will not consider this observation as a personal attack upon his integrity, or any depreciation of his professional learning, for both of which I have always had the highest respect. The truth is, when the mind has long been engaged upon a particular subject, and has happened to look upon it in a particular point of view, it is its natural infirmity to draw into the vortex of its own ideas whatever it can lay hold of, however unsuited to their support. I cannot account upon any other principle for the doctrine maintained by so very learned a person. . . . (ST 25T: 266)

By a pleasant irony, in 1800 Erskine found himself opposed once again to Mitford in the trial of the brain-damaged James Hadfield who had discharged a pistol at George III in Drury Lane Theatre. In his defence of Hadfield, Erskine describes the nature of his insanity at great length, and in terms which more or less repeat the description he had given of Mitford's obsessions and delusions in the trial of Horne Tooke (ST 27: 1307–30). Holcroft, in his letter to Scott, extends the charge of madness to him: 'I know you must have been deceived; . . . by that dereliction of mind which, if not insanity, I know not by what name it can properly be called' (Holcroft 1795a 91–2).

The justification for this charge lay most clearly, as far as the defence was concerned, in the extraordinary accumulation of evidence, written and verbal, presented by the Attorney General in an effort, according to the defence, to perplex and bewilder the imagination of the jury. It was impossible for the defence, Erskine and Gibbs maintained, to give detailed consideration to such a mountain of data. Only in the obsessive imagination of the Crown Lawyers, they argued, could what Holcroft described as 'a mass of heterogeneous facts, vague but perplexing assertions and stupefying readings and recapitulations' be conceived of as linked together (Holcroft 1795a 21); only in their infatuated understandings could it be seen as the huge and intricate web they saw it as, the vast plan for the subversion of the constitution itself and of every institution of government (see for example ST 24H: 937, 1123–4, 1152; 25T: 292). But once that design had been conceived – in the imaginations of the accusers, not of the accused – it became (Erskine uses the term again: ST 25T: 298) a 'vortex', with a centripetal power to draw into itself every scrap of evidence, or of what was evidence at least to the Law Officers of the Crown, and to use it against the defendants.[21]

So much for the accusation that the treasonous imaginings with which Hardy, Horne Tooke, and Thelwall were charged were in fact the dark infatutated imaginings of the prosecution itself – and as Nicholas Roe has pointed out, a similar suggestion, that they were the imaginings of Pitt himself, were entertained by Godwin, but not by Wordsworth or Coleridge, who regarded Pitt as a man entirely without the imagination necessary for the task (Roe 200ff.). In the context of that general charge, I want to turn again to the question of constructive treasons, considered as – in Godwin's phrase – 'imaginary treasons'. In a passage much quoted in the treason trials (see for example ST 24D: 126; ST 24H: 892), Sir Matthew Hale had argued that the history of the law of treasons showed

how dangerous it is, by construction and analogy, to make treasons, where the letter of the law hath not done it; for such a method admits of no limits or bounds, but runs as far as the wit and invention of accusers, and the odiousness and detestation of the persons accused, will carry men.   (Hale 1: 259)

This argument, and the clause in the statute itself which was interpreted as a prohibition of treasons made by judicial construction, are the two key texts which in almost any trial for treason the defence will adduce. In response to this argument, the prosecution, as in the cases of Hardy and Horne Tooke, will always be obliged to argue that they are not attempting to 'invent' constructive, accumulative, consequential, or analogous treasons, 'like cases of treason', or crimes 'enhanced' into treason (see for example ST 24H: 251–2; 25T: 501); and it is precisely of inventing 'analogous' treasons that the Lord Chief Justice and the Crown Lawyers are accused, by Godwin and by the lawyers for the defence (Godwin 1794 18).

But since Hale had sat on the bench, the history of the imagination had developed, by 1794, to the point where the defence was able to argue that virtually any charge of treason in the form of compassing or imagining the king's death was an analogous, and therefore an imaginary treason, or what Hamilton intriguingly described as a 'constructive imagination' (ST 23W: 1332). It had come to be very generally accepted that in a system of Common Law the task of the court was to look for and to argue over the 'analogies' between the instant case and the possible precedent cases. As Paley puts it, 'the greater part of legal controversies may be resolved' into 'the competition of opposite analogies. . . . It is by the urging of these different analogies that the contention of the bar is carried on' (Paley 401). According to Coke (12) and Hale, these analogies were discovered by the 'wit'; but to Hume and Bentham, for example, they were now discovered by its eighteenth-century successor, the imagination, considered as the faculty which discovered, or as the power of discovering, resemblances. It may have been a desire to signal his differences with Hume on this as on so many other issues that led Paley to argue that such analogies were discovered neither by the wit nor by the imagination, both of them no doubt too frivolous for the task, but by 'the sagacity and wisdom' of the court (Paley 402).

'Many of the reasonings of lawyers are of this analogical nature,' wrote Hume, 'and depend on very slight connexions of the imagination.' This was not, for Hume, a matter of regret; rather, it was of the very nature of jurisprudence, which was 'in this respect, different from all the sciences' in that

> in many of its nicer questions, there cannot properly be said to be truth or falsehood on either side. If one pleader bring the case under any former law or precedent, by a refined analogy or comparison; the opposite pleader is not at a loss to find an opposite analogy or comparison: and the preference given by the judge is often founded more on taste and imagination than on any solid argument. (Hume 1966, 196, 308–9, and see Postema 128–34)

This common-law habit of analogising, Bentham pointed out, could be taken so far that Sir Edward Coke was delighted to be able to unravel a knotty legal problem with the help of an analogy not between one case and another, but between the Common Law itself and the laws of dynamics:

> When in justification of an article of English Common Law, calling uncles to succeed in certain cases in preference to fathers, Lord Coke produced a sort of ponderosity he had discovered in rights, disqualifying them from ascending in a straight line, it was not that he *loved* uncles particularly, or *hated* fathers, but because the analogy, such as it was, was what his imagination presented him with, instead of a reason, and because, to a judgment unobservant of the standard of utility, or unacquainted with the art of consulting it, where affection is out of the way, imagination is the only guide.
> (Bentham 1948 137n; and see Bentham 1970 191)

For Bentham, however, it was crucial to any properly conducted system of law that the judge should pay no attention to the analogies suggested by his imagination.[22] The fact that the system of Common Law was entirely based on the imaginative perception of analogies was a part of its 'imaginary' and *'ex post facto'* character (1970 187n.; 1977 119, 49–50).[23]

For Godwin, all law is *ex post facto*, because it cannot do what it pretends to do: it cannot foresee what actions will be performed in the future (Godwin 1976 684–8). For Bentham similarly, but more specifically, the Common Law is an *ex post facto* and a 'merely imaginary' system because it was not a system of general commands but a collection of particular decisions. Whereas by consulting a properly drafted code of statute law, we would be able to know in advance whether an action we contemplated would break the law or not, the Common Law offered no guidance at all, but simply waited for us to perform an action, and then decided, by a process of the imagination, whether what we have done is more analogous to an action which has previously been regarded as legal, or is more like an action previously adjudged illegal. Precedent was no adequate guide, not simply because the body of precedents was no more than a collection of particular decisions about past events, but because (according to Blackstone for example) previous judicial decisions which a judge chose to regard as 'contrary to reason' were 'not law' (1 Comm. 69–71). Judges were thus permitted, if they saw fit, to set precedents aside, which as Paley pointed out (see Lieberman 79–80), made the law entirely uncertain. It was a permission of course that no one else could claim: only judicial reason was competent to decide that previous instances of judicial reason were contrary to reason, and no lay persons could estimate what attitude the law might take to their actions.[24]

Under such a system of analogous justice, as Bentham, Godwin, Erskine point out, it is impossible to know in advance how to act; and to appropriate to such a system a statute whose 'single object', as Erskine insists, 'was to guard against constructions' (ST 24H: 902) is among other things to appropriate to the terrain of the imagination what should be a matter for the reason and judgement. The attack launched in these trials on 'analogous' and 'imaginary' treasons, in terms of a discourse which concedes no role whatsoever to the imagination in the determination of truth, amounts, once again, to an attack on the whole institution of English Law. And a version of the same attack is launched by Erskine's insistence, many times repeated, that in trials for treason the statute must always be followed to the letter, must always be interpreted literally; which is to say, it must not be interpreted at all, must be treated as if – as Coke (23) had put it – it has no 'IMPLICATIONS OR INFERENCES WHATSOEVER' (for example ST 24H: 889–92, 902). If within the discourse of the Common Law the 'letter' of a statute is opposed to what can be alleged as its 'spirit', so within the discourses of aesthetics and rhetoric which the repeated references to the imagination have brought within the discursive orbit of the trials, the 'literal' is opposed to the 'figurative', and the plain language of the statute of treasons, and ideally of all statute law, is opposed to the figurative, imaginative, mysterious language of the Common Law and of the discourse of custom (and see Godwin 1794 17–18). The relation between the binaries letter/spirit and literal/figurative (and Barrington's variant, 'explicit'/figurative) is nicely pointed out by Holcroft, who invents the personification 'Constructive Treason' as an assistant for Scott – the spirit of the statute, and in clear contradiction of the letter (Holcroft 1795a 63).

These binaries form part of a much longer list of binary oppositions in terms of which the defence and those who write as defendants or in support of them construct their argument:

> matter of fact as against matter of law
> the jury as against the judge
> the written as against the unwritten law
> the sovereignty of Parliament as against the usurpations of the judiciary
> the reason or judgement as against the imagination
> principles as against analogies
> being in one's senses as against being infatuated

and so on and so on. And it is not simply the length of this list, or the ground it appears to cover, which makes it so much a threat to the institution of the law in England. It is rather the damaging relations of contrast and analogy that it proposes: the analogy, for example, between the Common Law and madness; the contrast it generates between a concern for the judgement of fact and the role of the judicial imagination, or between reason and an insane system of law which was itself claimed to be 'the perfection of reason'.

V

It may be helpful if I end by recapitulating my argument. I am suggesting that, especially in the London treason trials, the institution of the law itself was put in question. Not *just* because the function of the law was always liable to be questioned in state trials; not *just* because the nature and function of the law were always at issue in arguments about constitutional reform, for the unwritten law was a crucial component of the unwritten constitution; and not *just* because the terms in which the institutions of government were being defended in the 1790s were borrowed from those which had traditionally been used to extol the Common Law. In addition to all those factors, there were two aspects of the law of treason itself which especially facilitated the process by which the trials of Hardy and Horne Tooke became trials of the Common Law itself. The first was, that at the heart of the law of treason was a statute, and one which expressly stated that it left nothing to judicial construction; the second was that one specific treason was defined in the statute as 'imagining the king's death.'

In the first place, the clause against construction enabled the defence to attack, in the terms of the discourse of philosophical radicalism, the appropriation of a declaratory statute by Common Law, claiming it to be a usurpation of sovereign legislative power by the judiciary; and to attack also the accompanying process by which what the statute represented as matters of fact, to be decided by the jury, were represented instead as matters of law, to be determined by the judge. In the second place, the fact that the defendants were charged with 'imagining' the king's death made possible the riposte that the prosecution was doing the imagining, and that its imagination was hopelessly disordered. In the context created by that riposte, it was possible for the defence to give a particular and a pejorative point to the fact that the Common Law proceeded by the search for analogies, and to the argument that analogies were discovered by the imagination: the Common Law, it seemed, had usurped the functions of reason and judgement. The particularly capacious and ambiguous character of the term 'imagination' in the 1790s had made it possible for the defence to question the authority of the law, by refusing to cooperate with its tendency to expel all discourses from the court other than its own. It did this, however, not in the name of a notion of a legal process that might be more dialogic, or of a legal discourse that might be more or less insulated from the language of the world outside the court. It was not the monologic character of law that the defence chose – or found itself obliged – to attack, but the fact that it was insufficiently monologic, compared with an ideal of written law so thoroughly proof against semantic change and the ill-treatment of usage, and so purged of the ambiguous and the figurative, that it could claim – or so it was imagined – the virtue of having 'NO IMPLICATIONS OR INFERENCES WHATSOEVER.'[25]

7

The Birth of Pandora
and the Origin of Painting

I

In a letter from Rome addressed to his patron Edmund Burke in about
1770 (1: 178), James Barry discusses the shortcomings of Raphael's
Cupid and Psyche frescoes in the Villa Farnesina. The subject of one
of these frescoes, *The Council of the Gods* (Figure 22), required Raphael
to represent a gathering of all the deities of Olympus; but the work,
Barry argues, shows Raphael to have had only the most uncertain
understanding of the different physical characters of the Olympians.
This was not, however, his fault: the greatest antique statues were yet
to be discovered when Raphael was painting, and the knowledge of
classical literature was not what it had since become. Indeed, so great
had been the advancement of classical knowledge since the early
sixteenth century that a modern painter could now hope to challenge
Raphael in the representation of the pagan divinities, if he could find
a similar subject, one in which 'all the gods and goddesses of antiquity'
could put in an appearance. And Barry claims to have found just such
a subject: it was (though he does not say so) the story of the birth of
Pandora, as described by Hesiod in the *Works and Days* (lines 57–101).
In 1775 he exhibited at the Royal Academy a drawing, now lost,
entitled *Pandora*; the exhibit was no doubt both an invitation to
prospective patrons, who might consider commissioning the large
picture of Pandora that Barry had in mind, and an attempt to warn
off other painters from a subject which, he believed, 'included the
whole of the art' of painting (2: 383).[1]

The story, as it appears in the translation by Thomas Cooke which
Barry probably used, is as follows. In the period before women were
invented, when mortal men reproduced themselves by copulating with
nymphs, Prometheus stole the fire of heaven and brought it to earth.

This essay is published here for the first time. Citations not preceded by an
author's name refer to Barry 1809.

22. Nicolas Dorigny, after Raphael, *Deorum Concilium* ('The Council of the Gods') 1693. Approx 37 × 66 cm

23. Luigi Schiavonetti, after James Barry, *The Birth of Pandora*, 1810. Approx 41.6 X 93.2 cm

The first woman, Pandora, was intended by Jupiter as a punishment to men for accepting Prometheus's gift. Her manufacture was entrusted to Vulcan, who was required to mould clay and water 'to frame a Creature exquisitely fair', a creature with the voice and vigour of a human, but as beautiful as a goddess. All the other Olympian deities were then to give her some gift or skill peculiarly their own. Minerva adorned her mind 'with every female Art', and in particular taught her 'the secrets of the Loom'. Venus taught her 'the Wiles of Love', and how to make the most of her beauty. Mercury was required to 'form her mind': to teach her 'soothing Language, and the treach'rous Smile', so that she could be alternately kind and cruel to men. Her dress, coiffure and toilet were entrusted to Persuasion and the Graces; and she was named 'Pandora' because she had received a gift from each of the Olympian deities. Jupiter then ordered Mercury to escort Pandora to earth and present her to Epimetheus, who ignored the warning of Prometheus his brother and accepted the gift. But Pandora had a 'Casket . . . Full of Diseases and corroding Cares'; she opened the lid of this casket, and evil escaped into the world (Cooke 37ff., lines 84–147).

Like Cooke, who pointed out that *'Pandora's* Box may properly be took in the same mystical Sense with the Apple in the Book of *Genesis'*, Barry thought of Pandora as the 'Heathen Eve' (Cooke 119, Barry 1775a). But unlike most earlier artists who had treated the subject of Pandora, he had no great interest in depicting the moment when Pandora opened her fatal casket, box or jar.[2] The episode Barry chose to illustrate was the ceremony of endowing Pandora with divine skills and qualities, and this, he declared in a letter published in the *Morning Chronicle* in May 1775, was 'altogether a virgin subject, and perhaps one of the finest remaining of the ancients' (Barry 1775a). According to Pausanias and Pliny, the pedestal of the chryselephantine statue of Athena Parthenos in the cella of the Parthenon had been decorated with a bas-relief of the subject by Phidias, but beyond Pliny's observation that it represented no less than twenty gods and goddesses (S. Jones 82), no description of this work has come down to us, and as far as Barry knew, no modern artist had attempted the subject.[3] It was only this moment in the story of Pandora that provided the opportunity to represent a large company of Olympians, as Raphael had done in *The Council of the Gods*. And it was a moment which required the painter to pay the most careful attention to the differentiation of the deities one from another, in terms of their physical character. They are each of them to be depicted giving Pandora something which it was uniquely theirs to give – some skill which they have invented or which they oversee; some quality which they quintessentially possess; something constitutive, in short, of the different divine nature of each of them. Thus they must all, male and female, be carefully differentiated, so that they will all severally appear as the perfect embodiment of the various activities and qualities they exist to embody.

'I had this work so much at heart', wrote Barry in 1783, 'that the whole of my studies, whilst I was abroad, were but one continued preparative to the painting of it' (2: 383). It was a subject so valuable to him that he tried first to keep it secret, and then to claim it as his exclusive intellectual property.[4] But apparently because he could find no one to commission the painting, it was not begun until 1791, twenty years after it was first conceived, and was not finished until 1804. As far as we can judge, his conception of the form of the work did not change to any great extent: the 1775 drawing is lost, but an engraving survives by Luigi Schiavonetti of another drawing by Barry of the birth of Pandora, presumably not very dissimilar from the exhibited one (Figure 23); like Raphael's fresco, it is arranged as a frieze, and so eventually was the painting itself, and for the most part the Olympians occupied the same positions in 1804 as they had thirty years earlier. Throughout this period, as far as we can judge from the numerous writings by Barry which refer to the subject or discuss it in detail, he seems to have regarded *The Birth of Pandora* as the most complete statement he had to make about painting and society, more important even than the cycle of six paintings he produced for the Great Room of the Society of Arts at the Adelphi, on no less a subject than 'the progress of human culture'.[5] But almost every time he attempts to describe the significance the subject has for him, it turns out to have changed: the sense of its immense importance never disappears, but quite what is so important about it is curiously hard to pin down.

The Birth of Pandora, in short, comes to look like a subject as much in search of a meaning as of a patron, and the meanings that Barry thinks up for it provide a fascinating chronicle of the development of his ideas about the social and political functions of his art. But as we follow through this narrative of change, it comes to seem that, whatever else the proposed picture is required to do, it has one task which never changes: to define and to preserve the difference between male and female, as if for Barry that difference is felt to be confused and blurred. None of the various meanings which accrue to the subject can be reduced to this function alone, but each can be understood as an attempt to perform this task and at the same time to disavow it; and each new attempt to define the meaning of the subject can be seen as necessitated by the failure of the previous one to segregate men from women in adjacent but separate compartments. As each connecting door is shut and locked, a new one swings open; and it

is the repetitive nature of this scenario that my own narrative will try
to put across. And as we shall also see, Barry's seemingly endless
involvement with the Pandora project reveals how the question of
sexual differentiation is inseparable from that other, no less intractable
question, of the origins and the political function of art.

The writings and images that make up Barry's project attempt to
perform this task mainly by the discussion and representation of the
body; and it makes convenient sense to think of the project as an
attempt to produce a more and more definitive – more clearly defined,
more tightly sealed, more leakproof – image of *homo clausus*, as Norbert
Elias termed it, or of what Bakhtin thought of as the classical body
(Elias 249–63, Bakhtin 25–30, 317–22). In fact whatever is imagined or
projected as the nature of the classical body – its cleanliness, its
impermeability, its emptiness, the distance it keeps, its refusal to
acknowledge its sexual character, its 'finished' quality, its entirely
abstract nature – all that seems to be somehow *especially* true of the
form taken by the neo-classical body in late eighteenth-century Britain.
It is not hard to think of reasons why this should have been so: the
very late, and so very academic attempt to establish the British school
as one of the great European schools of art; the discourse of civic self-
denial in which that attempt was conceived; the traditional protestant
suspicion, which survived even in the Anglican church, of artistic
representation. But for the moment I want to defer a consideration of
the reasons for the phenomenon, and to focus on the phenomenon
itself. No artist before Flaxman, I suggest, had succeeded in depicting
the body so thoroughly eviscerated and drained, and no earlier theorist
of painting had attempted to dematerialise the human figure to the
same degree as had Joshua Reynolds, who argued that images of the
body were more to be admired the more general and abstract they
were.

For Reynolds, what the body lacked in detail and specific character
by being depicted according to the average, the 'central form', it gained
in universality: the emptier the space enclosed by the body's outline,
the more it was enabled to represent the body in general, the body
of the public; while the more detailed the form, the more it became,
merely, *a* body.[6] As we shall see, in his own writings on art Barry
developed a theory which attempted to restore to the body the
precision of anatomical detail that Reynolds had denied it, but at the
cost of representing the neo-classical body as constituted by a different
kind of limitation. For Barry, every body became *a* body, or rather a
type of body, its differences from other bodies codified according to
the contemporary discourse apparently best able to account for such
differences, the discourse of the division of labour. According to that
discourse, the body was shaped by what it did; and thus, inevitably,

it was also shaped, in all its details, by the multiplicity of things it could *not* do. In the Pandora project, this constitutive limitation comes to be imaged as a dismemberment; and in this context the body of the woman can be seen as a means of disavowing the thought that the male body (too) might be incomplete, and equally, as in any such mechanism of disavowal, of representing to view the possibility of such incompleteness.

In Barry's writings on Pandora, this question of the body and its completeness is raised also by his evocation of the abundance and multiplicity of the figures in Egyptian and Hindu art, which come to fill the space of the 'grotesque' body against which the closed, the neo-classical body is defined. But as we shall see, what seems to be at stake in Barry's contemplation of 'oriental' art is that it seems to threaten or destabilise the category of maleness. This essay tries to describe the relation between the disavowed concern to protect the male body, and the overt meanings and functions that Barry attributes to history painting in general, and to *The Birth of Pandora* in particular.

II

The story can begin with an account of Barry's disagreement with Reynolds on the nature of the neo-classical body. In the *Morning Chronicle* letter of 1775, published to help publicise the drawing of Pandora then on show at the Academy exhibition, Barry repeats the claim that the primitive state of classical learning in the early sixteenth century had prevented Raphael from understanding the distinctive characters of the different divinites. It is no wonder, he writes,

> that through the whole range of Deities in his History of *Cupid and Psyche* at the Ghigi Palace, he has mistaken and improperly treated almost every one of them . . . his Jupiter, with his hair like white wool, is not Homer's, but is in the common-place idea of God the Father, and originating from that passage in the Prophet Daniel of the *Ancient of Days*. The Mercury likewise is so far from being the delicate, beautiful youth described in the Odyssy [*sic*], that he is musculous enough to supply, upon occasion, the place of his grand father Atlas. The same fault is observable in the female figures, they all of them seem to be cast in the same gigantesque mould, by which means the Minerva, Juno, &c. are not of larger proportions than Venus and the Graces.

When Barry next writes about his Pandora-subject, in his essay of 1783 on the sequence of paintings he had produced for the Great Room of the Society of Arts, he repeats this critique of Raphael almost verbatim, and he repeats too some sentences which may have seemed uncontentious enough eight years earlier, but which must now have been understood as a direct challenge to the authority of Sir Joshua Reynolds. 'The Greeks', he had argued, 'by a most ingenious refinement, have admirably distinguished the different Deities by such peculiar proportions and formations as belong properly to the idea of such characters.' But 'many of our modern painters and sculptors'

> appear to see nothing further in those Deities that [sic] certain attributes and insignia; by putting on an helmet and gorgon any girlish proportion is made to signify a Minerva; the petasus and caduceus make a Mercury; and the eagle, Jupiter. Nothing can be more ridiculous than this error. (Barry 1775a)[7]

In his tenth discourse, on sculpture, delivered at the Academy in 1780, Reynolds had argued that in sculpture 'the figures are distinguished by their *insignia* more than by any variety of form or beauty.' There is little or no difference in the characters, he claims, of sculpted representations of Apollo, Bacchus, and Meleager – it is the lyre, or the thirsus, or the boar's head, that tells us who is who. 'In a Juno, Minerva, or Flora, the idea of the artist seems to have gone no further than representing perfect beauty, and afterwards adding the proper attributes, with a total indifference to which they gave them' (Reynolds 1975 181–2).[8]

It is of such importance for Barry to affirm the contrary position that in his essay of 1783 he develops his notion of the distinctive character of the Olympian divinities in an abstract language which announces that the issue is to be understood not simply as a matter of fact, but as a question of theory. As so often in such questions, the correct practice is attributed to the Greek painters, whose vanished works can be adduced in support of almost any critical position. Those painters, Barry insists, were

> skilled in the sublime and elegant practice of personifying the abstract perfection of human nature, in all the different species of characters of which the Grecian mythology consisted, embodying and adapting a form and system of adequate proportions to the abstract idea of wisdom, in the character of a Minerva; of majesty in that of a Juno; of beauty in Venus; in Jove, in Mars, and in Hercules, admirably distinguishing through the whole suite of their male and female divinities, that peculiar formation, and that system of proportions, which naturally coincided with the idea of each character, and which altogether comprehended the whole exterior of male and female perfection. (2: 377)

There may at first sight seem to be nothing much at issue here, between Reynolds and Barry. Reynolds, after all, is talking about sculpture, and is making a careful distinction between the degree of characterisation which has been attempted, or which can be achieved, in sculpture, and what may be done in the more expressive art of painting. The main task of sculpture, according to Reynolds, is to represent 'faultless form and perfect beauty'; to represent character and expression as well is desirable up to a point, but the more marked and striking these are allowed to become, the more a work must risk departing from the exhibition of 'the perfection' of 'abstract form' which is its primary concern, and from the gravity, the austerity, the uniformity which are the primary characteristics of the art. Thus the chief danger for sculptors, according to Reynolds, is to imagine they enjoy the variety of styles, genres and objects of imitation that are available to painters, who are as free to concentrate on the characteristic differences between one divinity, one kind of body, and another, as Barry would claim (Reynolds 1975 175–7).

But if Reynolds seems to be attempting to define the uniform nature of sculpture by distinguishing it from the variety available within the art of painting, he can think of no clearer way of describing that uniformity than by comparing sculpture with the grand style of painting, to which, he argues, sculpture 'has a relation so close, that it may be said to be almost the same art operating upon different materials'. And like sculpture, the grand style of painting has as its primary aim the representation of perfect beauty, which in each species is 'invariable'; and Reynolds can never rid himself of the notion that this aim will be compromised if we allow, as Barry does, that there may be different kinds of bodies, different physical types or characters, each with their own abstract standard of perfection (Reynolds 1975 175, 49).

'It may be objected,' Reynolds acknowledges, 'that in every particular species there are various central forms . . . that in the human figure, for instances, the beauty of Hercules is one, of the Gladiator another, of the Apollo another; which makes so many different ideas of beauty' (Reynolds 1975 46–7). And up to a point, the force of this argument must be acknowledged, if painting is to be saved from the obligation to represent, over and over again, the same body, the same abstract standard of perfection: narrative paintings in the grand style must be able to include figures of different types, sexes and ages if their stories are to get told. But he is not willing to budge from his belief in a single aesthetic standard governing the forms taken by the neo-classical body. The Hercules, the Gladiator, the Apollo, may each be 'perfect in their kind'; but

the perfection of human beauty . . . is not in the Hercules, nor in
the Gladiator, nor in the Apollo; but in that form which is taken
from them all, and which partakes equally of the activity of the
Gladiator, of the delicacy of the Apollo, and of the muscular strength
of the Hercules. For perfect beauty in any species must combine all
the characters which are beautiful in that species.

(Reynolds 1975 47)

For Reynolds, then, perfect beauty is an invariable standard; and
however the exigencies of narrative require the painter to represent a
variety of physical forms, the highest aim of painting remains the
representation of that standard. It might perhaps have been more to
the point for Reynolds to describe painting in the grand style as an
art which aspires to the condition of sculpture rather than the other
way round: the greater possibilities for narrative that painting enjoys
are for him something of a liability. For Barry, too, beauty is to be
regarded as an invariable standard; but just because it is, it is 'tasteless
and insipid' (1: 401), of no particular interest to the artist; and the
highest aim of painting is the representation, with a precision and
detail which for Barry do not interfere with idealisation, of all the
various classes of physical character as they are variously differentiated
from perfect beauty. The value, as a subject for painting, of the birth
of Pandora, was that if offered an opportunity to produce just such a
representation, and so to produce a complete statement of all that the
art should aim to do. For Reynolds, the equivalent opportunity would
have been, perhaps, a group of three male graces, seen from
different angles, and each a perfect combination of mutually exclusive
perfections.

Much more is at stake in this disagreement than an aesthetic
question about the relation of beauty and variety. It is also a
disagreement, if not about the proper function of painting, then
certainly about how painting should perform that function in late
eighteenth-century Britain.[9] For both Reynolds and Barry, the function
of painting is to convert its 'audience' into a 'public', and not simply
a public for painting, but a political public. Properly pursued, the art
of painting attempts, we could say, to make men citizens, aware of
the grounds of the affiliation by which they and others are constituted
as members of a polity. And for both of them painting does this by
representing images of the human body which by some means attempt
to produce this civic awareness in those who examine them. For
Reynolds, the only image of the body that can be imagined as having
this effect is the image of perfect beauty, which is the same thing as
the 'central form' of the human body. By the careful comparison of

body with body, the artist observes how they differ from each other, and thus arrives at an understanding of what they have in common. It is this that he must paint: general form, purged of the detail that is the sign of the particular; for his task is to 'represent in every one of his figures the character of its species.' (Reynolds 1975 44, 50) The spectator, contemplating such images, is encouraged to believe that the ways in which one person differs from another are of far less importance than what they have in common. What they do have in common is their humanity, and to be human is, according to the civic discourse, to be, potentially, a 'political animal'.

The inadequacy for Barry of such a political aesthetic is that it refuses to acknowledge difference. It produces an image of the ideal citizen, whether as represented in the picture, or as looking at it, which is rigidly uniform; and it can regard difference only as a mark of failure in the civic character, the sign of a refusal or inability to subordinate oneself fully to one's identity as citizen. For Barry, on the other hand, such an image of citizenship is anachronistic: we cannot expect to discover a civic uniformity of character in modern commercial nations, which are not theatres for the performance of acts of heroism, but vast diffused market-places where the products of the division of labour are exchanged. What characterises a society as modern is the division of labour, which, by enabling everyone to specialise in one particular task or another, makes them dependent on others to provide them with the goods they themselves cannot produce. In such a society, the social structure becomes the structure of mutual interdependence created by the division of labour; like Adam Ferguson and Adam Smith, Barry considers that difference itself can be thought of as the ground of social affiliation in modern society.

One disadvantage of this form of social unity was thought to be, of course, that it made no appeal to the social affections; it gave no sense of belonging to a collective social or political unit. Those who worked away at their divided labours could be thought of, certainly, as working for others as well as for themselves, and as working also therefore for the public interest, by participating in an economic and social structure whose strength was the result of the interdependence of its parts. But for the most part they were concerned only with their own interests, and were unaware of, and unattached to, any such notion as the interest of the public. And so it comes to be the task of painting, in Barry's view, to overcome the sense of alienation, the occlusion of social perspectives, that is produced by the division of labour.

To do this, the nature and meaning of the difference between one body and another would have to be reconceived. For Barry, these differences should be regarded as 'deviations from the general standard for the better purpose of effecting utility and power' (1: 400); and the different physical characters apparent among the members of a society at any time could be understood by asking such questions as these:

> Is he bred at Wapping or at St James's? Is he bred a smith, a mercer, or a soldier? Does he till the land? Is he a waterman, common-council-man, or is he a waiter at a tavern or coffee-house? If a woman, does she sell fish or millinery-ware? Is she a fat greasy cook, or has she the delicacy, vapours, smelling-bottles, flirt, giddiness, and low spirits of higher life?   (Barry 1775b 82–3)

Difference of physical character may be regarded as the cause, or as the effect, of the division of labour – we may do a particular job because we are built that way, or we may come to be built that way because we do a particular job. But either way physical difference can be understood as the image of occupational difference, and occupational difference can be understood in terms of the different contributions made by different kinds of work to the achievement of a common social object.

For Barry, however, the strength of a society was not a simple function of the degree of its economic or occupational interdependence. Many of the occupations performed in modern commercial Britain – those involved in the production of luxury goods, or in the provision of immoral services – were the causes or symptoms of disease rather than of health, and their moral character was not to be redeemed simply by recognising their participation in an economy of exchange. The bodies of all those who perform manual or intellectual labour depart from the standard of perfect beauty; but those who were 'well employed' (2: 333) – who produced or provided socially useful goods or services – were to be represented in painting as diversified into various forms which could be seen as sublime; while the 'ill-employed' were to be represented as deformed. The variously admirable bodies of the Olympian gods and goddesses, therefore, were the ideal representations of the physical and so of the occupational differences among those who performed work of genuine social utility; and the co-operative activity of the Olympians, in the creation and education of Pandora, can be regarded as a figure for the unity and the shared objectives of a society apparently divided by the fact that, in a complex national economy, those who performed different kinds of useful work were for the most part invisible to each other. In representing the story of the birth of Pandora, painting thus fulfils its highest function in modern society, to make visible a community of social purpose which, in extensive commercial societies, would otherwise be invisible.

To give as much room to displaying the various bodies of the pagan divinities as is consistent with the maintenance of some kind of pictorial – and therefore of social – unity, the subject is organised in Schiavonetti's etching (and so presumably on the drawing on which it is based) into a frieze-like structure, similar to that of *The Council of the Gods*. At the centre of the picture, Pandora, seated, is being adorned by the three Graces. To the left, and from the left, are Apollo ('singing the Hymeneals', according to Barry's account of his drawing of 1775), Bacchus, Pan, and Mars. The recumbent Vulcan has been moved from the inconspicuous position allotted to him by Raphael, to a place in front of the wall of deities which had been filled in Raphael's painting by a river god; but in Barry's version, he has turned away from Pandora, and looks out of the picture, so as to suggest his status as an outsider on Olympus. Venus, helped or hindered by Cupid, is removing her cestus to give it to Pandora. The goddess to the right of Pandora is Minerva, who holds a piece of woven cloth, and with her other hand is presenting Pandora with a shuttle. To her right, just as in Raphael's picture, sit Pluto, Neptune, Jupiter (to whom Hebe is offering a cup of nectar),[10] Juno, and Diana, with Ceres and Vesta behind them. In the right foreground sits Mercury, 'putting on his Talaria to carry her [Pandora] down to Epimetheus, her husband.' The figures in the air are the Horae, 'strewing flowers'; absent from Schiavonetti's etching are the Fates, who were represented in the 1775 drawing; one of them was carrying 'that well-known casket which contains her portion' (Barry 1775a). But even in the 1775 drawing, they were clearly in the background, somewhere behind Jupiter, for as we have seen it was not the evils brought by Pandora that interested Barry in 1775 or in his essay of 1783: it was the different processes involved in her production, and it was the idea of Pandora as a figure for the unity of those processes.

The composition is thus unified around the body of Pandora, which is the same thing as to say that the various Olympian deities are represented as unified by this perfect product of their joint labour; and their unity – this is the final point of painting them – is to be taken as a model or pattern of the unity of divided labour in a modern commercial society. Because both gods and goddesses are shown as participating members in the unified society of Olympus, the picture seems to constitute its audience, too, as composed of men and women, as if it seeks to make them aware of themselves as all equally members of a public open to all who engage in useful work, irrespective of their sex. But a further look at the conditions of viewing implied by this picture, in the light of Barry's accounts of the function of painting, will suggest that the sexual difference which, at the edges of the picture, is dissolved in the name of occupational differentiation, is reconstituted at the centre in the name of civic unity.

For what is the effect of Barry's choice of a story, and an arrangement of figures, which place an image of ideal feminine beauty at the centre of the composition? The body of Pandora can perform its unifying function only so long as it is not also taken as an image of a possible or an ideal identity for the individual subjects who contemplate it. The audience must not identify it with their own, must not receive it as a representation of that ideal and uniform civic identity which is to be achieved by learning to disregard or to transcend individual differences and aspirations. It was of course essential to Reynolds's theory that the ideal body should be a male body: only educated males were capable of performing the processes of abstraction necessary to enable them to recognise and identify with that ideal form. But if the body of Pandora is to perform the very different task assigned to it by Barry's theory, it must negate the possibility of such an act of identification, and deflect the spectator into identifying with one or other of the physically differentiated bodies of the Olympians; and it can perform this task only if Barry's spectator, too, is conceived of as male. For a female spectator, the body of Pandora would be the central form of all the female bodies on display, the image of a unity that would abolish their difference; only for the male can if function as a symbol of the unity that only difference can produce. It is by virtue of the fact that the men in the audience *are* men that Pandora can legitimate the differences in their physical characters (and therefore in their social and economic roles and functions), by standing as an emblem of what they have, or do, in common.[11]

But at this very point, where the appropriate spectator seems to have been constituted as masculine, a paradox opens up. It is Pandora's identity as female which enables her to function as a symbol rather than as focus of identification, but it also risks the collapse of that very function. If only the male spectator can be trusted to read Pandora's body correctly, he is also especially liable to misread it; for though he is intended to find in Pandora a purely formal and ideal representation of civic unity – that is why her body is represented in such an abstract and linear style – he may find instead an object of desire, and the provocative pose she has adopted, passive, ornamented and displayed, does nothing to discourage this. Indeed, it seems that to find the one he must find the other: Pandora must appear as an object of desire, to encourage him to desire what, as symbol, she represents. For political economists, the mutual dependence created by the division of labour was a matter of fact, not of value, or it was a matter of economic rather than moral value: the greater the division of labour, the more productive a society would become, though its members would not therefore become morally better. For Barry, that mutual dependence was of value only if it was recognised and desired as a matter of *moral* value – only if the participants in a social economy were able to understand their private virtues as public virtues, and their private interests as identical with the public interest; to become aware of themselves, in short, as citizens, different but the same. It is the desirability of this awareness that painting especially could impress upon the spectator, and which is to be discovered in the desirability of Pandora.

It was an essential article, however, of the civic theory of art that it was committed to a republican critique of sexual indulgence and of the dangers it posed to civic virtue. If painting was to persuade men to recognise themselves as citizens, it must teach them to pay no regard to the private gratification of their appetites, which would anyway have the effect of making them effeminate and incapable of performing their civic duties (see above, 65). If it was essential to Pandora's symbolic function that she should be an irresistible object of desire, it was no less essential to the civic unity she symbolised that the spectator should not desire her. Barry has attempted to detach the good beginning of Pandora's story from her bad end, so as to use her beauty to stand for the ideal civic unity which, he believed, could still be envisaged in commercial society, in spite of the cupidity encouraged by commerce. But for the picture to work on Barry's terms, the spectator would have to be able simultaneously to desire and not to desire Pandora. He can only desire what she symbolises by desiring her body: but if he does desire her body, he cannot have what it symbolises. Far from being an image which offers some self-evident position for a male spectator, Schiavonetti's etching sets up conditions of viewing for such a spectator which it simultaneously renders inoperative or undermines.

These problems become less salient in Barry's later images of Pandora and his explanations of them, but not because they are acknowledged and addressed. For the next time we hear of the Pandora project, the body of Pandora has ceased to be the principle focus of attention. Barry's main concern has come to be Minerva, who is the very opposite of Pandora, in this at least, that according to Freud (18: 273) she 'repels all sexual desires'; and that was her reputation, too, at the end of the eighteenth century.

III

Barry's attempts to secure a commission to paint the birth of Pandora attracted the attention of the Duke of Richmond, the reforming politician, and of the bourgeois collector William Locke. But neither was happy with the size of the projected canvas, which in 1783 Barry estimated at 8' 10" by 17' 8", and nothing came of their interest (2:

383–4). They may also have objected to Barry's plans for the sizes of the figures relative to each other – in the final painting they are sized in order of Barry's sense of their rank in the Olympian hierarchy, with Jupiter and Juno drawn on a quite different scale from Mercury, for example. The work seems finally to have got started in 1791: a note in the *Morning Post* for 28 April of that year records that Barry was busy on 'a great design . . . called "The Birth of Pandora;" in which the whole Synod of the gods and goddesses are convened in full Olympic state.' The early interest of possible patrons had come to nothing: but Barry 'has now his own size, his own price, and his own time' – a claim probably not so much misinformed (as far as we know, Barry had no commission) as ironic, for virtually throughout Barry's career his time was very much his own, and the price of all his major works was whatever he himself was prepared to pay, in terms of effort and deprivation. 'Much expectation is formed', the note concludes, 'from the sweep and firmness of his classical pencil.'

In 1798, some years before the painting was finished, Barry published another account of its subject, in his *Letter to the Dilettanti Society*. The main point of this letter, as William Pressly has summarised it, was that the Royal Academy was 'no longer capable of accomplishing its original intention of improving public taste,' and that therefore Barry 'was appealing to another society, the Dilettanti, to undertake this patriotic duty in its place' (Pressly 1981 137). The controversy that followed the publication of the letter is beyond the scope of this essay: it led, the following year, to Barry's expulsion from the Academy.

Throughout his career Barry had argued that the improvement of taste in the visual arts was a matter of public concern and should be a matter of public policy. Artists, he insisted, should behave as the teachers and the servants of the public, and not as self-employed businessmen; and his was the most urgent of the many late eighteenth-century voices urging that painters should regard themselves as members of a learned profession. As a part of his attempt to promote the dignity of painting, Barry argues at one point in the *Letter* for the superiority of the art of painting over the arts of literature, by claiming (among other things) that while the several modes and genres of writing were thought of by the Greeks as entrusted to the supervision of the various Muses, they believed that the goddess of wisdom herself presided over painting. 'The employment,' he writes,

> for which Minerva is peculiarly distinguished from all the celestial personages, is her skill in the labours of the loom . . . she was sovereignly skilful in the art of painting in tapestry . . . . by the skilful labours of the loom the ancients always understood the art of making pictures in tapestry . . .   (2: 585)

Minerva was entrusted with responsibility for the art of painting, Barry argues, because painting, which exhibits 'actual' things, things themselves, is 'the real art of wisdom', whereas poetry, which employs only the names of things, is 'only an account or relation' of wisdom. But the immediacy of painting is not all that entitles it to the protection of Minerva. 'It is . . . not the merely copying of actual, casual, ordinary nature, but the new moulding and imitation of it . . . was the true reason why the ancients placed this art in the hands of Minerva herself'; for her art can 'call to our view . . . a new creation, where . . . objects, sublimated and purged from all dross and alloy, appear before us in *gala*, in all conceivable and possible splendour.' The ideal nature of Minerva's art was a part of her concern that painting should be didactic – she 'could employ that universal language of forms . . . to all the grand ethical purposes of information, persuasion, and instruction' (2: 585–7).

'These observations,' as Barry describes them, 'respecting the patronage and presidency of Minerva in our art' (2: 595) were Barry's own: it does not appear that any earlier writer had chosen to regard the weaving in which Minerva was skilled as 'the art of painting in tapestry'.[12] But having developed the conceit, he now rewrites the long history of his intention to paint the birth of Pandora, by claiming that 'the moment I came to ask myself what it was that Minerva was teaching to Pandora, it opened upon me all at once, that she was teaching her to paint' (2: 595). Whether or not the subject is losing the meanings attributed to it in 1775 and 1783, it is now acquiring another meaning: it is attaching itself to a flourishing eighteenth-century sub-genre, of paintings depicting the origin of painting.

In the eighteeth century, paintings about the origin of painting are almost always to be read as about its *function* as well, for what has come to be known as the 'genetic fallacy' was so ingrained within the cultural philosophy of the period, that enquiries as to the function of any cultural practice – government, language, poetry – were almost always answered by statements about its origin. The standard myth of the origin of painting was the story, from Pliny, of the daughter of Dibutades, the 'Corinthian' or 'Sicyonian' maid, who with Cupid guiding her hand had traced on the wall the shadow of her parting lover's profile. This story was probably more often chosen than any other by British artists of the late eighteenth century. In the 1770s it was the subject of a print by John Hamilton Mortimer, and was painted by David Allan and Alexander Runciman, who had both been contemporaries of Barry at Rome. Before the end of the century it was treated also by Joseph Wright, Edward Burney and Thomas Stothard. There is a drawing of the subject by Barry, dating probably from the 1790s (Figure 24), and he had included the imaginary portrait of the

24. James Barry, *The Sicyonian Maid*, or *The Origin of Painting*, date unknown. Pen and brown ink over pencil
13.6 × 22.7 cm. Ashmolean Museum, Oxford.

Sicyonian maid, who 'gave a beginning to the art' (2: 384) among the
company of the saved in the final picture in his Adelphi cycle, *Elysium
and Tartarus or the State of Final Retribution*.[13]

But from Barry's point of view, it would be difficult to think of a
myth of origin more calculated to degrade the function of painting
than this one. Everything is wrong with it. It represents the original
genre as portraiture, not as history; it valorises servile copying –
tracing – at the expense of idealising invention; and it ascribes a
priority to the private over the public function of painting, in terms
both of where painting happens – in a private house, not in a public
building – and of what it is used for – the expression of personal
feelings, the memorialisation of personal attachments, rather than the
creation and celebration of public spirit. We could sum all this up, I
want to suggest, by saying that Pliny's myth, in attributing the origin
of painting to a woman, would have been interpreted in late eighteenth-
century Britain as attributing a feminine function to the art. Women
were generally assumed, by men at least, to prefer portraiture to
history painting; their inability, whether by nature or nurture, to
generalise, and so to idealise, was a crucial mark of their difference
from men; and the range of their interests and concerns was taken to
be confined, and properly confined, to the private sphere and to

domestic space. By contrast, the highest kind of painting, the epic and heroic, had always been represented by Barry as the masculine art *par excellence*. The 'sublime and daring genius' of the Greek artists, who provide the standard of perfection in the noblest branches of the visual arts, was the result of their 'public spirit', their 'love of virtue and liberty', which they owed to 'the manly philosophy of Socrates' (1: 364–5); and the comprehensiveness of vision, the public spirit, and the self-denial necessary to the creation of great art – the republican, masculine virtues – are also those which art, if it is to be great, must communicate to its audience.

The argument Barry has been developing in the *Letter to the Dilettanti Society* has reinforced the notion that painting, in its highest manifestations, is by comparison with poetry a masculine art. To argue that painting could still perform a cognitive function, as opposed to the consolatory function which was increasingly being attributed to the arts in late eighteenth-century Britain, was inevitably to argue also that it should be thought of as a masculine activity, outside and above the feminised realms of feeling and sentiment. So is the claim that it can be employed 'to all the grand purposes of information, persuasion and instruction': painting here appears to be credited not simply with a cognitive and a didactic, but with a large-scale ('grand') rhetorical ('persuasion') function which attaches it to the public and so to the masculine sphere. The concern of painting with the ideal, too, is a concern that demands on the part of the artist a comprehensiveness of vision and a 'penetration' (a favourite word of Barry's – see for example 1: 456; 2: 398, 586), which are regarded in the late eighteenth century as characteristically or even exclusively masculine capabilities. And yet it is precisely these aspects of painting, Barry claims, 'the new moulding' of nature 'according to the more perfect and wiser views of completeness, utility, and ethical adaptation', that led the ancients to place painting 'in the hands of Minerva herself' (2: 586–7).

The irony of attributing the origin of a masculine art to a female deity is not missed by Barry. The Greeks, he writes, 'reserved this Master Art, this Art *par excellence*, to employ the . . . exertions and skill of the mistress of all, of Minerva, or Wisdom itself' (2: 586). Painting is described as a 'Master art', presumably, not primarily to gender it as masculine, but to distinguish if from poetry which, by virtue of the lower degree of skill it involves, can be thought of as apprentice-work. But the rhetorical contrast, 'Master art' and 'mistress of all', must certainly represent an acknowledgement that there is a question of gender at stake in the new myth that Barry has invented for the origin of his art – and that to invent a feminine origin for painting is to risk feminising its function. In so far as the origin of painting has become a part of the complex subject of *The Birth of Pandora*, the painting itself has accumulated another layer of contradiction. The threat posed to the conception of painting as a masculine art by attributing its invention to a female goddess was hardly an unforseeable, but it was certainly an awkward by-product of Barry's determination to upgrade painting at the expense of the arts of literature: however much more prestige may attach to the goddess of wisdom as compared with the daughters of memory, she remains female.

To a degree, of course, the threat is contained by the manly character and physique traditionally attributed to Minerva. In a lecture on 'design' which Barry delivered at the Royal Academy sometime in the 1790s, he had considerably revised his earlier account of how the body should be represented in history painting. The marks of occupational differentiation, by which the body departed from the standard of ideal beauty, were now acknowledged to be visible in the male body only; the sublimity, indeed, of the male body, consisted in the fact that it was adapted for the performance of heroic or useful tasks dedicated to the general good. The female body, incapable of aspiring to what was, for Barry no less than for Burke, the exclusively masculine category of the sublime, was henceforth to become a protected site of ideal beauty. It was to be entirely innocent of labour and untouched by history (with the implication, of course, that women did not therefore perform useful labour, and so could no longer be regarded as citizens on the same terms as men).[14]

Minerva, however, was the exception that proved the rule: no learned painter could represent her as anything other than the manly antitype of ideal feminine beauty. As Joseph Spence, for example, had pointed out, though Minerva has dignity, firmness, composure, even beauty, she has none of 'the little graces, or of the softness and prettiness of Venus': the ancient artists represented her as 'more apt to strike one with awe and terror, than to charm'. She is also the most civic, the most public-spirited of goddesses, so that the image of Virtue herself is very like, or even based upon, the image of Minerva. She is, in short, Spence says, a *masculine* goddess (Spence 59). And because the body of Minerva was not conventionally regarded as an object of desire, to advertise the special importance of Minerva might have the advantage, when the canvas was finally exhibited, of distracting attention from the problems created by placing the languid body of Pandora at the centre of a work whose official concern was to promote public spirit over private appetite.

But she remains obstinately female, and the manner in which she becomes the patroness of painting must still have the effect of feminising the art. For the story of the birth of Pandora does not enable Minerva to be shown instructing men in the practice of painting as a part of their public duties: she is to be shown teaching the art to a woman, in the form of weaving, and as part of Pandora's 'domestic duties' – the duties, indeed, 'of a wife' (2: 595). The questions raised by Barry's own myth of origin persist, and when eventually he addresses them, it is only to recommend that we apply elsewhere for the answer. The recommendation needs to be quoted at length.

> If any one should start a query, why the ancients, who reasoned so deeply, should, in their personifications of the sovereign wisdom, have chosen Minerva a female; why the Muses, who preside over the several subordinate modes of intelligence, &c. are all females; and why the conversation of the serpent was held with Eve, in order that her influence might be employed in persuading Adam; such queries could have been well and pertinently answered by the eloquent, generous, amiable sensibility of the celebrated and long-to-be-lamented Mary Wolstonecraft, and would interweave very gratefully with another edition of her Rights of Woman. Her honest heart, so estranged from all selfishness, and which could take so deep and generous an interest in whatever had relation to truth and justice, . . . would find some matter for consolation, in discovering that the ancient nations of the world entertained a very different opinion of female capabilities, from those modern Mahometan, tyrannical, and absurd degrading notions of female nature, at which her indignation was so justly raised.   (2: 594)

It was modestly courageous of Barry thus to evoke the memory of Mary Wollstonecraft, in a year (1798) which had begun with the publication of the notorious *Memoirs of the Author of a Vindication of the Rights of Woman*, by his good friend William Godwin.[15] And in terms of the argument he is elaborating, it was certainly convenient for Barry to be able to evoke her at this point, as the appropriate person to solve the problems produced by his own speculations. As the *Letter* continues, however, it is not too hard to see why it might also be convenient that she is now unable to give her answers. In the terms of a late eighteenth-century economy of gender-attributes, a female, whether woman or goddess, who insists upon the importance of wisdom and of virtue as especially public or civic virtue, can only be a masculine woman; and in the 'introduction' to her *Vindication*, Wollstonecraft's assault on the 'Mahometanism' which treats woman as 'subordinate beings' (Wollstonecraft 1975 8) obliges her to confront this problem directly:

I am aware of the obvious inference: – from every quarter have I heard exclamations against masculine women; but where are they to be found? If by this appellation men mean to inveigh against their ardour in hunting, shooting, and gaming, I shall most cordially join in the cry; but if it be against the imitation of manly virtues, or, more properly speaking, the attainment of those talents and virtues, the exercise of which ennobles the human character, and which raise females in the scale of animal being, when they are comprehensively termed mankind; – all those who view them with a philosophic eye must, I should think, wish with me, that they may every day grow more masculine.   (Wollstonecraft 1975 8)

Wollstonecraft's point, of course, in this passage and elsewhere, is to suggest that the virtues called 'manly', and the values regarded as 'masculine', are universal human values which have been appropriated by men and expropriated from women. Her refusal, however, to admire any of the attributes which her society regarded as properly and exclusively feminine could certainly be read as valorising that civic notion of masculinity ('laborious and self-denying', 1: 365) that Barry regarded as the very foundation both of public spirit and of the art of painting. Barry is able to take advantage of this construction of the *Vindication* to find in Wollstonecraft a modern Minerva; and so, if he has encumbered himself with a myth of origin that threatens to feminise his art, he can still protect himself against the worst consequences of the myth, by evoking an account of femininity which is as little feminine as possible – which is indeed the negation of femininity by any contemporary understanding of gender-difference. If the art of painting is feminised, then the feminine itself must be made masculine.

A year after the publication of the *Letter*, during the proceedings to remove Barry from the professorship of painting at the Royal Academy, and finally from the Academy itself, Francis Bourgeois RA suggested that among the grounds for expulsion should be included the fact that 'He has highly commended *David*, & Mrs Wolstoncraft & commended their principles' (Pressly 1981 180). But in point of fact, Barry's attempt to use the principles of Wollstonecraft is much less than whole-hearted, and turns out to create as many problems as it had seemed to resolve. For those principles could be used to defend Barry's art from the feminisation that threatened it, they could not so easily be relied upon to reassure him that the true character of his art was to be masculine; for their aim, and Wollstonecraft's 'earnest wish', was 'to see the distinction of sex confounded in society' (Wollstonecraft 1975 57), and so to dissolve the very categories by which Barry's own notions of gender, and so – as we shall see – his own masculinity, are constituted.

Indeed, so potentially disastrous is Barry's own invocation of Wollstonecraft, that no sooner has it been uttered than he hurries to retract it: better to accept the logic of his myth of origin, to attribute to art just that feminine function which he has been trying so hard to push away, than accept an account of human capacities which does not treat them as gender-specific. His account of *The Birth of Pandora* now takes a quite extraordinary turn: Pandora must learn to paint, not so that she can introduce into the world an art capable of being employed to 'grand ethical purposes', but simply so that she will acquire an appropriately feminine accomplishment. The transition, from a sternly republican account of the function of art to one which is its exact opposite, occurs within the space of a single sentence. Minerva, writes Barry, is teaching Pandora to paint:

> teaching her an art which was capable of being made subservient to all the social duties, and where it was impossible to excel in it, without the acquisition of such information, respecting all the concerns and dearest interests of humanity . . .   (2: 595)

– so far, it may seem, so civic; but the word 'dearest' seems to provide a pivot which enables Barry to turn his back on the unfamiliar identity of male feminist that, a page earlier, it had seemed in his interests to assume; and he continues:

> . . . dearest interests of humanity, as could not fail, when joined with the superior sentiment and graces of feminine softness, to become the solace and anodyne against the numberless and unavoidable miseries of life; and as wives, mothers, daughters, sisters, citizens, and above all, as friends, these endearing accomplishments . . . could not fail of rendering them the graceful ornaments of all stations.   (2: 595)

The point of Minerva's 'interference in *female education*' turns out to be that, by learning to paint, women will learn to make themselves more agreeable to men – to the men who define the identities of women by their mode of relation with them, as husbands, sons, fathers and so on. The suggestion that among the possible identities of women they may be 'citizens' is all that is left either of Barry's or of Wollstonecraft's civic concerns, and nothing that follows seems to know what to do with that notion. The duty of women, it seems, is to become 'graceful ornaments', offering solace to men returning bruised from the collisions of public life; and they can do this, presumably, either by inviting these men to glance at their home-made watercolours, in which the 'superior sentiment and graces of feminine softness' will be apparent, or by employing the fund of information they have acquired in the study of the art of diverting their menfolk with conversation. The 'wish', as well as the 'destination' of women, it seems, is 'to excel each other in pleasing, and to create a superior interest in the other sex', and so an education in the fine arts is of particular value in helping one woman to get the start of another. And a knowledge of painting will be especially becoming to the women of Britain, where it will be set off by 'the beauties and graces' which 'it is the pride and glory of our mild and genial climate to produce', and so on and so on (2: 595–7).[16]

That all this should be passed off as of a piece with Wollstonecraft's account of 'female education' is of course extraordinary: virtually everything said here is contested by, or is a contestation of, the *Vindication*, whether Barry's belief that women are naturally more capable of sentiment than men, or that they should wish to be ornamental or graceful, if grace implies softness, or that, if they compete for the attentions of men, it is their 'destination' to do so.[17] No less extraordinary is that this passage represents a complete abandonment of all that Barry had stood for, in his many attempts to redefine the public function of painting. Essential to those attempts was his insistence, continued over twenty years, that art has a public function because it has a cognitive function: its task, as we have seen, is to discover and to represent the nature of social and political affiliation in a commercial society apparently divided by the division of labour. Now, suddenly, painting has moved indoors, from a public to a private and a domestic space. Its function is no longer cognitive, but, at best, consolatory: it has no purchase on what I have called the collisions of public life, and its concern is not to understand or represent or change them, but to kiss them better. Whatever we think about this new account of the function of painting, we can probably agree that, within the terms of Barry's notions of gender, it is a recognisably feminine function; and that Barry seems to have been forced into producing it in order to protect those very notions. Painting may no longer be a manly activity; but manliness itself has survived.

IV

The last and longest account Barry produced of his Pandora project is the essay known as the 'Fragment on Pandora'. This seems to have been written in 1805 (1: 295), the year after the painting had been completed, and it was intended as an explanatory note to be published with the large mixed-method print that Barry himself had made of the painting; it was eventually published in 1809, in the posthumous edition of his writings. The essay begins by reaffirming the aims of the project as they had been set out in the *Morning Chronicle* in 1775, and in the 1783 *Account* of the paintings in the Adelphi cycle. Once again Barry declared that, when Raphael was painting, the primitive state of learning had given him a most inadequate knowledge of the 'peculiar characters' which the Greeks had assigned to their several deities, 'those emphatical qualities, which constitute the essence of whatever is beautiful, graceful, or sublime' (2: 143, 145); that the discoveries of the last three centuries, however, had made it possible for modern artists to believe that they might excel Raphael in the representation of the members of the Greek Pantheon; and that the birth of Pandora was a subject which offered Barry the chance to do just that.

Indeed, the subject now seems an opportunity to excel the Greeks themselves, or what we know of their art. The statues which have survived from antiquity are not their best: the Venus de' Medici, for example (Figure 12), has 'something of the mother . . . about the breasts and abdomen', and the Jupiter at the Verospi palace 'comes infinitely short of that perfection' which the father of the gods should display. Such statues are of value less for what they are, than for the hints they give of the perfection that must have been evident in the lost works of the finest Greek sculptors. The 'restoration of this perfection,' writes Barry, 'has been the business of my life'; and, defending this ambition against an as yet unidentified adversary, he argues that, as nobody now believes in Jupiter, Juno and the rest, these 'vestiges of paganism' may be appreciated simply on account of 'whatever they may afford of beautiful, graceful, sublime'. They are now available to be used as 'mere symbols of attributes, elements, abstractions of virtues and dispositions', and, in this light, their representation may be innocent enough, and may even be made 'most subservient to the cause of Christian piety and virtue' (2: 146–8)

It may seem unlikely that in 1805 the representation of the pagan deities by an academic painter would be at all controversial or in need of justification. In fact, however, what was still probably the standard text-book of classical mythology, Tooke's *Pantheon*, missed no opportunity, as Godwin (v–vi) put it, to calumniate the divinities of Greece 'in the coarsest thoughts and words that rancour could furnish', and in particular to inveigh against the 'filthy loves of gods and goddesses' which did so much to mould the character of Byron's Don Juan (I, xli). Godwin's own *Pantheon*, published pseudonymously in 1806, was attacked by the *Eclectic Review* for failing to acknowledge the baseness of the heathen religion; and in order to win a contract from Charles Burney, who was considering adopting the *Pantheon* as a text-book in

his school in Greenwich, Godwin was obliged to replace the engravings
showing Apollo, Venus and so on, with images of them decently
clothed (P.H. Marshall 269, St Clair 287). The 'infamous example of
. . . imaginary deities' (Jenyns 4: 29) were always an embarrassment
to schoolteachers, so that Lemprière made it a selling point of his
Bibliotheca Classica that it had been inspected for purity 'by several
gentlemen in that line' (Lemprière, 'Preface'). Among evangelicals,
especially, the immorality of the pagan gods called into question the
advisability of giving children an education in classical literature: thus
for Hannah More, for example, girls were at a considerable advantage
as compared with boys when it came to the reception of 'serious [i.e.
religious] impressions', because they were not obliged 'to learn by
heart', as boys were, the poetical fables of the less than human gods
of the ancients' (More 2: 383).

Barry is, in fact, quite happy to join this assault on the morality of
the Greek divinities, so long as it takes the form of an attack on Greek
literature. The 'imperfect nature of mere words', he argues – he has
in mind, it seems, the fact that language employs arbitrary, not natural
signs, and that it is obliged to privilege diachronic over synchronic
representation – means that the ancient poets had no other means of
expressing the similarities and differences of function and character
between one divinity and another, than by having 'recourse to
such genealogies and impious Titanic relations and perversions, as
constituted the very essence, abomination, and yet absurdity of idolatry
and polytheism' (2: 148). The 'Grecian artists', however, 'had no
occasion to sully their works with deeds of abomination and turpitude';
their aims

> were fully obtained by selecting from the general mass of human
> nature those specific perfections which are still traceable in the
> works of the Almighty Creator; the relish and pursuit of which he
> had planted in our nature, finally to bring us to Himself, where
> *only* all those perfections of the exterior figure, the intended signs
> of the interior dispositions, can be found united in their most
> sovereign completeness.   (2: 148)

The value of Greek representations of the Greek gods and goddesses
– and the point of Barry's attempt to restore the lost perfection of
Greek art – are here defined in such a way as to give a new clarity,
and a clearer justification, to the Pandora project. The bodies of the
Greek divinities are the exterior and ideal images of interior dispositions, of the different interior dispositions which define the differences between the various character-types of humanity; as Barry had
put it in his lecture at the Royal Academy on the history of painting,

the characters and forms of their several deities were copied after the abstract ideas of whatever was found to be most majestic, most beautiful, graceful, or interesting in human nature . . . all those several perfections, male and female, that were particularly adapted to each walk of character.   (1: 366)

But in so far as each of us belongs to one of these types or another, the identity of each of us is the sign, also, of a multiple lack; and this lack operates as a 'relish and pursuit' (2: 148), implanted in us by God, to know and to desire *all* the exterior and interior forms of perfection that elude us, and which can be found united and complete, however, only in God himself. The taste for Greek nudity and polytheism thus finds its justification as a God-given taste, as a taste, a relish, a desire for God, and for a God who is beyond representation, except *via* images of his various constituent perfections.

This part of Barry's argument is primarily directed against what had become, by 1800 or so, a commonplace of mythography, that the polytheism of the ancient world was a corruption of an earlier monotheism, and that the Greeks were the people chiefly responsible for that corruption.[18] In his defence of the highly differentiated deities of Greece, Barry contrasts them with the 'ancient symbolical figures' of Egyptian religion, and of the Hindu deities who had recently become known in Britain[19] – figures in which heads, hands or other parts of the body were multiplied, and in which human and animal forms ('the horse's head, serpents, dolphins, dove, &c.', 2: 149) were mixed. He had already discussed such figures in his Academy-lecture on the history of painting (1: 351–8), in which he had borrowed from the argument developed by d'Hancarville in his remarkable *Recherches sur l'origine, l'esprit et le progrès des arts de la Grèce* of 1785. Like other scholars of ancient art, d'Hancarville regarded the *'figures monstrueuses'* (d'Hancarville 1: 54) of Egyptian and of early Greek art as hieroglyphs, as attempts to convert natural into arbitrary signs, so as to express ideas – of divine wisdom or power, for example – which had no equivalents in nature. In classical Greece, however, *'l'esprit emblématique'* of pre-classical art was replaced by *'l'esprit de l'art'*; to the various qualities which earlier ages and peoples had attributed to the gods, the Greeks added one more, beauty; and they permitted nothing to be represented in images of the gods which was incompatible with beauty. Thus they no longer sought to represent divine strength, for example, by multiplying the arms or hands of the god, but portrayed him instead with an exaggerated, but still harmonious and well-proportioned musculature. In the sublime beauty of Greek sculpture, writes d'Hancarville, 'the artistic spirit reached the limits of possibility; it achieved all it could achieve of perfection' (d'Hancarville 1: xv–xxiii).[20]

In Barry's lecture, it is the Greeks' attempt to attribute to their gods 'whatever was . . . most majestic, most beautiful, graceful or interesting in human nature' which led to the 'mixtures and incongruities of form' of Egyptian art being 'thrown aside as . . . disgusting' (1: 365). But in the 'Fragment on *Pandora*', he represents himself as rather less appalled than some of his contemporaries by the composite images of 'oriental' religion.[21] He is now willing to acknowledge the advantages of what he calls the 'more ancient complex figures' by which the divine principle had originally been embodied. One advantage was that the sheer grotesqueness of the forms that resulted from 'the monstrous mixture, or multiplicity of parts' made them less likely to become the objects of 'idolatrous perversions'; and a second, no less important from Barry's point of view, was that 'such a figure as the Hindostan Brumha' (sic),[22] for example, 'with his multiplied heads, hands, and attributes [Figure 25], must appear more conformable to the idea of unity and the identity of all powers in the same being' than could 'the more improved figures' of classical sculpture, 'appropriated to the several class or species of character, male and female'.[23] Essential to this notion was the fact that from the body of Brahma had proceeded all the castes that composed Hindu society, in which difference of caste was conceived in terms of the division of labour. As the historian William Robertson had explained,

> The *Brahmin* [proceeded] from the mouth (wisdom): To pray, to read, to instruct.
> The *Chehteree*, from the arms (strength): To draw the bow, to fight, to govern.
> The *Bice*, from the belly or thighs (nourishment): To provide the necessaries of life by agriculture and traffic.
> The *Sooder*, from the feet (subjection): To labour, to serve.
> The prescribed occupations of all these classes are essential in a well-regulated state.   (Robertson 412)

Barry's appeal to Brahma, as the unity of those labours which he has also divided, is of particular importance to the Pandora project. If, as his meditations on the phenomena of difference and social division have suggested, the ideas of unity, and of 'the identity of all powers', which are communicated both by the Judaeo-Christian concept of divinity and by these 'ancient complex figures' (2: 152), can be understood also as ideas of the *social* unity produced by the combination of divided labour, then he seems to be suggesting that those grotesque figures are also more efficacious as images of the collective, the common social body, than the statue of any Greek divinity could possibly be. Barry is acknowledging, in short, as

25. Engraver unknown, *Brahma*, from d'Hancarville's *Recherches*, 1785, vol. 3, plate 3.

Reynolds acknowledged, that the forms of Apollo, Hercules, the Gladiator, each falls short of the central form in which the mutually exclusive perfections of each of them would ideally be united. And yet he is still insisting that however 'mistakenly' the Greeks 'had divided the Divine Essence' into the numerous 'partitions or gods' who inhabit the classical Pantheon, we are still indebted to the Greek artists for their 'pursuit of the beautiful and the perfect', by which they purified and reformed the grotesque images of divinity into the classical forms of Jupiter and the rest, each of which, paradoxically, is perfect, only by virtue of being somehow incomplete (2: 149).

One purpose of the Pandora project had always been to make visible the form of social cohesion available to the members of a nation divided by the division of labour. But the painting was to do more than simply to reveal to us that we were members of a social collective, whether we knew it or not, and whether we felt it or not. The task of the painting was to stir the social affections, so that whatever the differences between our characters, dispositions, occupations, we should *wish* to participate as citizens in the collective life of the polity; it was to teach us that the united pursuit of the public interest is an aim more admirable, and more rewarding, than the furthering of our private interests. But if within the repertoire of classical bodies there was none which could stand, by virtue of the range of 'attributes, elements, . . . virtues, dispositions' it represented, for 'the body of the public', still the grotesque bodies of Egyptian or oriental monotheism, however abundant, could not be preferred, because they could not be admired (2: 147). No one, feels Barry, would be moved to identify with the image of a collective life if it was, as it would be, a monster. Faced with the choice between the classical and the grotesque body, the Greek artists had turned away from the 'mixture of forms' and 'multiplication of parts' that must make everyone of 'true taste' disgusted by the image of common life they represent (1: 358). They preferred the perfect but differentiated forms of the Olympians, and so must we; and if our choice leaves us unable to represent the unity either of God or the state, at least it will not destroy the desire to participate in both.

We are invited by Bakhtin to discover, in the sealed orifices of the classical body, the fear that our individuality will be invaded and dissolved by contact with the popular, the common, the collective, the undifferentiated. A preference for the classical over the grotesque is thus effectively a preference for a life lived within a properly organised and regulated *polis*, where the boundaries that distinguish you from me and mine from yours are clear and secure. As Peter Stallybrass and Allon White have put it.

the grotesque body stands in opposition to the bourgeois individualist conception of the body, which finds *its* image and legitimation in the classical. The grotesque is emphasised as a mobile, split, multiple self . . . and it is never closed off from either its social or ecosystemic context. The classical body on the other hand keeps its distance. (Stallybrass and White 22)

We have already seen that Barry's notion of the public is one in which difference – difference of occupation, and so of character, represented as physical difference – is approved and made constitutive of the commonwealth; and that his whole purpose in attempting to represent each of the classical divinities as accurately as possible is to insist that what may be seen, from one point of view, as a lack, may from another be valued as difference. In the light of the Stallybrass-White account of Bakhtin, the different classical bodies of the Greek and Roman gods may seem to stand for the discrete and private selves of bourgeois individualism, who participate in a public, certainly, but one which, like God, is abstract, invisible, and mercifully incapable of being represented except as an arrangement of individuals. It may seem, in short, in the terms at least of bourgeois individualism, a positive blessing that the classical as against the Hindu Pantheon (or Barry's notion of it) is unable to provide a single image of the collective life, just as it had been an advantage to the male spectators constituted by the early drawing of the Pandora subject, that the company of the Olympians could provide no single, central form of perfection.

The history of the Pandora project so far, however, has suggested that the differences Barry is determined to preserve, the boundaries he is anxious to police, are not simply or primarily those of character or occupation or even of the self more abstractly considered, but those that distinguish male from female, masculine from feminine; and it may have been exactly here that his concern to defend Greek polytheism from the accusations of contemporary mythographers was at its most urgent. We have already noticed that contemporary writers on myth were arguing that all the divinities of the ancient world had originally been one; and they had been so, it was generally agreed, 'nothwithstanding . . . the distinction of sexes' (Elton 1812 11). According to Thomas Maurice (1793–1800, 5: 933), for example, the divine nature in all religions is originally androgynous; and according to William Jones (3: 353), 'the invisible cause, eternal, self-existing', in Hindu religion, is *'neuter'*; but it is redundant to exemplify so ubiquitous a notion. The story told by virtually all the mythographers is of a perpetual theogony, in which divinities are continually changing sex, and often manage to exhibit the physical characteristics of both sexes at once, so that, according to Bryant (1775 1: 510), 'we must not regard sexes . . . when we treat of ancient deities'. Here, for example, is Jones on Venus, who presided

> over *generation*, and, on that account, exhibited sometimes of both sexes (an union very common in the *Indian* sculptures), as in her *bearded* statue at *Rome*, in the images perhaps called *Hermathena*, and in those figures of her, which had the form of a *conical marble;*

"for the reason of which figure we are left, says TACITUS, in the dark:" the reason appears too clearly in the temples and paintings of *Hindustan;* where it never seems to have entered the heads of the legislators or people that any natural thing could be offensively obscene . . .

(W. Jones 3: 367)

The term 'Hermathena' suggests that Minerva, too, could turn up in the same kind of indeterminate or androgynous forms: according to Liddell and Scott, it is disputed whether a hermathena was '(1) *a terminal figure like a Hermes with the head of Athena,* or (2) *a figure with a Janus-like head both of Hermes and Athena,* or (3) *a figure compounded of both deities.* Knight compares Minerva with 'the Indian Gonnis': he acknowledges that Gonnis is male, and Minerva female, but argues that 'this difference of sexes, however important it may be in physical, is of very little consequence in metaphysical beings, Minerva being, like the other Greek deities, either male or female, or both,' and he quotes Orpheus on the point (Knight 57).

We have already seen how much of an embarrassment Minerva's masculine character had become to Barry, however much, in the first instance, it had allowed him to contradict the implications of his own account of the origin of painting, and to reassert the masculinity of his art. The suggestion that Minerva's biological sex was no more determinate than her gender was hardly less embarrassing.[24] It is no surprise, therefore, that when he attempts to vindicate the polytheism of the Greek artists by exemplifying the *process* by which they sought to 'weed out . . . incongruities of monstrous mixture' and to produce 'the more improved figures' of the Olympians (2: 149, 152), the image he fixes upon is the sculpture of Minerva made by Phidias for the Parthenon, the Athena Parthenos – Figure 26 shows what is thought to be a copy in miniature of the lost original.[25] His discussion of that statue, however, refers us first to another, recently discovered representation of the goddess in which two sphinxes are shown 'clambering up her shoulders', surmounted by two lions, and the whole supported by two cavaliers, or men on horseback' (Figure 27). Barry does not find the image too offensive – Minerva's body is still distinct, and his greatest disgust is reserved for 'Egyptian and Asiatic' art. Nevertheless, 'to an eye cultivated by good taste', these symbols weigh down the figure instead of adorning it, and so he congratulates Phidias and his followers, who 'ingeniously transplanted these symbols into the more eligible situation of her helmet; where, instead of encumbering, they became graceful ornaments in addition to their apposite signification' (2: 150). On the top of the helmet of the Minerva on the Acropolis, between a pair of supporting gryphons, Phidias placed the sphinx, a symbol which:

26. Minature copy of the *Athena Parthenos* (the 'Varvakeion'). Height 1.05 m. National Archaeological Museum, Athens.

27. Warner, after James Barry, *Bronze Figure of Minerva found in the Tomb of Achilles*, from Barry's *Works* (1809), 2: 149. Height of image 10.9 cm.

comprehends more than a mere union of even the bodily force of Ajax and the intellectual provident skill of Ulysses; for the head and breasts show it to be feminine, and consequently endowed with all the interesting advantages derived from the superior sensibilites and affectionate tenderness of heart, which so happily and necessarily accompany the female or maternal character through all animal nature ... this discrimination in the matter of sexual sensibility was not overlooked by the penetrating wisdom of the ancients ...
                                                                    (2: 150 – 1)

The main advantage, Barry seems to suggest, of the 'improved forms' produced by the Greek artists, was that they enabled a careful discrimination of the sex and gender of the Greek divinities. Phidias's achievement was not simply to disburden Minerva of many of her grotesque and complex attributes, but to retain, and to give pride of place to, the one which would, according to Barry, most clearly emphasise her femininity. She has thus been pronounced feminine by the greatest of Greek artists; and if the cost of determining her gender is that painting is once again to be affirmed as a feminine activity, that may be better than contemplating the possibility that the distinctions of sex and gender are less than entirely stable. This is suggested specially by the fact that the sphinx, the symbol that apparently determines the goddess's gender, is itself one of those complex and monstrous forms which Barry has been writing against. If his preference for the classical over the grotesque body was largely dictated by a belief that the distinctions of sex and gender were more respected by the former, he is not above enlisting the help of grotesque forms, where he can claim that their sexual character is unambiguous.

V

At this point it will be best to have before us Barry's own description of *The Birth of Pandora*, or rather, his description of the mixed-method (etched and engraved) print that he made of the completed painting. The plate was too large to be printed on Barry's own press – to obtain proofs of it he had to take it elsewhere (Pressly 1981 280) – and this perhaps explains why Barry's description starts off back-to-front: he seems to be describing the image as it appeared on the plate, in reverse, so that 'the Apollo Lyristes' is 'sitting in the right end of the picture', though he is the leftmost figure in all versions of the subject. Apollo, then, on the left as we see him,

> in all the energies of the enthusiasm of poetry and music, of sense and sound, is celebrating the assembly and the occasion in a hymeneal song, to which Bacchus, his great rival in beauty and enthusiasm, is attentively listening, as is also Pan, who is affectionately leaning on Bacchus. Mars, who is sitting next, is looking up to Venus, who is coquetting with him, whilst she is taking off, though seeking to retain, her cestus from Cupid, who is assisting in the decoration of Pandora, seated on his right [Barry here reverts to describing the composition as we see it]; whilst the three Graces are severally employed, two of them in pouring ambrosia and plaiting her hair, and the third putting on her sandals. While Pandora is thus dressing by the Graces, her head is attentively turned towards Minerva, who with one hand is shewing her a shuttle, and earnestly exhorting her to the performance of those respectable matrimonial duties, the essence of which depends on the acquisition of that intimate

knowledge of manners and things, which will enable her to design and fabricate such tapestry (truly feminine work) as the famous Peplon, or covering, which Minerva is holding up in the other hand. Hymen is standing on the right of Minerva; on her left is Pluto, Neptune, and Jupiter. Hebe is kneeling, and with the most profound veneration is presenting the festal bowl of nectar to Jupiter, who seems as if he were going to hand it to Juno, behind whom sit Vesta, Ceres, and Diana, attentive to what is going forward. In the advanced space Mercury putting on his talaria is preparing to carry down Pandora to her destined husband, and in the cave of clouds some distance behind Jupiter, are the Parcae or Fates; one of whom is spinning and singing the future destiny of Pandora; the second is writing down what is sung; and the third is coming forward holding that fatal vase, in which those evils and calamities of life are concealed, which Jupiter had prepared as the secret portion of dowry which should accompany the beautiful exterior accomplishments of this fascinating present with which he intended to entrap mankind. . . . Calliope (the most advanced figure of the muses, who attentively surround Apollo) has her hand on the shoulder of Vulcan, as it were (agreeably to her office) pointing him out as the ingenious, sublime artificer of that Pandora, whose education and interests occupy the attention of the whole assembly.

(2: 153–4)

Partly as a result of a change in the proportions of the design, the composition of the painting, when it was finally completed in 1804 (Figure 28), was rather less frieze-like than the drawing on which Schiavonetti had based his etching, and this difference is still more marked in Barry's print of the painting. In 1783, Barry had estimated that the canvas would measure 8'10" x 17'8" (see above, 159), which is to say that (like Schiavonetti's etching) it would be twice as wide as it was high. The finished painting measured 9'2" x 17'0½", rather less than twice as wide as it was high, and, no doubt mainly for technical reasons, Barry's print (Figure 29) was further contracted, to a ratio (height to width) of 1: 1.45. The effect of these contractions is to emphasise what we can think of as the second element of meaning in the subject at the expense of the first – that is to say, the print reinforces a concern which had already become evident in the painting, that we should focus more on the transactions between Minerva and Pandora, where the new myth of the origin of painting is being generated, and between Hebe and Jupiter, and correspondingly less on the rest of the panorama of divine perfection, from Apollo on the left to Diana on the right.

This shift of emphasis is reinforced by another compositional change by which the original frieze-structure has been attenuated – the provision of a *repoussoir* in the left foreground, made by the recumbent figures of Vulcan and three muses. As Pressly puts it, 'the general format is now that of a shallow semi-circle, within which the gods and goddesses are arranged around a series of slightly receding, crisscrossing diagonals' (Pressly 1981 148). Vulcan in particular has been moved forward and turned round, so that instead of being portayed in his traditional role as the outsider among the gods, as he is in Schiavonetti's etching – the only Olympian who looks out of the picture, away from Pandora – he has become crucial, by virtue both of his position and of the direction of his gaze, to the new stress on the importance of the central actions. And two further changes have had much the same effect: Barry has considerably increased the size of the figures, relative to the picture-space as a whole, and in an attempt to outdo Phidias as well as Raphael he has increased their number by four: in addition to the muses, Hymen now peers over Minerva's shoulder in an effort to find out whose wedding it is that he has been asked to bless.

The effect of both these changes is to cramp the composition, and to give much less room for the exhibition of the various but perfect bodies of the Olympians. Thus Apollo, for example, the paragon of masculine grace, had been able to offer us the profile of his whole body in Schiavonetti's original etching; now he gives us the merest flash of his chest and shoulders. The full frontal image of Venus now stops above the waist, though her breasts have been left visible to show us how far Barry has excelled the sculptor of the Venus de' Medici. Some of the deities have all but disappeared: Mars, whose physique in the original etching might lead one to suspect him of popping steroids, becomes no more than a face and a helmet in the painting, and in the print, almost ludicrously in view of Barry's original aims, he has been reduced to a selection of facial features sandwiched between the horns of Pan and the armpit of Cupid. And also in the print, Ceres, who in no version had been allowed much space, has been whittled down to an eye, a mouth, and part of a nose, and Hymen has become just a torch and half a face. The general effect of the print, especially, is to suggest that most of the Olympians have fallen back into the Orphic soup of undifferentiated body-parts from which the classical aesthetic had rescued them, and from which now only Pandora, Minerva, Hebe, Jupiter and Juno seem to have escaped.

There are some further crucial differences between the painting and Barry's own print. I have already remarked how, in both, the figures of Minerva, Hebe and Jupiter have become more salient than they were in Schiavonetti's etching, relative to the other deities. Of these

28. James Barry, *The Birth of Pandora*, begun c. 1791, completed 1804. Oil on canvas 279 × 519 cm. Manchester City Art Galleries.

29. James Barry, *The Birth of Pandora*, c. 1804–5. Etching and engraving 63.8 × 92.7 cm.

three, however, it is the figures of Hebe and Jupiter that are particularly emphasised in the painting; in the plane they occupy, most of the light not required to illuminate the body of Pandora herself is used to illuminate theirs, while the blue drapery worn by Minerva seems to hold her back among the general mêlée of the other divinities and divine fragments. In the print, where the light is more equitably distributed, Minerva is a far more visible presence. What is more, in the painting Minerva is made to appear *pretty*, in a way which seems intended to feminise the seriousness of her expression, in line with Barry's attempt, in the 'Fragment', to attribute to her a greater degree of femininity than the iconographic tradition allowed. In the print, however – and it is this, of course, that Barry is describing in the 'Fragment' – that prettiness has gone, and she has become positively burly, of a size to match the huge proportions of Jupiter and Juno.

This new pictorial emphasis on the centre of the picture, and, in the print, on Minerva, must have seemed of especial importance to Barry as his work on the Pandora project was nearing completion, for by the end he had found a way of extrapolating a function for painting from the new myth of origin he had invented for his art in the *Letter* of 1798. The myth provided by the tale of the Corinthian or the Sicyonian maid, it will be recalled, seemed to prescribe a function for the art which fell far short of Barry's notion of what painting should be and should do. But the alternative myth based upon Minerva's patronage of 'the art of painting in tapestry' (2: 585) was still one which placed a female, woman or goddess, at the origin of the art. Faced with the choice of representing that female as masculine, or feminising and thus weakening the power and scope of his art, he chose the latter option. We can sum up the argument of the *Letter* in the form of two sequential and conflicting propositions: if painting is to be feminised, the feminine must be made masculine; and if masculinity is to be protected, painting must be feminised. The task of painting, it seemed by the end of the *Letter*, would from now on be to offer a form of feminine consolation, in private, to men exhausted or disappointed in the public world of affairs. But by 1805, as we shall see, he has developed his myth of origin to the point where he can show that painting, though its origin may lie in the 'truly feminine work' of tapestry (2: 153), has recovered the grand and public function that he had attributed to it in all his earlier writings.

In 1798, Minerva had been described as having, in her left hand, 'a tapestry robe . . . in which is represented . . . the story of Jove fulminating the Titans, or the punishment of that pride and arrogance which was likely soon to become apparent in the descendants of poor Pandora' (2: 595). In 1805, the robe has become the 'famous Peplon' (2: 144, 153), and the change must have seemed to Barry to solve almost all his problems with the subject of Pandora. The peplus was the centrepiece of the great quinquennial Panathenea, the festival instituted, according to one account, by Orpheus, but 'renew'd and amplify'd by Theseus, when he had united into one City the whole *Athenian* Nation' (Potter 1: 419 – Barry's main source for his knowledge of the festival). The festival was thus a celebration of the unity, the wholeness (*panathenea*) of the Athenian state, and came to celebrate, also, its republican constitution, for 'in the Songs us'd at this Time, they rehears'd the generous Undertakings of *Harmodius* and *Aristogiton*, who oppos'd the Tyranny of *Pisistratus*'s Sons; as of *Thrasybulus* also, who deliver'd the *Athenians* from the *thirty Tyrants*' (Potter 1: 420).

The peplus was 'the principle ornament' of this festival. It was a robe embroidered by virgins of the city, and on it was represented

> the battle of the gods and giants. Amongst the gods was Jupiter hurling his thunder-bolts against that rebellious crew, and Minerva seated in her chariot, appearing the vanquisher of Typhon, or Encalladus. . . . The names of those Athenians who had been eminent for military virtue, were also embroidered on it; Potter says, had their effigies on it, whence men of true courage and bravery were said to be Αξιοι του πεπλου, i.e. worthy of the Peplus.   (2: 158)

The peplus was carried from the Acropolis where it was made, and paraded through Athens in the Panathenaic procession – the procession depicted in bas-relief on the Parthenon frieze, generally ascribed to Phidias, and which, Barry reminds us, was among the works which 'the tasteful attention of the Earl of Elgin . . . has now secured to this country.' The peplus ended where it had begun, on the Acropolis, where it was carried to the Parthenon and there 'consecrated to Minerva'; according to Potter it was draped upon the chryselephantine statue of Minerva in the cella of the temple. It was in his design for this statue, it will be recalled, that Phidias had rescued Minerva's body from the grotesque attributes that had clambered upon it before, and in the process had rescued her femininity. But, equally important, it was on the base of this statue, as Barry earlier informed us, that the only previous representation of the Birth of Pandora could once have been seen.[26]

The symmetry, the circularity of all this seems to promise an end to the numerous difficulties Barry has had in producing a meaning for the Pandora project, a meaning adequate to his sense of its enormous importance.[27] To find such a meaning, since 1798 at least, had become especially urgent – had become the same thing as to find a meaning, a function, for painting itself, and to rediscover its cognitive and its didactic purposes at a time when both had been put in question. The identification of the embroidered robe as the peplus, which Minerva is teaching Pandora to weave, and which will finally be draped around a statue of which the painting itself is effectively the base, provides the art with an origin and an end both equally civic, both equally dedicated to 'the grand ethical purposes of information, persuasion, and instruction'. The notion that painting might have a private, consolatory, and feminine function, is now reduced to the fine print of a footnote (2: 153n). The art now has a far more dignified task to perform: to represent, like the peplus itself, the religion of the republic, the heroes of the republic, the unity of the republic. Once again it can occupy, or can claim to occupy, the psychic centre of the public sphere.

As Marcia Pointon has pointed out to me, the solution thus proposed to the problem of gender can equally be read as a new version of the problem itself. What had been a function of the body in history painting has simply been displaced onto an item of clothing, and an item of female clothing at that: and we shall see in a later section that the narrative of reparation that Barry came to attribute to the painting is inseparable from the narrative implied in a psychoanalytic account of fetishism. In the meantime, however, the 1805 'Fragment' asks to be read as a text which has provided painting once again with a masculine function; and the account of Vulcan offered in the same essay seems to provide it at last with a masculine origin. The achievement of the Greek artists, as we saw, was to produce the perfect bodies of the classical divinities; and they did this by boiling down, as it were, the formless Orphic and Asiatic soup in which human and animal, male and female forms had been jumbled promiscuously together and run into each other. This, as we shall see, is exactly what Barry will claim Vulcan has done, in the creation of Pandora. In making this claim plausible, he was helped by the efforts of late eighteenth-century mythographers to rehabilitate Vulcan, who by the consent 'of all the old poets', according to Spence, had been 'a meer mortal blacksmith . . . blackened and hardened, from the forge' (Spence 80–1). But the investigation of the role played by Vulcan or his equivalents in Egyptian and Orphic theology had meant that, by the early nineteenth century, no mythographer would have disagreed with the spirit of Barry's claim that

> whilst the fascinating manners and mental qualities of Pandora are made to be the gift of other gods, yet the substratum or material fabrication, organization, and vitality, are obtained from the complicated energies and skill of Vulcan, whose character (instead of the mere blacksmith) is by this ingenious and most apposite

fable, exalted into the more sublime symbol of the active principle, the busy element of fire, the great operator even of the other elementary energies which counteract the torpor and inertness of mere material things. (2: 154)

The immediate source of this account of Vulcan is probably an essay of 1792 by Francis Wilford, in the *Asiatic Researches* (3: 360), 'On Egypt and other Countries . . . from the Ancient Books of the Hindus'. But Jones, Maurice, Bryant and a number of other mythographers had all rehabilitated Vulcan as more than 'the blacksmith, who . . . forged iron in Mount Aetna' (Bryant 1775 1: 140), and associated him with a range of Orphic, Egyptian and other Asiatic divinities endowed with supreme creative power. At the very least he was the 'demiurgic mind' (Maurice 1793–1800 4: 321) immediately responsible for the creation of the universe; at best he was 'the chief of the Gods the same as the Sun', and indeed *'the Father of the Gods'* (Bryant 1775 1: 140). More important for our purposes, however, will be the association that developed between Vulcan and a range of Orphic, Egyptian and other Asiatic divinities endowed with supreme creative power.

'Vulcan is sitting,' Barry continues, 'with certain residue near him, which might be supposed to have resulted from the experiments for his master-work of Pandora' (Figure 30). The residue in question is a range of animal forms – from right to left, a snake, 'with an egg issuing from his mouth', encircling 'a vase of water'; 'a frog on the edge of the vase'; 'the Psyche, or butterfly, held by the fingers of Vulcan, and the sluggish cast of the Chrysalis underneath' a bunch of grapes and a bird peeping out of a broken egg, one of a number apparently, of different sizes, on Vulcan's anvil. These various components of the residue left to Vulcan were all well-known components of the Orphic, Asiatic or pre-classical religious imagery out of which the Greek artists had created the bodies of the Olympians, as Vulcan has created that of Pandora. But Barry intends them as symbolic representations, also, of the process of cosmic creation, and of the 'progressive melioration', the ascending progression of life forms, by which creation operates: 'the egg and the bird; the seed and the plant' (2: 154–5).

The egg, as Knight points out, 'was a very proper symbol of Chaos, containing the seeds and materials of all things, which, however, were barren and useless, until the Creator fructified them by the incubation of his vital spirit.' The 'Creator', in this passage, is the Orphic Eros, a type of Vulcan, who 'delivering the fructified seeds of things from the restraints of inert matter by his divine strength, is represented . . . by the . . . wild Bull, in the act of butting against the Egg of Chaos, and breaking it with his horns' (Knight 21).[28] The frog sitting on the edge of a vase of water, 'the agency of which is so necessary in organic

30. James Barry, detail of Figure 29: Vulcan and his residue.

and other combinations', is adapted from the image of a frog sitting on the edge of a lotos blossom which decorated the base of the statue of Apollo at Delphi (Bryant 1810 41, and see 1775 2: 393); the frog is visible in the print but not in the painting, where the vase, however, is prophetically filled with what appear to be tadpoles. The lotos, because its seeds germinate while still attached to the plant, can be thought of, as Knight again points out, as 'productive of itself, and vegetating from its own matrice,' and it was therefore 'naturally adopted as the symbol of the productive power of the waters, upon which the active spirit of the Creator operated in giving life and vegetation to matter' (Knight 50).[29] The butterfly emerging from the chrysalis is, Barry explains, another figure of 'progressive melioration', in this case the soul escaping from 'a degraded organisation' in which it 'had been so long imprisoned' (2: 155, and see Bryant 1775 2: 385–6; Darwin 1791 57; Knight 100). And as Barry may have known from the *Asiatic Researches*, many of these forms were symbols for the process of the cosmic creative power of Brahma, another type of Vulcan.[30] Writing of 'the triple divinity VISHNU, SIVA, BRAHMA' Jones tells us that the Hindus,

> when they consider the divine power exerted in *creating*, or in giving existence to that which existed not before, they call the deity BRAMA in the masculine gender also . . . The first [viz., the creative

as opposed to the destructive] operations of these three *Powers* are variously described in the different *Purana's* by a number of allegories, and from them we may deduce the *Ionian* Philosophy of *primeval water*, the doctrine of the Mundane Egg, and the veneration paid to the *Nymphaea*, or *Lotos*, which was anciently revered in *Egypt*, as it is at present in *Hindustan*, *Tibet*, and *Nepal*.

(W. Jones 3: 351)

The most crucially significant of the symbols which litter the foreground of the painting, however, is the snake disgorging the egg. This snake, Barry explains, is 'the Egyptian Cneph or Cnuphis'. 'The Egyptians,' according to Porphyry, 'call *Kneph*, intelligence, or efficient cause of the universe. They relate that this God vomited an egg, from which was produced another God named *Phtha* or Vulcan (igneous principle, or the sun), and they add, that this egg is the world' (quoted from Volney 153).[31] The general doctrine concerning the snake-deity Cneph, his analogues, and the mundane egg, was to be summed up by Faber like this:

the great father, under the name of *Phanes* or *Brahma* or *Eros*, is represented as having been born from an egg; while, under that of *Cneph*, he himself produces an egg from his own mouth, which again produces the god Phtha or Vulcan, who, nevertheless, if his character be analysed, will prove to be the very same person as Eros or Brahma or Cneph or Phanes.

(Faber 1: 198, and see Bryant 1775 1: 59–60, and Elton 1815 xvii)

Thus the symbol of the serpent with the egg represents the birth at once of the world and of Vulcan, and in so far as Vulcan and Cneph are one (and Barry would certainly have known the research that suggested they were), it represents Vulcan as, at once, the creator of the world, and as self-originated: Vulcan is the beginning of all things. He is also, as we have seen, the first artist, senior, by all accounts, to Minerva, in age if not always by rank: it was only with his help that she was able to emerge from the forehead of Jupiter. As the first artist, his task is the 'progressive melioration' of forms, the production, as I have suggested, of more improved figures from figures relatively monstrous; and so he is a type of Phidias and, of course, of Barry himself, who has always conceived the Pandora subject as an occasion to improve on the figures of Raphael, and, he has now claimed, on the surviving works of the Greeks. If the (mere) practice of painting is still to be thought of as originating with Minerva, the creative power exercised in the art originated with Vulcan; the originator of the origin of painting is a masculine god, with whom Barry has apparently identified himself.

Pandora is leaning back in a golden chair of complicated design, with lotos leaves forming the legs, and an egg-and-dart pattern running along the side of the seat. Whether we are to attribute the chair as well as its occupant to the creative genius of Vulcan is not clear, but earlier in his career Vulcan had indeed made a golden chair for a woman. It was for his mother Juno; and 'was so contrived by springs unseen, that being seated in it she was unable to rise, till the inventor was prevailed upon to grant her deliverance' (Bell 2: 319). The analogies suggested in the 1805 essay, between Vulcan, Phidias and Barry, as representatives of a primary masculine creative power, seem similarly to have been invented in the attempt to keep a troublesome and unruly femininity in its place. The feminine, it seems, will no longer cause trouble, will no longer threaten to blur the definition of masculinity.[32] In a painting of Pandora (of all women), that must be regarded as quite an achievement, though it is one that has been looked forward to, throughout the long history of the project, by the decision to place Pandora's 'well-known casket' (1775a) or her 'fatal vase' (2: 154) deep in the background of the picture.

Or that, at least, is where Barry has four times assured us it is to be found. As the Panofskys pointed out, there is some disagreement among writers and artists of the renaissance and after as to exactly what kind of a container it was that Pandora was destined to open. In Hesiod, it was a πιθos, a storage-jar; and it was not described as a 'box' by anyone before Erasmus. Thereafter, in northern Europe where the influence of Erasmus was stronger, it generally became a box or casket – it is a 'casket' in Cooke's translation of Hesiod – while in southern Europe it remained a vase or some such vessel (Panofskys 14–26). At some time between writing the *Account* of 1783 and the *Letter* of 1798, Barry too learned that the pithos mentioned by Hesiod might be better translated as 'vase' than as 'casket'.

A large part of the Panofskys' interest in the iconography of the Pandora subject is in recording which artists represent Pandora with a box, and which with a vase or jar; and they were particularly pleased with Barry for representing it, as they believed, with exemplary erudition, in the form of 'a kylix enormously magnified and transposed into metal but admirably correct in shape' (89). At this point, however, their own erudition is a little less than exemplary, for the figure they interpret as 'one of the Fates "coming forward holding the fatal vase . . ."' is, according to all Barry's accounts of the project, Hebe, presenting Jupiter with a festal bowl of nectar, which he will shortly pass on to Juno (Panofskys 89). The Panofskys were misled, of course, not only by their own desire to find vases rather than boxes, but by the tradition which, as they point out themselves, has no foundation in Hesiod, that it was Jupiter who gave the pithos to Pandora. What I take to be the current standard edition of the *Works and Days* continues this tradition, though, as the Panofskys again suggest, it seems more reasonable to believe that the Pithos – usually a large, barrel-sized affair – was part of the furnishings of Epimetheus's household, rather than something which Pandora and Mercury had between them been obliged to lug down from Olympus (Panofskys 8).

But there was something else, of course, that misled the Panofskys, and which in some sense vindicates their understanding of the picture. In a painting of the birth of Pandora, we quite reasonably expect the casket, vase or jar to occupy a central position, as it does so meretriciously, for example, in Picart's engraving, where one box of mischief both hides and stands for another, the true centre of picture and myth alike (Figure 31).[33] In Barry's painting, the 'true' vase is effectively invisible: it appears as no more than a dark smudge on a dark background, and must certainly pass unnoticed by those who are not familiar with Barry's own accounts of the Pandora project. But the transaction between Jupiter and Hebe is indeed central, and is further thrown into prominence by the dramatic lighting of the picture, which seems to pick them out for special attention. If we look at the painting, as most spectators will, with no knowledge of Barry's descriptions of it, it is highly likely that we will believe that Hebe is passing the vase to Jupiter so that he may give it, not to Juno, but to Pandora. And for Barry to make this transaction so central and so prominent, after he had learned that the 'casket' was really a 'vase', seems almost to be an unconscious invitation, disavowed of course by Barry's descriptions, that we should misread exactly as the Panofskys did. The fatal vase, the sign of a bad, uncontrollable femininity, is hidden not only in the dark background of the picture: it is also hidden, like a purloined letter, in full view, at the very centre. And as we shall see, the threat of the bad feminine remains, despite all Barry's efforts, as a part of the unconscious of the painting, its unacknowledged and yet – as Barry's continued attempts to expel it make clear – its most resilient subject.

VI

The peplus carried in the Panathanaic procession, Barry has told us, was embroidered with 'the battle of the gods and giants'. Jupiter was shown hurling his thunder-bolts, and Minerva appeared as 'the vanquisher of Typhon, or Encalladus'; and it exhibited also the names, and perhaps the portraits, 'of those Athenians who had been eminent for military virtue.' The peplus which Minerva is presenting to Pandora is described by Barry as an 'exemplar' (2: 157) of the kind of tapestry she must produce, and so, more generally, of art as performing a civic function, and of the subjects proper to such art. It is too closely folded for much of the design to be visible, but in the painted version we can make out, towards the top of the peplus, a hand, certainly Jove's, clutching a thunderbolt; towards the bottom, a foot, extended outwards from the leg and with toes pointed; and below that, part of the contorted face of what must be a falling god or giant. In Barry's etching and engraving, the hand is still there, though less easily visible in the lower contrast of the print-medium (Figure 32). The foot, however, is no less salient – it is a less delicate affair now, and it has changed position, so that the sole is visible; and to the face has been added a thigh, buttock and torso.

There is a certain appropriateness, of course, in the fact that, faced with the challenge of representing the great antique exemplar of what a civic work of art should be, a modern painter has shown us little more than the hand of a god and the foot of a giant. The designs on Barry's peplus may remind us of Fuseli's drawing, *The Artist in Despair over the Magnitude of Ancient Fragments* (Figure 33; c. 1770–80), in which a modern artist bewails – or can be interpreted as bewailing – his pygmy stature, unable to conceive of works of art on the sublime scale of the ancients, or denied the opportunity to create them. Either way, the *disjecta membra* of antique art seem both to point out, and to stand for, the incompleteness of the modern artist. In a self–portrait tucked away in a corner of his Adelphi painting *Crowning the Victors at Olympia*, Barry identifies himself as the Greek painter Timanthes, who managed to represent in a small panel the gigantic stature of a sleeping Cyclops, 'by painting at his side some Satyrs measuring the size of his thumb with a wand' (Figure 34; Pressly 1981 98). Here the enormous thumb of the Cyclops seems to function also as a figure for the gigantic stature of Timanthes's genius, and, by association, of Barry's. Read in the light of these two analogues, the images on Barry's peplus may be read as a claim that he is an artist of comparable stature with the artists of antiquity, or as an admission that he is not, but either way they seem to associate themselves with the issue.

I want to forget about the hand for a while, and concentrate on the foot, and in particular on the attitude of the foot as it appears in the painted version, extended, and with toes pointed. It is an attitude which appears a number of times in Barry's small *oeuvre*. We come across it first in his early painting of *Philoctetes*, the Greek hero who suffered unendurable agonies after his foot had been bitten by a snake (Figure 35). Philoctetes had been painted by the great Greek artist Parrhasius, whose version of the subject was the subject of an epigram

31. Bernard Picart, after Abraham Blomaert, after Abraham van Diepenbeeck, *Pandora's Box*, from Antoine de la Barre de Beaumarchais, *The Temple of the Muses*, 1733. 34.5 × 25.2 cm.

32. James Barry, detail of Figure 29: Minerva and the Peplus.

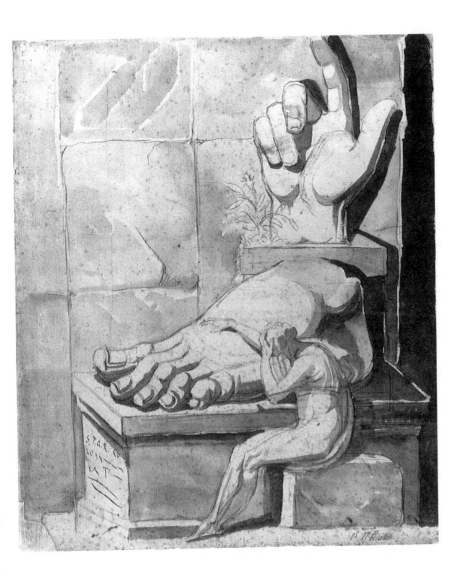

33. Henry Fuseli, *The Artist in Despair over the Magnitude of Ancient Fragments*, c. 1778–80. Red chalk and sepia wash 42 × 35.2 cm. Kunsthaus, Zurich.

34. James Barry, detail from *Crowning the Victors at Olympia*, 1777–84 (with later retouching). Oil on canvas. Royal Society of Arts.

35. James Barry, *Philoctetes on the Island of Lemnos*, 1770. Oil on canvas 228 × 157.5 cm. Pinacoteca Nazionale, Bologna.

by Glaucus, which Barry had found in Daniel Webb's *Inquiry into the Beauties of Painting*; and as Pressly says 'Barry obviously wished to rival' the Greek Painter (Webb 162, Pressly 1981 22). His own Philoctetes is shown sitting on a fragment of bas-relief, and apparently unwinding a soiled bandage from his wounded foot. The pose is clearly reminiscent of another victim of the serpents, Laocoon; and the position of the wounded foot, and the tensed toes of the sound one, seem to respond to Webb's remark, that had only the foot of the Laocoon been discovered, still 'the swelled veins, the strained sinews, and the irregular motion of the muscles, might have led us into a conception of those tortures, which are so divinely expressed in the face, so wonderfully marked through the whole body' (Webb 157–8). Certainly Barry paid special attention to the position and attitude of the wounded foot. The other versions of the subject illustrated by Pressly show Philoctetes's foot supported, on a bench or a rock, but Barry thought such an attitude less than entirely sublime: on the back of a preparatory drawing for the painting (Figure 36) he wrote, 'There will appear more Agony & yᵉ disorderd leg will be more distinctly mark'd by having it

36. James Barry, study for *Philoctetes on the Island of Lemnos*, 1770. Pen and ink 21 × 28.7 cm. The Oppé Collection.

37. James Barry, *Portraits of Barry and Burke in the Characters of Ulysses and a Companion Fleeing from the Cave of Polyphemus*, c. 1776. Oil on canvas 127 × 100.8 cm. Crawford Art Gallery, Cork.

stretched out in air & without any support from ye rock he sits on' (Pressly 1981 23).

The attitude reappears elsewhere in Barry's painting. We find something like it in the blinded Polyphemus who fills the background of the extraordinary historical portrait of around 1776, and from whose cave Burke, Barry and a stone-faced companion are shown escaping (Figure 37). The comparable, if not precisely similar attitude of the mortally wounded hero in *The Death of General Wolfe*, of about the same date (Figure 38), was particularly noted by the critic for the *Morning Post*: the position of the general's legs and thighs, he wrote, 'is meant, we suppose, to give us an idea of the pliancy of human limbs when life is at her lowest ebb; but Mr Barry, to effect this, has bow'd them out in so awkward a manner, as must disgust the eye of every observer' (Pressly 1981 61). Orpheus, too, in the first picture of the Adelphi cycle (1777–84) is swinging his unsupported foot at the very centre of the composition (Figure 39). Unlike the others, he has not yet been wounded, though his wife, of course, was another snake-bite victim; and it may turn out not to be irrelevant here to recall that in time Orpheus would be dismembered by the women of Thrace.[34]

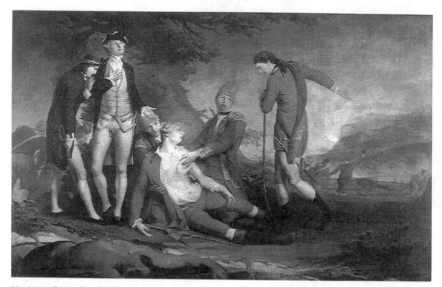

38. James Barry, *The Death of General Wolfe*, c. 1775–6. Oil on canvas 148.6 × 236.2 cm. New Brunswick Museum, New Brunswick.

39. James Barry, *Orpheus*, 1777–84 (with later re-touching). Oil on canvas approx. 362 × 464 cm. Royal Society of Arts, London.

40. James Barry, *St Patrick and the King of Cashel*, 1760–3. Oil on canvas 136 × 202 cm. Terenure College, Dublin.

41. James Barry, *The Education of Achilles*, c. 1772. Oil on canvas 103 × 129 cm. Yale Center for British Art.

Barry's paintings of Philoctetes and Wolfe are a part of what seems to have been a more general interest in depicting men, heroes and gods – many of them artists of one kind or another – with wounded or otherwise troublesome feet. The first historical painting by Barry that survives (Figure 40; 1760–3) is of St Patrick – he who expelled the snakes from Ireland – who when he baptised the King of Cashel was careless enough to drive his crozier through the royal foot; the crozier, it seems, 'according to the manner of the times, was armed at the lower extremity with a spear'. The painting was remarkable, noted one of Barry's obituarists, for 'the heroic patience of the king', and 'the devotional abstraction of the saint.' 'Few stories . . . have been selected with greater felicity, or with greater scope, for the skill and the ingenuity of the artist. . . . The monarch neither changes his posture, nor suffers the pain from the wound for a moment to interrupt the ceremony' (1: 8). It was this work which first brought Barry to the attention of the polite world of Dublin, Burke included. It was believed to have been burnt in the fire at the Irish House of Commons in 1792, and a few years later Barry made another, oil on paper version, which he apparently kept himself. The pentimento of this version, Pressly tells us, shows the crozier in the act of piercing the king's right foot, but if finally came to be positioned, 'in a less sensational manner', behind it (Pressly 1983 144).

One of the first paintings exhibited by Barry at the Royal Academy was *The Education of Achilles* (Figure 41), in which an avuncular Chiron is teaching the young tenderfoot the Orphic hymns; Achilles's legs, explains Pressly, are 'entwined', so that 'the vulnerable heel is covered' (Pressly 1981 35). And of course there is Vulcan himself, the god who according to some accounts was lamed from birth, and according to others was lamed by the brutality of one or other of his parents, Jupiter or Juno. In Schiavonetti's etching of Barry's early drawing of Pandora, nothing seems to suggest Vulcan's lameness except perhaps his recumbent posture. In Barry's own print, the god seems to have concealed his feet by burying them in the ground, behind what may be a lotos, just to the right of the snake with the egg in its mouth; though in the painting, one of his feet is still partly visible.

We should consider here too another early history-painting, *The Temptation of Adam* (Figure 42; 1767–70), of which Pressly points out that the serpent who has already beguiled Eve 'is shown close to her raised foot in anticipation of God's prophecy: . . . Her seed shall bruise thy head, thou bruise his heel' (Pressly 1981 18). Though it is Eve's heel, not Adam's, that is threatened in the painting, the effect is to represent Eve as, metonymically, her own male descendants, so that the picture seems to belong with the other paintings about men with problem feet. And certainly Barry came to convert the subject into just that, in his mixed-method print of 1792–5, *The Discovery of Adam and Eve* (Figure 43), where the snake has moved over to threaten Adam's heel, and Eve's recumbent body seems to recapitulate the curves of the snake. The painting thus reinforces the connection, between bad feet and snakes, that has been suggested one way or another by the figures of St Patrick and the King of Cashel, of Philoctetes, and of Vulcan. But it also opens a counter-motif, in which feet (usually good ones) trample upon bad snakes. In the fourth painting of the Adelphi cycle the Prince of Wales had appeared with his foot on a bale of imported cotton; around 1790, Barry painted a full-length portrait of the future George IV in the same pose, but by replacing the bale of cotton with a serpentine dragon he made him into St George (Figure 44). The motif first entered Barry's repertoire of motifs with his Adelphi picture, *Crowning the Victors at Olympia*: at the far left of this painting, just next to Barry's self-portrait as Timanthes that we have already glanced at, is a sculpture of Hercules treading down envy in the form of a snake.

42. James Barry, *The Temptation of Adam*, 1767–70. Oil on canvas 233 × 183 cm, National Gallery of Ireland, Dublin.

43. James Barry, *The Discovery of Adam and Eve*, c. 1792–5. Etching and aquatint 58 X 41.6 cm.

44. James Barry, *The Prince of Wales as St. George*, c. 1789–91. Oil on canvas 238.7 × 147.3 cm. Crawford Art Gallery, Cork.

45. James Barry, *Self-Portrait*, head c. 1780, remainder completed 1803. Oil on canvas 76 × 63 cm. National Gallery of Ireland, Dublin.

The extraordinary self-portrait (Figure 45) which Barry began in 1780, but which he did not complete until 1803, is virtually a blow-up of the bottom left-hand corner of the Olympia painting. Barry appears once again as Timanthes – though this time in modern dress – with the painting of Cyclops and the satyrs, the thumb-measuring picture. Above him and behind him is a portion of the same Hercules statue, now reduced to a large foot, which crushes a writhing snake into the statue's plinth; the open mouth of the snake is threatening Barry's ear, and no doubt saying something venomous. By being included thus in a self-portrait, the most heroic that Barry had attempted, the motif is made as much a part of Barry's self-representation as is the self-comparison with Timanthes. This complex of imagery might want to say, I suppose, that Barry is an artist of heroic stature, whose *porte-crayon* can almost stand being measured against the crozier-like staff of the Cyclops, which projects from between his thighs. Only Envy will deny this; and Envy will be crushed. And if this is the statement the picture seeks to make, it also negates it, of course, as soon as we ask why the artist should choose or need to make such a representation of himself.

That Barry might have intended the painting as a vindication of his own greatness (in one sense or another) certainly seems to be suggested by the comment he had made, in 1783, on the statue of Hercules in the Olympia painting. In tones of pious resignation, he wrote:

> it is no doubt a good and wise distribution, that Envy should continually haunt and persecute the greatest characters; though for a time, it may give them uneasiness, yet it tends on the one hand to make them more perfect, by obliging them to weed out whatever may be faulty, and occasions them on the other, to keep their good qualities in that state of continued unrelaxed exertion, from which the world deserves greater benefit, and themselves in the end, still greater glory. (2: 331)

We have come across some of these phrases before: the artist, we have seen, by 'weeding out' the monstrosities of pre-classical, sexually undifferentiated forms, produces 'more perfect' figures, and becomes himself of course greater, more perfect, more complete – and more masculine.

There are a good number of other works by Barry where feet come into close, but not *very* close contact with snakes; or where the monsters are not quite as serpentine as those we have looked at so far; or where a kind of visual pun seems to place the foot not next to a snake, exactly, but to a serpentine form of one kind or another. But in an essay which has promised to talk about Barry's art in terms of fetishism, the evidence had better not be too oblique, or the fetishism will come to seem my own – and it is more important than I care to explain that I should appear here as diagnostician and not as co-analysand. But no pedestrian tour of Barry's *oeuvre* would be complete without a quick look at the foot of Pandora herself (Figure 30), which seems to be extended in the same attitude as are the feet of Philoctetes, Wolfe, Orpheus, and Polyphemus. She had adopted much the same pose in the earlier drawing which is the original of Schiavonetti's etching; and Pressly suggests that it derives from the pose of Venus in a painting of the goddess, then in Kensington Palace, by the studio of Guido Reni, which appears to be the source also for the pose so awkwardly adopted by the Sicyonian maid in Barry's sketch of the origin of painting. In the figure of Pandora, however, Venus's pose is reversed, which leads Pressly to suggest that Barry may have been using Robert Strange's engraving of the painting (Figure 46: 1759), rather than the painting itself (Pressly 1981 29 and 208 n. 94). And reversed, of course, the whole attitude of Venus resembles not only that of Pandora, but of Philoctetes.

The two subjects seem both to have become important to Barry in Rome in 1770, and I am suggesting that the figures of Philoctetes and Pandora are twins, children of the same moment in Barry's life, of the same image of Venus. It may be worth recalling here that Barry's next picture, after the Philoctetes, was *Venus Rising from the Sea*, the painting in which he first attempted to banish the maternal idea of the goddess that he saw in the Venus de' Medici, in favour of the fresh, the virginal (Pressly 1981 black and white plate 21; National Gallery of Ireland, Dublin). At the same time, however, the two figures, male and female, seem to belong on opposite sides of a series of related paradigms. Philoctetes (Figure 47 is Barry's own print after his painting) appears to be unwinding the soiled dressing from his foot, which Barry has left 'without any support' so as to mark more emphatically the agony he suffers. Pandora's foot, like Venus's, is supported by one of the Graces, who, as in the Guido painting, is binding her foot into a sandal. Barry, incidentally, had a great admiration for sandals in the classical style. Around 1770, at Itri 'in the Neapolitan territory' he was delighted to discover what he described in a letter to Burke as a 'monument', a 'vestige', of the 'old Romans'. It was

> a piece of raw hide, a little broader than the sole of the foot, tied on in the manner of the ancient sandal. I bought a pair of them, which I will put on to shew you the villainy of our cursed gothic shoes, which by separating the foot from the leg by the line, which the terminatiion of the upper leather makes upon the stocking, cuts off the foot from the leg, and loses that fine idea of one limb, which is kept up in this vestige of the sandal.   (1: 109)

46. Robert Strange, after the studio of Guido Reni, *Venus Attired by the Graces*, 1759. Approx. 48.1 × 36.2 cm.

47. James Barry, *Philoctetes*, 1777. Etching and aquatint 45.4 × 37.1 cm.

The strange violence of the language here seems to entitle us to add
to the paradigms that differentiate Pandora from Philoctetes. Not only
woman/man; supported/unsupported; and bound/unbound; also the
idea of a limb which is whole, in one piece; and the opposing idea
of the foot 'separated', 'cut off' from the leg.

In his paper on fetishism of 1927, Freud describes that perversion
as the symptom of a mis-match between what is believed and what
is perceived, and as, at the same time, a mechanism which enables
both the belief and the perception to be credited. The boy-child at
first believes that his mother has a penis, and subsequently sees that
she does not have one. He believes the evidence of his eyes, but he
also disbelieves it; and he sustains this structure of contradiction by
fixing on something that she certainly does have – a part of her body
(a foot would do, and it sometimes does), or some inanimate object
related to her – and by making it a substitute for what she is perceived
to lack. The substitution has the effect of giving her back the penis
she has lost, and it must be made, of course, because the mother's
perceived lack of a penis could be explained only by the assumption
that she had been castrated; and if she has been, then one day the
boy might be similarly dismembered. The fetishism is presumably
reinforced by the fact that the fear of castration produces also an
aversion to the female genitals – and so to the female sex – because
they have come to represent that fear.

According to Freud's brief essay on the head of the Medusa (written
1922; published 1940), it is quite appropriate that Minerva, the 'virgin
goddess', should wear the Medusa's head as an ornament on her dress,
'for thus she becomes a woman who is unapproachable and repels all
sexual desires'. The abundance of snakes on the Medusa's head, Freud
invites us to believe, is an emblem of the female pubic hair, and thus
of the place where the penis is not. Minerva is unapproachable because
she displays 'the terrifying genitals of the mother'; she is a woman
'who frightens and repels because she is castrated' (Freud 18: 274).[35]
Freud's essay is perhaps a little too confident in its attribution of so
fixed, so emblematic a meaning to the Medusa; but it may help us to
think about the anxiety that first surfaced in the 1798 *Letter*, at the
prospect of the 'masculine' woman, whose archetype was Minerva,
and who called into question the masculinity of the artist and of the
entire male sex. And it may do so, because it helps us to think about
the phenomenon we noticed earlier, that snakes seem to bear a
particular responsibility for the problems that heroes have with their
feet.

In the light of Freud's remarks on the Medusa, Barry's discussion
of the masculine goddess can be read as suggesting, paradoxically
enough, that her manliness is in the first place the result of what she

does not have. It is the snake as an emblem not of the penis but of its absence that produces the vulnerability of the male; and in this light, not only *The Birth of Pandora*, but a large part of Barry's *oeuvre*, literary and artistic, can be read as a series of meditations on how that absence could be abolished, and of attempts to abolish it. In these terms, the image of the man, say Philoctetes, with his wounded and unsupported foot, would come to express the fear of castration; but because that fear derives from the belief that the woman is castrated, it can be allayed only by restoring to the woman (the fetishised substitute for) the penis she has lost. The representation of Philoctetes with his wounded foot produces the need for the companion representation of Pandora with her healthy foot, supported, dandled and sandalled. The two figures are children not only of the same moment and the same mother, but of the same need. And if the visual parallel between the Cyclop's staff and Barry's *porte-crayon* (Figure 45) suggested there a connection between his manhood and the instrument of his art, it may be we should understand Minerva's action, in presenting Pandora with the shuttle, as a part of the same act of restoration. With it, Pandora is to weave the peplus, which has its own place, as Marcia Pointon has suggested, within this ubiquitous economy of fetishism, and which will restore a lost masculine function to a feminine art.

This fetishistic strategy may however be complicated by the suggestion that seems to arise when we put *The Birth of Pandora* alongside a number of the paintings we have been considering, that it is the woman herself, that it is Minerva, who threatens the male with castration. In the 1798 *Letter*, Barry devotes a digression of several pages to demonstrating that the serpent was, like Minerva herself, an emblem of wisdom. Minerva's breastplate, Barry begins,

> is a large serpent's skin, hanging from her right shoulder across her breast . . . The edges of this skin appear bordered with smaller living, and, as it were, embryo serpents, twirling about in different ways; but upon a more attentive inspection they are found to be only the several necks and heads of the great serpent, whose skin is thus wrapped round Minerva; and there is generally on the top of her helmet an entire serpent, as it were, couchant, and just launching . . . Now, as Minerva is . . . the sovereign mind, and issuing full-formed from the head of Jove himself, . . . we suppose these serpents to represent thoughts or acts of the mind (2: 588–9)

The whole digression is remarkable, not just for the knowledge of recent mythographic research it displays, but for the fact that so much space is devoted to proving what no contemporary mythographer would have dreamed of questioning. One point of the digression, however, seems to be to produce an entire identity between Minerva and her emblem: she is, Barry tells us, 'always so enveloped with this breast-plate, or broad-belt of the living skin of this many-headed serpent, as to denote the same identity with the serpent itself' (2: 590). To this end, he proceeds to identify Minerva with as many grotesque, serpentine monsters as he can think of. They include, alongside the Medusa, 'the dragons or winged serpents' who draw Medea's chariot (two of Barry's lost history-paintings are of Medea – see Pressly 1981 230, 233); the 'woman or sorceress' who was the origin of the Scythians 'with her lower limbs terminating in two serpents'; 'the serpent with five heads, which so frequently occurs in the Hindoo antiquities'; 'that terrible image in the Bagvat Geta, swallowing whole armies and nations' (see Wilkins 92); the Hydra of Lerna; the serpent enveloping the lingam; and so on (2: 590–2).[36]

It is by establishing Minerva's identity as snake that Barry seems to identify her also as the bearer of the threat of castration; for as we have see, what most threatens the feet of men is the bite of the serpent. Hence, perhaps, the images of retaliation: the contests between foot and serpent which the foot is sometimes allowed to win: the serpent-killing represented in the images of the Prince of Wales as St George, and of Hercules treading down the serpent of envy. And hence too a more subtle strategy, glanced at in the 1805 *Fragment* but never developed, which attempts to de-phallicise Minerva by erasing the snake as her identifying emblem, and replacing it with the sphinx. The task of Phidias, and of the Greek artists, was to produce, from the unruly and polymorphous Orphic and Asiatic grotesques of an earlier monotheism, the 'perfect' figures of classical art, which were also acknowledged to be incomplete. The particular example Barry offered was of Phidias removing the sphinx from Minerva's shoulders, and locating it on the top of her helmet – and the sphinx, we were assured, was an emblem of Minerva's femininity, of the 'superior sensibilities and affectionate tenderness of the heart, which so happily and necessarily accompanies the female or maternal character through all animal nature.' But Phidias's real achievement, it may seem, was to substitute the sphinx for that 'entire serpent', 'couchant, and just launching', which, however, in his painting and print of Pandora, Barry retained, the only ornament of Minerva's helmet (Figure 32; 2: 150–1, 588).

The same fear, of woman as the imagined agent of castration, may assert itself in the form of the body Minerva acquires in the final print: huge, muscular, masculine. It may also be discovered in the determined effort made in the painting itself to change Minerva's character and function: to represent her, against all the injunctions of iconography, as pretty rather than as severely beautiful, and to celebrate her, at the same time, as herself a killer of snakes, the destroyer of Typhon, the polycephalous serpent-monster whose name is the name also of the castrator of Osiris. The strategy of course can only repeat the problem it attempts to resolve, for in the story Barry has to tell, the serpent appears both as the subject and object of castration, what does it and what it is done to.

VII

To end the matter there, however, would be to trivialise a project that preoccupied Barry for more than thirty years of his life. The point of this excursion into the psychoanalytic is not to explain *The Birth of Pandora* as, in the last analysis, an encoded account of Barry's personal psychic anxieties, nor is it to treat those anxieties as if they were the true, the deep ground of all his endeavours, to which his concerns with the political, the economic and the aesthetic are all equally reducible. Thus Barry's concern that painting should perform a public and a political function, should teach the virtues of disinterested citizenship, is not simply to be ignored, or simply to be regretted, on the grounds that he could imagine that function only in gendered terms. My concern is rather with the way in which, at a historically specific time, psychic and social determinants may intermesh within a given discourse or discursive practice. And I want to suggest that the anxiety which finds expression in *The Birth of Pandora* is a constituent of a fully articulated late eighteenth-century discourse on the representation of the body, which, though it does not enter Barry's writing until the 1790s, had been present to his consciousness throughout his career as an artist.

To make the point, I want to look again at the figure of Vulcan (Figure 30), but this time at his head. According to Bell's *New Pantheon* (2: 321) the Phrygian cap worn by Vulcan was blue, 'which is symbolical of the celestial or elementary fire, in its own nature clear and unmixed; whereas common fire, such as that used on earth, is weak, and wants continual accessions of the essential element to support it'. But Barry has chosen – the point is made, of course, only in the painting, not in the print – to colour it red, at a time when it would certainly therefore be taken as the *bonnet rouge*, the cap of liberty. The gesture – especially in the light of Barry's self-identification with Vulcan – could hardly have been more provocative; it must represent a deliberate decision to embrace the republican, and Jacobin character attributed to him by Francis Bourgeois, during the period leading up to Barry's expulsion from the Academy (see above, 166). It is also an act which associates the civic, republican tradition of painting, of which Barry was by now the most forceful advocate in Britain, with the revolutionary classicism of David; and, more than that, it identifies the classicising enterprise of the painting itself – the production of ideal and bounded forms out of an undifferentiated chaos – as a revolutionary enterprise.

It does not cease to do any of those things when we remember that Neil Hertz, in his much discussed and much responded-to essay on the head of Medusa, suggests that 'the cap that meant "liberty" could also mean "castration"', or the *fear* of castration. It was worn, he points out, by a group of *semivirs*, devotees of the Eastern cult of Attis in second and third-century Rome, 'who had castrated themselves in fervid emulation of their god'. As a result, its 'Asiatic' and therefore effeminate character, and its drooping shape, 'phallic but not erect', could elicit 'uncertainties about the stability of sexual difference, uncertainties that could resonate with those developing out of the blurring of differences in social status – between, for instance, citizens, freedmen, and slaves'. Hertz quotes a pamphlet of 1796 by the painter Esprit-Antoine Gibelin, which denounces 'this effeminate cap' as the badge of Asiatic servitude, entirely inappropriate as a cap of Liberty (Hertz 184–7). The dangers, Hertz notes, that seem to threaten Gibelin are

> indeterminately political, sexual, and epistemological. Enslavement, seduction, the loss of manhood, and the unfixing of determinate ideas of what things mean are upheld as equivalent threats, and these baleful consequences inhere in the overly refined turn of the top of a cap, or . . . in the possibility that, looking for Liberty . . . , we may find, exposed to our glance, the droop of the Phrygian cap.
> (Hertz 188)

It does not matter to me whether Hertz's playful excursion into the archaeology of headgear has come up with the truth about the Phrygian cap; the cap as he describes it will do to introduce the notion of dangers which are 'indeterminately' political and sexual, and which are the inventions of a collective male hysteria that in and after 1789 could afflict equally ('fraternally', perhaps I should say) those who supported and those who attacked the revolution in France.

For a painter with the concerns and connections of Barry, the revolution raised a very specific issue in aesthetics. In his *Philosophical Inquiry*, as is well known, Burke had described the distinction between the categories of the sublime and beautiful in gendered terms. An object which is sublime, according to Burke, is a 'modification of power' (Burke 1968 64) and, in the contemplation, at a safe remove, of such an object, the subject of aesthetic experience (always assumed to be male; see for example Burke 1968, 91) experienced a delight which suggested that he took on its power himself. Sublime objects produced

> a sort of swelling and triumph that is extremely grateful to the human mind; and this swelling is never more perceived, nor operates with more force, than when without danger we are conversant with terrible objects, the mind always claiming to itself some part of the dignity and importance of the things which it contemplates. Hence proceeds what Longinus has observed of that glorying and sense of inward greatness . . .　　　(Burke 1968 50–1)

Beautiful objects, on the other hand, were beautiful by virtue of 'that quality or those qualities in bodies by which they cause love, or some passion similar to it.' Though Burke explicitly distinguished the love inspired by beautiful objects from 'lust' and 'desire', he was happy to admit that love and desire may operate together, and in respect of the objects (for that is how he invited his readers to think of women) which he regarded as the most beautiful, desire might be found without love, but not apparently love (or beauty, therefore) without desire (Burke 1968 110, 91). There was no question of a beautiful object being a modification of power: 'the beauty of women is considerably owing to their weakness', and 'Beauty in distress is much the most affecting beauty'. It was for this reason, no doubt, that 'love approaches nearer to contempt than is commonly imagined' (Burke 1968 116, 110, 67).[37]

The system of aesthetics set out in the *Inquiry* thus presupposed a powerful, or a potent masculinity, and a femininity which is, or should be, another word for feebleness. It is this system, that was put in question by the role played by women in the revolution in France, and particularly in Burke's own reconstruction of the events of 6 October 1789, when Louis XVI and Marie Antoinette were conducted from Versailles to Paris in the noisy company of 'furies of hell, in the abused shape of the vilest of women'. These women, far from being objects of affecting weakness, like the queen, were both terrifying and powerful, and threatened to appropriate to themselves the category of sublime which the *ancien régime* had reserved for men, and to which women were admitted only as personifications of the sublime passions.[38] It is this threatened and threatening appropriation Burke hints at when he talks of the events of 6 October as 'Theban and Thracian orgies' (Burke 1964 69). Thebes and Thrace were the two places in Greece where a king's resistance to the cult of Dionysus had resulted in his dismemberment: Pentheus, in Thebes, at the hands of maniac women, and Lycurgus in Thrace by wild horses. Orpheus, of course, was dismembered by the women of Thrace 'while they celebrated the orgies of Bacchus' (Lemprière, article 'Orpheus').

Among intellectuals in Britain 'sympathetic', as we say, to the revolution – in its early stages at least – both Mary Wollstonecraft and James Barry seem to have registered the fact that Burke's account of the events in France may have put in question his own gendered system of aesthetics, and his belief that nature had made women '*little, smooth delicate, fair* creatures'. In her reply to Burke's *Reflections*, Wollstonecraft refers scornfully to his feminisation of beauty as 'weakness', as an other than 'manly' quality which 'melts', which 'relaxes the *solids*' of the body (Wollstonecraft 1989 5: 45–6), and in her *Rights of Woman* she attacks Milton, among others, for choosing to believe that physical strength was unnatural to women, who were formed 'for softness and sweet attractive grace' (Wollstonecraft 1975 19).

All this is very different from Barry's reaction. Before the revolution, as we have seen, Barry had (however carelessly) produced an account of the civic body which was not a gendered account; the bodies of both men and women were modified by the various tasks allotted to them in a modern economy, and both were thus inscribed with the distinguishing marks which were their credentials as members of a civic republic. But as we have also seen, in his second academy lecture, delivered in the early 1790s, Barry elaborated a very different theory of the representation of the body in painting. Only the male body, by being modified in the performance of some civic duty, could now aspire to sublimity; the female could be represented in painting only as beautiful and graceful, only with a proper regard to 'the superior softness and delicacy of their bodily frame' (1: 399–401). The effect of this revision is to distance Barry's thought from the civic republican tradition, and to allow it to accommodate a Burkean account of female beauty, as exciting not love only but desire, a desire that need not now be resisted or disavowed.

The revolution that Vulcan supports is a 'democratic' revolution, no doubt, but not therefore one which is to be taken as an opportunity to change the status or the 'sexual character' of women. Vulcan's concern, as we have seen, is to produce new forms from old: but whereas, for Wollstonecraft, the *ancien régime* had unnaturally divided the sexes, the pre-Olympian régime, for Barry, had blurred them unnaturally together, and the events of 1789 and after, instead of drawing a clear bounding line round male and female, masculine and feminine, had blurred them still more. In the 1790s, therefore, *The Birth of Pandora* became an opportunity to draw that line, but by virtue of the very urgency with which the opportunity was seized, the painting seems to betray more clearly the anxiety which finds more muffled expression elsewhere in Barry's *oeuvre*. It was not Barry's anxiety alone, however: a system of aesthetics which bases itself on a distinction between male potency and female weakness was one which could appeal to men on both, on all sides of the revolution controversy. It is also a system which has always already imagined its own destruction. Burke's fantasies of 'Theban and Thracian orgies' are foreshadowed, thirty years earlier, in the urbanity of the *Inquiry* and its careful discrimination between those capable of experiencing the swellings of the sublime, and those too weak to do so; in just the same way the threat represented for Barry in the 1790s by Minerva is anticipated in so many of his pre-revolutionary works. The good citizen, writes Burke in the 1790 *Reflections,*

> should approach to the faults of the state as to the wounds of a father, with pious awe and trembling solicitude. . . . we are taught to look with horror on those children of their country, who are prompt rashly to hack that aged parent in pieces, and put him into the kettle of magicians, in hopes that by their poisonous weeds, and wild incantations, they may regenerate the paternal constitution, and renovate their father's life.   (Burke 1964 93)

The opposition here, of binding and dismembering, seems to repeat the opposition in Barry's work between Pandora and Philoctetes, images of a loss made good and a loss that is irreparable. However the revolution may have divided them in other ways, the Burke and Barry of the 1790s were in one respect the same men who first met in Dublin in 1763 (1: 7–10), when Barry complimented Burke on his *Inquiry*, and Burke praised Barry's painting of the King of Cashel with a wounded foot.[39]

When finally in 1793 the king of France was decapitated, so also, it could be argued, were the French people; for in the king's body was represented the body of the state, and the regal and 'paternal constitution' was the constitution of France. In this light the period after the execution of the king seems to ask to be read in terms of an attempt to find an image of the ideal or the typical body (Hercules, Marianne) which can claim to 'regenerate', to reassemble the body of the public by representing it metonymically (see for example Outram, esp. chapter 9). But there may be a problem in telling this story, as I have recently heard it very well told,[40] as a narrative of the attempt to construct a whole object out of disparate and dismembered part-objects; for, told that way, the story seems to admit only one kind of successful outcome, whether in the coronation of Napoleon or in the Restoration. Indeed, I was taught at school, and for some reason it stuck, that Louis XVIII was so diseased that, when his valet removed his stocking, parts of his foot came away too, so maybe there is no legitimate, or legitimist ending to the story at all. Napoleon or nothing.

In this context, one point of Barry's account of the state as composed of variously differentiated male bodies is to envisage the state as a republic which is not merely tolerant of but dependent upon the differences among its citizens, differences which therefore cannot be subsumed or reunited into the single representative body of a George III or Louis XVI. It would be difficult to believe that the same thought had not crossed the mind of some of those who voted for Louis's execution. And yet we have seen that the very perfection of those differentiated bodies is a function of their incompleteness, and that the idea of incompleteness is evoked everywhere in *The Birth of Pandora*, dedicated though it was to wishing it away. The restoration of what is lost may not have been the only successful, the only satisfying outcome of the story which began with the desire for a republic, but in the decades around 1800 it would certainly have been evoked by every other imaginable outcome, if only by its conspicuous absence. The perfect bodies in Barry's painting that evoke imperfect ones; the perfect bodies made imperfect by the superimposition of bits of others; the perfect bodies with imperfect feet; all can be read as evidence of how tenacious was the ideology that linked the idea of the monarchical state with the ideas of physical completeness and of male potency, and of how difficult it was therefore to think the republic.[41]

Notes

FOREWORD

1. The term 'civic humanism' is borrowed from J.G.A. Pocock, *The Machiavellian Moment: Florentine Political Thought and the Atlantic Republican Tradition*. For an account of civic humanist theories of literature, see Meehan, *Liberty and Poetics*; for an account of civic humanist theories of the fine arts in eighteenth-century Britain, see my *The Political Theory of Painting from Reynolds to Hazlitt*.
2. The passage is from the 5th book of *Liberty*, lines 99–109, Thomson 1986 129–30; for its use in the trial, see ST 24 387, 1238.
3. There are two short pieces which were originally conceived as part of the essay on Rowlandson, but which, because they would have made the essay too long, were detached and published independently. One is on Thomas Gainsborough's drawings, which became part of a review of the Gainsborough exhibition at the Tate Gallery in 1980; it appeared as 'Gainsborough's Woodmen' in the *London Review of Books*, vol. 2, no. 24 (18 December 1980 – 21 January 1981). The other is Barrell 1982. Both may be of interest to those who find the Rowlandson essay of interest.
4. 'Geographies of Hardy's Wessex,' in *Journal of Historical Geography*, vol. 8, no. 4 (1982).
5. '"Who Ever Perished, Being Innocent?" Some Plates from the *Songs of Innocence*', *Style*, vol. 22, no. 2 (Summer 1988).
6. Wollstonecraft 1975, 110–12 (beginning 'Let me now as from an eminence survey the world stripped of all its false delusive charms', and continuing (111–12) 'I descend from my height, and mixing with my fellow-creatures, feel myself hurried along the common stream').

1: THE PRIVATE COMEDY OF THOMAS ROWLANDSON

1. See Barrell 1980 especially 53–88; for the transition from Gay and Goldsmith to Crabbe, see in particular 73–80. The starting-point for the present essay was my sense of having failed, in that book (see 118–20), to account for the relation between Rowlandson's comic representations of rural life and changes in the representation of the poor in oil-paintings contemporary with him. Although I believe that much of this essay is relevant to Rowlandson's work as a whole, I have preferred to let the origins of my interest show, by restricting my comments to his images of the rural poor.
2. Yale Center for British Art, New Haven. All four pictures are illustrated and discussed in Barrell 1982 39–42; see also Webster 106, 153–4.
3. Date unknown; Yale Center for British Art, New Haven.

221

4. Huntington Museum and Library, San Marino, California. See Wark 1975 70; plate and cat. no. 187.
5. Compare her, for example, with the extremely desirable women who sit at a cottage-door in Gainsborough's *The Woodcutter's Return* (date unknown, Belvoir Castle), illustrated in Waterhouse ill. 227.
6. See Barrell 1980 97–114.
7. Kris and Gombrich, 'The Principles of Caricature', reprinted in Kris 1953. It should be noted that the authors use the term 'caricature' more specifically than I do, to refer to 'caricature portraits' of specific individuals. Kris and Gombrich expand the argument of this paper in *Caricature* (1940), which contains a brief comment on Rowlandson (19).
8. James Thomson, *The Seasons*, ed. James Sambrook; quotations from Thomson, except when noted, are from this edition, and from this passage, a version of which first appeared in the 1730 edition of *The Seasons*.
9. See, for example, Roskill 157–69; or Paulson 1975 chapter 9.
10. Instances of these positions may be found in the third, fourth and fifth discourses: see Reynolds 1975 44–9, 51, 58, 59, 60–1, 78–9.
11. For a helpful comment on what to a landscape-painter constitute the 'accidents' of nature, see Francis Nicholson, SHG 1: 6–12 (1 November 1823).
12. Reynolds's willingness to admire the 'odd scratches and marks' character-istic of Gainsborough's style is not, of course, a qualification of his belief in the value of careful and distinct expression, but a crucial confirmation of it: for 'this chaos, this uncouth and shapeless appearance, by a kind of magick, at a certain distance assumes form, and all the parts seem to drop into their proper places' (Reynolds 1975 257–8); thus his work is more successful as an act of communication even than some works of Raphael, in which the 'expression of passions . . . has . . . by an indistinct and imperfect marking, left room for every imagination, with equal probability to find a passion of his own' (78–9). For taste and virtue, see 171.
13. See J. Hassell's comments upon an (unnamed) picture painted by George Morland for 'a very worthy character in the city': 'The pastimes and employments which constitute the subject of the picture are so very local, mean, and ridiculous, as to preclude it from being worthy a place in any gentleman's apartment' (Hassell 154).
14. My discussion of the arrangement of pictures by rooms in the eighteenth-century house is indebted to Mark Girouard's *Life in the English Country House*: for the relation of cabinet and saloon, see 129–30, 173–4; for the emergence of libraries, see 166–80, 234–5; for 'living rooms', see 234, 236–42.
15. SHG 2: 46 (1 May 1824); 1: 82 (15 November 1823); 1: 30 (18 October 1823); 1: 194 (3 January 1824).
16. By this phrase I mean to indicate a notion of government by which it is possible for any individual man to become enfranchised–if he can achieve the necessary qualification, in property or knowledge–but in which authority depends on the impossibility of many, or of most, achieving that qualification. Reynolds's notion of civic art, for example, as it strives to create a public, at the same time creates a private realm, of the 'ignorant', the 'vulgar', the 'common people', the 'untaught' (Reynolds 1975 43, 74, 79, 77) who do not grasp the principles of the arts, and who

seek in painting the gratification of the eye, not of the mind. The authority of the academy depends on the existence of this class, if its claim to be able to teach the principles of 'high' art is to be vindicated; see Uphaus, 'The Ideology of Reynolds's *Discourses on Art*'.

17. The tradition is continued by Coleridge's 'Frost at Midnight', a poem in which the 'blending of shapes' in a free play of fancy 'evokes childhood pleasures', to apply to it a phrase from Kris and Gombrich (1953 202).

18. 'What it's like to read *L'Allegro* and *Il Penseroso*', in Fish 112–35; it is as the 'brood of Folly' and as 'gaudy shapes' that the formless images of 'L'Allegro' are dismissed by 'Il Penseroso'. Fish says that he is writing against 'three hundred years' of criticism, but his examples of mistaken interpretations are all drawn from this century. I should make it clear that I find Fish's (brilliantly straightforward) reading of 'L'Allegro' most persuasive, at least to the extent that I agree that we are *offered* care-less and 'secure delight' by the poem; the problem, which his essay bears witness to but does not quite confront, is on what terms we are permitted to enjoy that delight. The pleasures of irresponsibility are illicit unless carefully licensed; certainly Il Penseroso seems to think so.

19. For a literary example of the notion that the comic is acceptable in the closet, but not in more public places, see Goldsmith's 'Preface' to *The Good Natur'd Man* (1768) (Goldsmith 5: 13–14).

20. 1796; with the Fine Art Society, London, in 1982.

21. Collection of Mr Paul Mellon, Oak Spring, Virginia; see Baskett and Snelgrove 28; plate and cat. no. 84; the drawing is assigned to the period 1805–10 by Reily (63, no. 90).

22. The distinction between a responsible art which excludes images of transient expression and gesture, and an irresponsible art which accommodates them, is well suggested by an anecdote recounted by Henry Angelo (1: 262), of the occasion when Rowlandson, a student at the Royal Academy schools,

> gave great offence, by carrying a pea-shooter into the life academy, and whilst old Moser was adjusting the female model, and had just directed her contour, Rowlandson let fly a pea, which making her start, she threw herself entirely out of position, and interrupted the gravity of the study for a whole evening. For this offence, Master Rowlandson went near to getting himself expelled

The anecdote probably requires no comment, but I shall comment anyway: it is not simply that the 'gravity' of the occasion is interrupted by Rowlandson's playful and irresponsible action; it is that the model, carefully directed into a frozen 'academy pose', is returned by Rowlandson's pea-shooter into a fugitive, a transient attitude of the kind continually represented in his own 'irresponsible' art.

It may be appropriate here to notice that, as well as attending the Academy schools, Rowlandson was awarded the silver medal in 1777, made early visits to Paris and Italy, exhibited twenty pictures at the Academy between 1775 and 1787 (but none thereafter), won the praises of both Reynolds and West (see his obituary in the *GM*, June 1827 565, and Angelo 1: 235), and so began his career in a most exemplary and orthodox manner. He was certainly able to get comic subjects accepted at the Academy in the 1780s, and it may be that his unwillingness, or failure, to exhibit there after 1787 is further evidence of the increasingly unacceptable status of 'comic' art in the last years of the century.

23. I have borrowed the phrase 'off-hand' from Angelo's account (1: 386) of the art of Gillray; Rowlandson's art is described elsewhere by Angelo (1: 233–5) in terms by now familiar to us: Rowlandson's 'powers' are 'versatile', his 'fancy' is 'rich'; 'every species of composition flowed from his pen with equal facility'; he could '"Build the lofty rhyme,"' even with a dash of his pen'; 'he has sketched' in his 'careless style', his 'rapid manner', more scenes of 'fun and frolic' than any ten of his contemporaries. The obituary in the *GM* (see previous note) is in the same vein (564–5); it speaks of the 'versatility' of Rowlandson's talent, the 'fecundity' of his imagination', his 'almost incredible despatch'; even his etchings, many of them, were 'the careless effusion of a few hours'. These phrases are worth comparing with the account, by Kris and Gombrich (1953 191, 202), of caricature as 'a casual scrawl, "dashed off" with a few strokes'; 'a scribbling style'. The best description of Rowlandson's style is in Hayes 34–9. For a literary example of the connection between privacy, 'scribbling', and the closet, see William Cowper, 'The Progress of Error', *Poems* 57.

24. Four items exhibited by Rowlandson at the Society of Artists in 1783 (the only year he exhibited with that society) were described as 'stained drawings'; for the attitude of 'watercolour painters' to this method, see next note; for an account of Wheatley's watercolour practice, see Webster 109, and, for examples of his drawings of Irish fairs, see Webster 49, 51.

25. The Society of Painters in Water Colour was founded in 1804. The developments described in this paragraph have been well described by Roget, *A History of the 'Old Water-Colour' Society*, by Hardie, *Water-colour Painting in Britain*, and by Clarke, *The Tempting Prospect*. In the interests of brevity, I shall select my instances of this development, in this note and the next, entirely from the *Somerset House Gazette*, a periodical edited and largely written by the watercolour artist and engraver W.H. Pyne; all references date from 1823–4, and all passages are apparently by Pyne, unless otherwise noted. 'Scornful of the older method': SHG 1: 193, and 2: 95 ('"You noticed them I presume–I mean Alfred Chalon's tinted drawings! Sir, they are magnificent paintings in small."'); 'Conscious of themselves as . . . a profession': SHG 1: 14, 47, 66, 81, 98; 2: 45, 47, etc.; 'gold frames' and 'cabinet pictures': SHG 2: 46.

26. 'Hostile to "sketchiness"', 'correct drawing', 'academic standards': SHG 1: 14 (John Varley), 72–3 (Francis Nicholson), 83, 144, etc., and, in particular, 132, where John Glover is granted a 'license' to use 'a fortuitous scumbling or blotting', 'Careless scramblings', 'the absence of defined forms', in his watercolour landscapes, for, like Gainsborough's works (see above, n.12), 'when viewed at a distance of a few feet, they are as nearly allied to reality as any scenes that were ever imitated by graphic means'; but this method is 'fallacious and unworthy of imitation' (145). 'Moral grandeur' and 'exquisite feeling': SHG 1: 12, 81, 103 (David Cox), 133 etc.; 'long apprenticeship': SHG 1: 72–3, 160, etc.; 'foresight': 104 (David Cox).

27. See SHG 2: 130 (5 June 1824), on a watercolour by Joshua Cristall, whose 'peasants', say the reviewer (presumably Pyne) 'though truly English, are not the slouching boors and slatternly ale-house maids of George Morland. They are selected from the sequestered village, yet uncontaminated by the vicinity of manufactories', and are 'the healthy offspring of retirement and content'.

28. Yale Center for British Art, New Haven. Baskett and Snelgrove 30; plate and cat. no. 95.
29. Private collection; see Hayes 38.
30. I am grateful to Peter de Bolla, Tim Clark, Harriet Guest and Anne Wagner, all of whom read a draft of this essay and commented most helpfully upon it.

2: THE PUBLIC FIGURE AND THE PRIVATE EYE

1. The text of the ode is taken from Collins 1979.
2. According to Wendorf and Ryskamp (Collins 1979 123) 'Collins' *Odes . . .* was published by Andrew Millar on 20 December 1746 (but was dated 1747, as was common with publications late in the year)'. The notes to the 'Ode to Evening' in this edition, and in Lonsdale's *The Poems of Gray, Collins and Goldsmith*, contain, among other valuable information, useful bibliographies of critical discussions of the poem.
3. A facsimile copy of the first (1730) complete edition of *The Seasons* was circulated. An excellent account of Tardieu's engravings of Kent's designs will be found in Cohen 269ff. Cohen however sees in these illustrations more of a unity than I do between sky and landscape, supernatural and natural, which Kent may certainly have intended but which I do not find achieved. Those who agree with Cohen may find a similarity between Kent's accommodation of the allegorical and the natural descriptive and Collins's, as I see it in the 'Ode to Evening'.
4. For a discussion of to what these 'gleams' are to be attributed, see Lonsdale 465.
5. I am thinking of I Corinthians 15: 44–5: 'It is sown a natural body: it is raised a spiritual body. There is a natural body, and there is a spiritual body. And so it is written, The first man Adam was made a living soul; the last Adam *was made* a quickening spirit.'
6. I am grateful to Harriet Guest for her help and advice when this essay was being written.

3: THE PUBLIC PROSPECT AND THE PRIVATE VIEW

1. For civic humanism in relation to Reynolds and landscape painting, see especially 120–3.
2. My remarks on Pope in this essay are adapted from my *English Literature in History* 1983 35–6.
3. See Pocock 390, Harrington 42–3.
4. The phrase is borrowed from Montaigne; see Diderot 236 n.312.
5. D.D. Raphael and A.L. MacFie (Smith 1976b 135n.) suggest a source for this passage in Berkeley's *New Theory of Vision*, Sec. 54. To me it seems closer to his *Discourse of Passive Obedience*, Sec. 28.

> . . . if we have a mind to take a fair prospect of the order and general well-being, which the inflexible laws of nature and morality derive on the world, we must, if I may say so, go out of it, and imagine ourselves to be distant spectators of all that is transacted and contained in it, otherwise we are sure to be deceived by the too near view of the little present interest of ourselves, our friends, or our country.

6. Spoken observation of Reynolds, recorded in Madame D'Arblay, *Memoirs of Dr Burney* (Burney 2: 281–2), quoted in Lipking 204–5.
7. I can make this point more clearly to those who have read David Solkin's recent essay, 'The Battle of the Cicero's: Richard Wilson and the Politics of Landscape in the Age of John Wilkes' (1983), in which he discusses Wilson's *Cicero and his two friends at his Villa at Arpinum* (1770). Solkin's brilliant account of the painting might be strengthened by pointing out that the image of Cicero as the guardian of the public interest is further defined by his being represented in an ideal, extensive prospect, and not in the kind of occluded landscape depicted, for example, in Wilson's *Solitude* eight years earlier.
8. This essay was first published in garbled form in Eade (ed.) *Projecting the Landscape*. When it was submitted for publication, it was imagined that it would be published before the publication of my *The Political Theory of Painting from Reynolds to Hazlitt*. A number of passages in that book are repeated from this essay. The first chapter of the book contains a more detailed account of the 'rhetorical' and the 'philosophical' aesthetic, and of Reynolds's thinking about the principles and place of landscape painting. Too many people gave help and advice with the essay to name them all individually: most influential on its development was Harriet Guest.

4: THE DANGEROUS GODDESS

1. For civic humanism see above, 221, n.1. The title of this essay has been borrowed from Arthur Young: 'After all I had read and heard of the Venus de Medicis, . . . I was eager to hurry to the *tribuna* for a view of the dangerous goddess. . . . In the same apartment there are other statues, but, in the presence of Venus, who is it that can regard them?' (*Travels in France and Italy During the Years 1787, 1788, and 1789*, quoted in J.R. Hale, 'Art and Audience: The "Medici Venus" c. 1750–c. 1850', 42. This invaluable article deals with (mainly British) responses to the Venus de' Medici, in the period after that discussed in this essay.
2. (1) 'A Notion of the Historical Draught or Tablature of the Judgment of Hercules', first published in French in 1712, in English in 1713, and included in the second edition of Shaftesbury's *Characteristicks of Men, Manners, Opinions, Times* (London, 1714), together with an engraving (see Figure 11) by Simon Gribelin of the painting by de Matthaeis, now in the Ashmolean Museum, Oxford; all references to the *Characteristicks* are to the fourth edition, cited as Shaftesbury 1727. (2) 'A Letter concerning Design', first published in the fifth edition of the *Characteristicks* (London, 1732), and reprinted in Benjamin Rand's edition of the *Second Characters* (hereafter cited as Shaftesbury 1914). (3) 'Plastics, or the Original Progress and Powers of Designatory Art', first published in Shaftesbury 1914.
3. For a fuller account of this matter, see Barrell 1986, 'Introduction', and especially 10–23.
4. On eighteenth-century treatments of the choice of Hercules, see Paulson 1975 38–40, 73ff.
5. For an account of this process see Hohendahl, *The Institution of Criticism*, or, for a briefer version, Eagleton 9–43.
6. The thought appears to derive from Plutarch's life of Marcus Caius

Coriolanus (Plutarch 4: 120); Gilbert West, 'On the Abuse of Travelling', in *The Works of the English Poets*, 57: 280–3.

7. The phrase is quoted from Ovid. *Tristia*, II, ix, 48.

8. The authority for representing Venus in these terms derives from Horace, *Ars Poetica*, line 42 ('Ordinis haec virtus, erit et venus, aut ego fallor').

9. See also Shaftesbury 1727 3: 185, where the vice of attachment to the forms of outward beauty prompts the exclamation 'O EFFEMINACY! EFFEMINACY!'

10. See also Turnbull 63, on the painting of Danae by Artemon, in which Venus was represented as smiling at the 'vain Precautions' taken to guard Danae: Turnbull quotes Horace, Odes III, xvi, 6–7: 'Jupiter et Venus / Risissent'.

11. Thomson to Dodington, 1730, quoted by Sambrook in Thomson 1986 39.

12. I am much indebted to Haskell and Penny for information on the Venus de' Medici, and on the other statues referred to in this essay.

13. D'Hancarville (1: 383–4, n. 240) says that the little putti around the dolphin of Venus are often interpreted as 'Amours', and Venus regarded as their mother. But Venus was, according to mythology, the mother only of Cupid, and d'Hancarville points out that the 'amours' are anyway much too small in relation to Venus to be her offspring, so that (he believes) the artist must have thought of them as accessories with at best a very remote iconographical relation to Venus. D'Hancarville does offer to interpret the dolphin, though not according to any mythological narrative: the statue represents Venus as (1: 402, n. 248) the female aspect of the one 'Etre *générateur*', and the dolphin specifies her identity as the mother of marine animal life.

14. See also Turnbull 86. Wright (2: 407) makes an epigram out of the pretence of being unable to tell whether the statue is of stone or flesh:

> Ex Petra num facta Caro est, ex Carneve Petra?
> Credo *Medusaeum* hoc, nullius artis, Opus.

('Is it flesh made of stone, or stone made of flesh? I believe it a work, not of art, but of the Medusa'). And see below, note 21.

15. See Spence 1755 67: 'if she is not really modest, she at least counterfeits modestly extremely well.' The fact that the Venus de' Medici's left hand was held a little away from her body enabled her to be seen, engraved, and painted, from angles which frustrated her attempt to conceal her sexual parts. Of numerous examples, see the engraving of the statue in Spence 1755 plate V; William Kent's and N. Tardieu's frontispiece to 'Summer' in Thomson 1730; and the painting of the Venus by Sir Godfrey Kneller presented to Alexander Pope, reproduced in Einberg and Jones plate 21.

16. For a thoughtful account of Shenstone's poem, see Pugh 111–12.

17. For copies of the statue in Britain, see Hale 43n.

18. See Paulson 1975 23ff. Gilbert West seems to have regarded the gilded statue as an emblem of modern corruption. He writes:

> Lo! in the *Center* of this beauteous *Scene*,
> Glitters beneath her *Dome* the *Cyprian Queen*:
> Not like to her, whom ancient *Homer* prais'd,
> To whom a thousand sacred *Altars* blaz'd:

> When simple Beauty was the only Charm,
> With which each tender Nymph and Swain grew warm:
> But, yielding to the now-prevailing Taste,
> In *Gold*, for modern Adoration, drest.
>
> (West 1732 13–14)

19. For Rousham see Pugh 102–21.
20. In an eclogue by Lyttelton, addressed to Cobham and offered to him as
    suitable to be read during a perambulation of the garden at Stowe, Venus
    is narrativised, and sanitised (as is appropriate in a private poem
    addressed to a relative) by being paired with Hymen:

> Beneath the covert of a myrtle wood,
> To Venus rais'd, a rustic altar stood.
> To Venus and to Hymen, there combin'd,
> In friendly league to favour human-kind.
>
> (Lyttelton 64: 262)

21. This is not the only occasion where Thomson shows himself unable to
    distinguish between flesh and marble. Musidora, in 'Summer', bathes in
    a stream unaware that she is being observed by Damon. He leaves, after
    a while, but leaves her a note to say that he will enjoy watching her
    bathe in future, and will protect her privacy from the 'licentious' eyes of
    others. Musidora is temporarily paralysed, perhaps in amazement at the
    effrontery of Damon's claim that his own gaze is less than licentious:

> With wild Surprize,
> As if to Marble struck, devoid of Sense,
> A stupid Moment motionless she stood:
> So stands the Statue that enchants the World;
> So, bending, tries to veil the matchless Boast,
> The mingled Beauties of exulting *Greece*.
>
> (Thomson 1981, 'Summer', lines 1344–9)

   A footnote by Thomson explains lines 1347–9 as a reference to 'The Venus
   of Medici'.
22. Compare, for example, Allan Ramsay's circumambulation of the statue,
    in Spence 1966 1: no. 1289.
23. I am most grateful for the advice and encouragement offered by Homi
    Bhabha and Jacqueline Rose in the writing of this essay.

5: VISUALISING THE DIVISION OF LABOUR

1. What is, as far as we know, the first extended discussion of the division
   of labour occurs in Book 2 of Plato's *Republic* (Plato 1: 149–71). Plato's
   account was imitated in the eighteenth century by Hume (1978 485ff.);
   and by James Harris, in 'Concerning Happiness, A Dialogue' (1744), in
   Harris 59ff. The fullest eighteenth-century elaboration of the discourse of
   the division of labour is Adam Ferguson's *An Essay on the History of
   Civil Society*, 1767.

2. Unless otherwise stated, all quotations from the *Microcosm* are from C. Gray's introduction to the first volume. For a brief bibliography, by A.E. Santaniello, of studies of Pyne's work, see Pyne 1971 17.

3. Compare with this sentence from Mandeville (360)

> But if we turn the prospect, and look on all those labours as so many voluntary Actions, belonging to different Callings and Occupations, that Men are brought up to for a Livelyhood, and in which every one Works for himself, how much soever he may seem to Labour for others: If we consider, that even the Saylors who undergo the greatest Hardships, as soon as one Voyage is ended, even after the Ship-wreck, are looking out and soliciting for employment in another: If we consider, I say, and look on these things in another View, we shall find that the Labour of the Poor, is so far from being a Burthen and an Imposition upon them; that to have Employment is a Blessing, which in their Addresses to Heaven they Pray for, and to procure it for the generality of them is the greatest Care of every Legislature.

4. See for example the definition of technology in Bentham's *Chrestomathia* 85:

> From two Greek words: the first of which signifies an *art* . . . a *connected* view is proposed to be given, of the *operations* by which *arts* and *manufactures* are carried on. . . . On this occasion will be to be shown and exemplified, the advantages, of which, in respect of *despatch* and *perfection*, the principles *of the division of labour* is productive.
>   Here will be shown how, by the help of this most efficient principle, as *art* and *science* are continually making advances at the expense of *ordinary practice* and *ordinary knowledge*, so *manufacture* (if by this term be distinctively designed *art*, carried on with the help of *the division of labour*, and thence *upon a large scale*) is continually extending its conquests, in the field of *simple handicraft art*–art carried on *without* the benefit of that newly found assistance.

5. Quoted in Barbier 112. Barbier's book is the best account of Gilpin, and an excellent guide to the early phases of picturesque theory.

6. Compare Archibald Alison (1: 121) on the same topic:

> The sublimest situations are often disfigured, by objects we feel unworthy of them – by traces of cultivation, or attempts towards improvements . . . The loveliest scenes, in the same manner, are frequently disturbed . . . by the signs of cultivation . . . [and] the traces of manufactures . . .

> Alison is not truly a theorist of the Picturesque, and bases his aesthetic on the association of ideas. The point of this passage is to prohibit the intrusion into aesthetic experience of mean associations, rather than to invite us to consider 'sublime situations' independently of the associations they may evoke.

7. In particular, Pyne edited, in 1823–4, *The Somerset House Gazette*, a periodical largely devoted to publicising the technique of painting in watercolour. See above, 224, notes 25–7.

8. For a list and discussion of Morland's sketch-books, see Buckley 211–20.

9. The history of Encyclopaedia illustration in eighteenth-century Britain is complicated by the fact that new encyclopaedias might buy or copy the plates of their predecessors, as well as from the Diderot/D'Alembert *Encyclopédie*. By and large, however, it seems fair to generalise that the *atelier*-scene more or less disappears around 1790. Such scenes appear, for example, in the first edition of *Encyclopaedia Britannica* (1771); in Hinde's *New Royal and Universal Dictionary of Arts and Sciences* of 1771–2; and in Middleton's *New Complete Dictionary of Arts and Sciences* of 1778; there are none in Howard's *New Royal Cyclopaedia* of 1788, or in Chambers's *Cyclopaedia* of 1791; and they are most uncommon thereafter.

10. See for example Pyne on the peasants depicted by Joshua Cristall, above 224, n. 27.

11. Basket Makers and Coopers, Brewing ($\frac{1}{2}$ sheet), Copper Smiths, Cottage Groups, Cottagers, Domestic Employments, Iron Foundry, Pottery and Leather Dressing, Slaughter-Houses, Statuary, Wheelwrights.

12. For some useful remarks on attitudes to gipsies in the last decade of the eighteenth century and the first decade of the nineteenth, see David Simpson 43ff. My thanks to him, and to Homi Bhabha, Tim Clark, Marcia Pointon and Jacqueline Rose for help and advice with this essay.

6: IMAGINARY TREASON, IMAGINARY LAW

1. For accounts of the trials, see Goodwin 307–59, Thompson 131–8, Veitch 291–318. For Watt, see Radicals 516–17.

2. On Bentham as a critic of natural law, see especially Lieberman 224–32. This is one of three excellent books (the others are by Green and Postema) to which this essay is indebted for most of whatever understanding it has of the legal questions it discusses. Whatever misunderstandings it displays are my own responsibility entirely.

3. 25 Edward III, st. 5, c. 2: 1351 according to most commentators; 1352 according to others; 1350 according to at least one; take your pick. Blackstone's account of the statute as a 'declaratory' act is challenged by Bentham 1977 133.

4. The 'ingenious writer' is so far untraced. The letters W, D, H and T after the numbers of the volumes of state trials refer to the trials respectively of Watt, Downie, Hardy and Horne Tooke.

5. The clearest analogy to the statute of treasons in this respect is the law concerning conspiracy, which can also take the will for the deed, but only where it can be claimed that the will was the will of more than one person. Gordon Wood writes of the law of conspiracy in terms illuminating to my following discussion of 'overt acts':

> In the years between the Restoration and the era of George III, the modern English notion of the criminal law of conspiracy was essentially formed. Basic to this notion was the belief that criminality of conspiracy lay in the intent, which was revealed by the acts done. A justice in *Rex v. Sterling* (1664) had suggested that 'the particular facts' were 'but evidence of the design charged.' A century later Lord Mansfield in *Rex v. Parsons et al.* elaborated the point by instructing the jury 'that there was no occasion to prove the actual act of conspiring, but that it might be collected from collateral circumstances' (James Wallace Bryan, *The*

Development of the English law of Conspiracy, Johns Hopkins University Studies in Historical and Political Science, XXVII [Baltimore, 1909], 77, 78–79, 81.   Wood 428n

6. For an informative though extraordinarily sanguine account of the process by which the construction put upon the specific treason of compassing and imagining 'grew gradually more and more extensive', see Holdsworth, 8: 307–18. Holdsworth sees this extension as inevitable and necessary, given the failure of the statute to specify as treasons the intention to depose the king or to put physical constraints upon him. The 'nation,' he says, 'acquiesced' in it, though he does not say who he means by the nation, or how he discovered its opinion on the matter.

7. Foster (204) repeats this doctrine twice more; it is accepted by East, 1: 58.

8. For more general accounts of the arguments of the defence in the London trials, see Cockburn 227–33, Goodwin 346–58; Twiss 1: 262.

9. For the reform of libel law, see Lubasz, Brewer, Holdsworth 10: 672–96, and (especially) Green 318–55, to whom this and the preceding two paragraphs are thoroughly indebted. Holdsworth (10: 604) refers to Erskine's argument in the 1791 debate on Fox's Bill that he 'considered the jury as the commons' house of the judicial system – the balance for the people against prerogatives which it was necessary to trust with the Crown and its magistrates, but which would often when unbalanced degenerate into oppression.' Quoting from Holdsworth, Mack (426) comments: 'For once Bentham found substance in rhetoric, and agreed tersely, "In a word, to undo what legislators and lawyers have done, is the great use of juries"' – Bentham 1843 9: 554. But Bentham, of course, had nothing like so high an opinion of the system of trial by jury as Erskine had–see e.g. Halévy 400–1, Mack 420–9, Dinwiddy 67.

10. This is an issue returned to repeatedly by the radical press throughout the 1790s, and especially by the publications of the London Corresponding Society (see e.g. LCS 1796–7: 207, 233, 313; LCS 1983: 14, 332). For a comment by Hardy, see Hardy 67.

11. According to Godwin, the statute of Edward III was 'one of the great palladiums of the English constitution' (Godwin 1794 4); for Coleridge on the clarity and wisdom of the statute, see Coleridge 1971 288–91.

12. According to Bentham (1843 10: 564) Erskine sought him out on the publication of the *Fragment on Government*.

13. For an account of law as fiction in Bentham see R. Harrison esp. 24–47; Leiberman 219–40; Postema 286–301.

14. For discussion of Bentham's notion of an entirely unambiguous legal code, see Dinwiddy 58–65; R. Harrison 47–75; Leiberman 241–56; Postema 421–34.

15. This was written in May 1989.

16. I have borrowed the phrase 'diseases of the imagination' from Hester Thrale, quoted by Engell 61; the phrase 'disordered imagination' is common throughout the late eighteenth century; for an example in relation to the treason trials, see Holcroft 1795b 16, where he writes to William Windham that his use of the expression 'acquitted felons' to describe Holcroft and others 'could only have been dictated by a disordered imagination.'

17. In this context we should also notice the extraordinary exchange between

Scott and Horne Tooke (ST 25T: 507–8). Scott gave a particularly colourful version of the 'Coronation Oath' argument, including the sentence, 'He [the king] ought to lose his life, and I trust would be willing to lose his life, rather than to govern contrary to that coronation oath.' Horne Tooke interrupts to ask, 'What! Is the Attorney-General talking treason?–I should be unhappy to mistake you–did you say the king ought to lose his life, if he took any other parliament [than a parliament constitutionally established]?' And as the Attorney General fumbled for a reply, Horne Tooke continued, 'I only wished to know whether in prosecuting me for high treason, the attorney-general intentionally said something far worse than anything he has imputed to me.' The specific treason that Horne Tooke was suggesting Scott might have committed, is that of 'compassing and imagining.'

18. According to Robert Hamilton, the case of the prosecution against Watt was a 'romance'; Watt was accused of 'a wild Don Quixote scheme', an 'absurdity' (ST 23W: 1349, 1351–2).

19. See Akenside *The Pleasures of the Imagination*, first version, Book 3, 380ff.; Gerard 29–76; Tucker 1: 1–32, 2: 1–25; for a general account of the theory of the creative imagination in the late eighteenth century, see Engell, especially chapters 6, 7, 12, 13; see also Abrams 161–3.

20. See Akenside, Book I, 46ff; Gerard 49–50, 65; Trotter 88–9, 218; see also Mackenzie, 32: '"delusive ideas . . . are the motives of the greatest part of mankind, and a heated imagination the power by which their actions are incited: the world, in the eye of a philosopher, may be said to be a large madhouse."'

21. This repeated suggestion that the Ministry and the Crown Lawyers, in believing they had detected a vast conspiracy, were vastly deluded, seems to qualify some of the larger claims made by Gordon S. Wood in his essay 'Conspiracy and the Paranoid Style', to the effect that 'conspiratorial interpretations . . . far from being symptomatic of irrationality . . . represented an enlightened stage in Western man's long struggle to comprehend his social reality', and that 'all enlightened thought of the eighteenth century' was 'structured in such a way that conspiratorial explanations of complex events became normal, necessary, and rational' (Wood 411, 421). On the relation between the spy-system of the 1790s and the 'tendency to interpret all evidence in the light of preconceived suspicions' see Ousby 49.

22. Or rather, this became Bentham's view very soon after he began writing on law: see Postema 203–5, 279, 441.

23. For a useful note on Bentham and the imagination, see R. Harrison 223.

24. For Bentham on the Common Law as able to be discussed in metaphors only, because itself a system of metaphor, see 1970 191; on the deficiency of the Common Law as a system of general rules, see for example 1970 184–5, 188, and Leiberman 232–40.

25. I am grateful to Colin Brooks, Nigel Leask and Jacqueline Rose for their help and advice during the writing of this essay.

7:   THE BIRTH OF PANDORA

As in the text of the essay itself, citations not preceded by an author's name refer to Barry 1809.

1. The development of Barry's Pandora project is discussed at some length

by Pressly (1981 26–9, 146–8, 208, 236), who also provides a useful account of writings about the project by Barry and others. My own essay is much indebted to the information and insight offered by this excellent book, as it in turn was indebted to the pioneering study by Wark.

2. The precise nature of Pandora's fatal vessel is discussed exhaustively by the Panofskys (see below, 190–1).

3. Pausanias's and Pliny's descriptions of the Athena Parthenos will be found together in Stuart Jones (81–3). Fragments of reliefs which appear to be imitations or replicas of the Pandora relief are illustrated by Boardman (plates 98 and 101, and see 106). The Panofskys for some reason place the Pandora relief at the foot of Phidias's Zeus at Olympia (Panofskys 9). More usefully, they also illustrate two seventeenth-century versions of the Creation of Pandora, a print by Jacques Callot and a drawing by Abraham van Diepenbeeck. Neither of these seems to have been known to Barry, by 1775 at least, despite the fact that an engraving by Abraham Blomaert after Diepenbeeck's version became the basis of Bernard Picart's engraving 'Pandora's Box' in *The Temple of the Muses* (de La Barre de Beaumarchais, plate IV), a popular and influential collection of illustrations of subjects from classical mythology–see Panofskys 71–8.

4. This, I take it, is the real point of Barry's apparent generosity in his 1775 letter to the *Morning Chronicle*: 'perhaps', he writes, 'I shall never be employed to put in execution' the Pandora project; 'therefore, if you should know any painter, of abilities, more fortunate than I have been, who may have *patrons* to countenance him, or some little independence to support him, you would do well to persuade him to set about this work . . . '

5. For the Adelphi cycle, see 2: 301–416, and Pressly 1981 86–122 and 285–98.

6. For Reynolds's account of central form in relation to representations of the body see Reynolds 1975 41–73.

7. In the 1783 version (2: 382) the last sentence is omitted.

8. Reynolds (1975 181–2) is discussing the means by which character is represented 'in a Bust, Cameo, or Intaglio', but his point is that the same means are used by sculpture.

9. The social and political ramifications of this issue, in the writings of Reynolds and Barry, are discussed at much greater length in Barrell 1986 (chapters 1 and 2), where detailed references will be found to the arguments attributed to the two writers in the rest of this section. See also Frances Ferguson 63–4 for an excellent account of the ambition of eighteenth-century theories of the sublime to produce the sublime subject as the 'representative', as a 'metonymy' of his culture: the aesthetics of the sublime is addressed towards the public, the political subject, not the unique individual.

10. Barry's representation of Jupiter is possibly an example of what he has in mind in suggesting that a fuller knowledge of literature has enabled modern artists to depict the Olympians with greater accuracy. Jupiter's pose and appearance seem to derive from a remark by Porphyry, that

> as philosophers differed in opinion respecting the nature and constituent parts of this god, and as they could invent no figure that should represent all his attitudes, they painted him in the form of a man. He is in a sitting posture, in allusion to his immutable essence; the upper part of his body is uncovered, because it is in the upper

regions of the universe (the stars) that he most conspicuously displays himself. He is covered from the waist downwards, because respecting terrestrial beings he is more secret and concealed. He holds a scepter in his left hand, because on the left side is the heart, and the heart is the seat of the understanding, which, (in human beings) regulates every action.   (Quoted in Volney 2: 162n–163n.).

11. Compare the role I have suggested for Pandora with that attributed to the Juno Ludovisi in Schiller's *On the Aesthetic Education of Man* (1795), 109, where the impassive harmony of the statue of the goddess, entirely undetermined by desire and undifferentiated by activity, is a unifying and recreative resource to all those who, stunted in one direction, over-developed in another, by the demands of the division of labour, repair to the statue in search of a lost wholeness.
12. Or so the Panofskys (89) claim.
13. For late eighteenth-century British treatments of the Corinthian or Sicyonian maid, see in particular Rosenblum 1957, and 1969 21n., and Allentuck. Mortimer's version, *The Origin of Drawing* (1771), is reproduced in Sunderland (figure 80); Alexander Runciman's *The Origin of Painting* (1773, private collection) in Macmillan (colour plate 16); David Allan's version (same title, 1773, National Gallery of Scotland) in Irwin (plate 91); Edward Burney's drawing (same title, Metropolitan Museum of Art, New York), in the *Burlington Magazine* 112 (1970), figure 64; Wright's *The Corinthian Maid* (1783–4, Paul Mellon Collection, National Gallery of Art, Washington) in Nicolson (vol. 2, plate 245). A version engraved by John Neagle, after Thomas Stothard (and kindly drawn to my attention by Marcia Pointon), appears on a trade card giving notice of the removal to new premises of the miniature and enamel painter Richard Collins (Banks Trade Card Collection, British Museum); James Barry's drawing of the subject (Pressly 1981 no. 20 in Catalogue of Drawings) is in the Ashmolean Museum Oxford; my thanks to David Solkin for supplying me with a reproduction, and with the tentative opinion that it is 'probably from the 1790s, though perhaps a little earlier'. For the 'portrait' of the Sicyonian Maid in the final picture of the Adelphi cycle see Pressly 1981 296, figure 149). Barry rejects this myth of the origin of painting as 'fabulous' (1: 359). See also below, n. 41.
14. For a discussion of this issue, see Barrell 1986 165–73.
15. The first edition of Godwin's *Memoirs* had been published in January 1798. For Barry's friendship with Godwin, see P.H. Marshall 67 and 416 n. 64, and St Clair 38.
16. We seem to see the dawning of Barry's awareness that the solution offered by Wollstonecraft will not work, in the last, extraordinary sentence of the paragraph in which she is evoked:

> Civil society has many obligations to that excellent woman, and would do well to discharge some of them, by kind attentions to the two female children she has left behind her, if ever they should need them, which I am happy to say is not the case at present, nor likely to be so, whilst God Almighty spares the life and health of the ingenious Mr Godwin, the father of one, and the kind and generous protector of the other.   (2: 594)

The obligations society owes to Wollstonecraft, it seems, are to be discharged by an attention to her children, an attention however which is not needed now, and is never likely to be, so long as Godwin looks after them. The more unnecessary it becomes to repay our obligations to her, the more the obligations themselves seem to fade from Barry's mind, to be replaced by the idea of his friend Godwin's paternal goodness: *more* than paternal indeed, for the point of praising him as the 'generous protector' of one of the two 'female children', Fanny Imlay, is presumably to remind us that she was Wollstonecraft's bastard. This reminder of the unusual nature of Wollstonecraft's life seems to wander into the *Letter* as an aside or afterthought, but once there it seems to function as a way of punishing Wollstonecraft for the solution she offers to Barry's dilemma.

17. For 'sentiment', see for example Wollstonecraft 1975 47 and 58; for 'ornamental', 'graceful', see for example 19; for 'destination', see 34, 36, 78, 120.

18. This syncretist argument that all pagan systems of polytheism were the corruption of an originally universal monotheism had the dual advantage of according with scriptural history (for all non Judaeo-Christian peoples had at some time 'deviated . . . from the rational adoration of the only true GOD': W. Jones 3: 320), and of enabling polytheism to be historicised in the characteristically late-eighteenth-century discursive structure of a primal unity endlessly differentiated. For an atheist account of the unity of religions, see Volney 2: chapters 21 and 22. The notion that the Egyptians had persevered in monotheistic beliefs, and that the Greeks were to blame for the corruption into polytheism, was particularly associated in this period with Jacob Bryant's *New System* (1775)–'new', I suppose, in relation to Ralph Cudworth's *The True Intellectual System of the Universe* (1678), the long fourth chapter of which had famously argued that monotheism was implicit in all systems of polytheism. Among mythographers whom Barry would probably have read, Richard Payne Knight also blamed the Greeks or their corrupting influence on religion (Knight 32, 45, 101–2, 109). See also for example Elton 1815 lxxvi. Also relevant here is the contemporary discussion of the Hindu religion and whether it should be classified as monotheistic or polytheistic (see for example Sonnerat 1: viii–ix, 2–3; Maurice 1793–1800 4: 21; Forster 29–30; Moor 1–3), and, more generally, the politics of the discussions of polytheism, which frequently oppose an aristocratic or élite, and secret monotheism, with a 'vulgar' polytheism: see for example Warburton 2: Book II, Section 4, Robertson 319–31, Knight 45 and 101–2, and Craufurd 1: 148.

19. For eighteenth-century awareness of Hinduism in Britain, see P.J. Marshall's introduction to his anthology *The British Discovery of Hinduism*.

20. For some account of d'Hancarville's writings and his extraordinary career, see Haskell, and for an endorsement of his account of the difference between Greek and Asiatic art, see Maurice 1793–1800 2: 395.

21. For examples of the extraordinary revulsion felt by many Europeans against the compound cult figures of Egypt and India, see for example Forster 1: 130 and 405, Volney 1: 190–1; the topic (among others) is dealt with at length by Mitter 73–186. This may be the appropriate place to note that Volney (2: 35n.), reflecting on the sacred books of the Hindus, calls 'the imaginary chest that contains them, the box of Pandora,' and

recommends that it be 'condemned . . . to the flames'. For examples of contemporary British illustration of the Hindu deities, see William Jones 3: 319–97, Maurice 1795–8 and Moor.

22. At 2: 152 Barry refers to Brahma (as the deity is usually named in Britain) as 'Brumha' at 2: 152, and as 'Bruhma' at 2: 590. This suggests there may also be a French source for his (modest) knowledge of the Hindu religion: see Volney's list of dialectic varieties of the name, 'Birmah, Bremma, Brouma' (2: 37n.), and Sonnerat's list of transliterations of the name of this divinity, 1: 4n., where 'Bruhma' occurs. Sonnerat himself prefers 'Brouma'. The most likely source however is d'Hancarville, who uses the form Brouma, which reinforces his claim to have identified Brahma with Bacchus or Dionysus, one of whose 'sirnames' was Bromius or Broumos: see d'Hancarville 1: 126–7, and 3: 66, Lemprière, article 'Bromius', and Mitter 83–97.

23. The best contemporary accounts I have found of the compound figures of the Hindu religion as expressive of the unity of powers (and so potentially of the social unity of the possessors of those powers) are by Knight, Forster and Maurice. Knight (60) writes that 'this mode of representing the allegorical personages of religion with many heads and limbs to express their various attributes, and extensive operation, is now universal in the East', which is, as Mitter (103) comments, an 'interpretation of multi-armed gods' which 'amounted to a direct challenge to the prevailing prejudice against the images of Indian gods as being irrational'. Forster (30) writes that

> those, and they compose a great portion of the people, who, from a want of requisite education, are not endowed with the ability of reading the praise of God, can with facility conceive an idea of his greatness, by contemplating a figure, sculptured with many heads and with many hands, adorned with every symbol of human power, and beheld by all classes of men with the utmost reverence and awe.
>
> According to Maurice (1793–1800 3: 355–6)

> The Indians worship the Deity by symbols; while his power extending through various nature, and his venerated attributes are represented by animals characteristic of them. Thus, for instance, his wisdom is symbolized by a circle of heads, his strength by an elephant, his glory by horns, . . . his creative energy by the male of animals of a prolific kind, . . . while the combinations of these animals, or parts of animals, were intended to designate his united power, wisdom and glory.

For Barry, it is an additional advantage of such compound figures that they can function as 'a kind of symbolical writing' (1: 359), though, 'like the Hieroglyphic or the Chinese writing', they have a tendency to collect too many attributes and meanings to be manageable (2: 149). For the argument that the 'fantastic compound' figures of the Egyptian religion were to be understood as hieroglyphics, see Warburton 2: 167 and 3: 199–200.

24. It could also be difficult to distinguish Minerva from Vulcan (Bryant 1775 1: 20, 22, and Elton 1815 lxviii), and I will have more to say about that in note 32. On Orphism, Hinduism, and bisexual or androgynous deities

see Mitter 98–101. On the question of the hermaphroditic or ambisexual nature of the heathen deities, note also Erasmus Darwin's remarks on the birth of Eve (Darwin 1803 Additional Note X).

> This part of the history, where Eve is said to have been made from a rib of Adam might have been an hieroglyphic design of the Egyptian philosophers [with whom Moses was educated], showing their opinion that Mankind was originally of both sexes united, and was afterwards divided into males and females: an opinion in later times held by Plato, and I believe by Aristotle . . .

Mythography here turns out to share the same preoccupations as natural science, or as the theory of evolution that is evolving in Darwin's poem. A part of the second canto of *The Temple of Nature* is concerned to argue that mankind and quadrupeds were formerly in an hermaphroditic state, that 'solitary' (i.e. asexual) reproduction, however, tends merely to perpetuate and not to improve the species, and that with the development of sexual reproduction among the 'most perfect orders of animals', creation benefited by a greater variety, a greater robustness, a greater resistance to hereditary diseases' (p. 53n. and Additional Note VIII). For Darwin, Eve represents the primal moment of sexual division, just as the picture of Pandora, 'the heathen Eve', can be read as representing for Barry an attempt to affirm the essential nature of that division.

25. There is a useful and well-illustrated summary account of the Athena Parthenos in Boardman 110–12.
26. Barry's account of the peplus derives also from Pauw 1: 303–4; both Potter and Pauw are elaborating the account in Meursius's *Panathanaea*.
27. For another view of the symmetry of the panathenaic procession and the 'programme of the Parthenon sculpture', see Boardman 172–4.
28. Though by the endlessly reversible interpretations of late eighteenth and early nineteenth-century mythography, which repeatedly seems to collapse together different cults and different periods into one unified system, the bull may also be what emerges from the egg, which may be broken by, or may produce, one of the various types of Vulcan (Pthas, Phanes, Eros, Brahma, Cneph and so on)–see e.g. Faber 1: 186.
29. See also Maurice (1793–1800, 3: 527ff.), and J.D. Patterson, *AR* vol. 8, 1805: 53, the lotos could also be an emblem of the preservation of life (Bryant 1775 2: 394).
30. For evidence of Barry's awareness of the *Asiatic Researches*, see 1: 348n.
31. For the representation of Cneph in the Adelphi cycle, see Pressly 1981 285–6: Barry's knowledge of the iconography on Cneph was probably derived from the version of Porphyry's account given in *An Universal History* (1: 13); and for fuller accounts of the iconography of Cneph, see Maurice 1793–1800 3: 529ff. and 4: 301–3; Volney 2: 42n.–43., 145.
32. There is a good deal more to say about the difficulties Barry might have encountered in staking the masculine character of the art of painting on the supremacy of the figure of Vulcan. That Vulcan is, like Minerva, associated with snakes, works towards identifying the two divinities rather than differentiating them in sexual terms; and in the Orphic hymns both Phanes and Metis could be understood indifferently as types of Vulcan *and* of Minerva (Bryant 1775 2: 25; Elton 1815, lxviii). I have made less of this than I would have liked, because the degree of Barry's knowledge of contemporary mythography is not clear; but it tends to

reinforce the general argument of the section that follows.

33. The reading, conscious or otherwise, of Pandora's box or vase as the vagina, certainly seems to have found its way into Barry's circle. The infidelity of husbands, warns Mary Wollstonecraft (1975 6), encourages wives to be unfaithful also; and 'the box of mischief thus opened in society, what is to preserve private virtue, the only security of public freedom and universal happiness?' The phrase 'in society' gives to the woman's body and its exposure some of the embarrassingly public character it has in Picart's engraving, where the gods all *point* at the box of mischief. Wollstonecraft refers to 'Pandora's pent up mischiefs' again on 13. In Picart's engraving, the Olympians seem to be making a pretext, almost, of offering their gifts to Pandora, in order to point to her nakedness; compare Ludmilla Jordanova's account of Pierre-Felix Masseau's *The Secret*, a late nineteenth-century wooden statuette of a woman 'incompletely covered by a long veil, holding to her chest a box'. Jordanova (93) comments 'In the specific sense of gift as an unsolicited present, surprise, pleasure and visual discovery go hand in hand. It is clear why the veiling of secrets seems to lead inexorably to femininity, the visual manifestations of which generate both excitement and fear.'

34. Though 'some maintain,' according to Lemprière (article 'Orpheus'), 'that he was killed by a thunderbolt'.

35. More reassuringly for men, however, Freud points out (18: 273) that the Medusa, by turning them to stone, is turning them *stiff* with terror; they rediscover their manhood at the very moment that they are threatened with losing it. There is a brief (three-sentence) article of 1923 by Ferenczi (360), 'On the Symbolism of the Head of Medusa', is which the head itself is 'the terrible symbol of the genital region', but 'the fearful and alarming starting eyes of the Medusa' have 'the secondary meaning of erection.'

36. Barry's inclusion in this list of the 'involutions' of the serpent 'round the Hindostan lingham' is apparently a reference to the miniature Hindu temple in the Townley collection, illustrated by Knight (plate xii) and discussed by him (49–50) and by d'Hancarville (1: 445–6)); the temple is also illustrated and discussed by Mitter (87, 101). As wearer of the peplus, Minerva is also associated with Typhon, the serpentine and dragonish giant who castrated Osiris: see Lemprière, article 'Osiris'.

37. For an excellent account of the sublime as 'swelling', see Furniss 82–4, 92–5.

38. For two excellent commentaries on the events of 5 and 6 October 1789, and on Burke and Wollstonecraft on the women who marched to Versailles, see Paulson 1983 72–3, 80–1, 86–7, 236, and Furniss chapters five and six, 198–240 and 241–91.

39. Apparently after he had written the 'Fragment on Pandora', the Pandora project acquired a quite new set of meanings for Barry, which seem to have developed out of his interest in mythography. According to his editor and biographer Fryer, the painting was now seen as the first part of an elaborate sequence, complementing the Adelphi-cycle.

> He had already painted the progress and moral qualities of mankind–those qualities which are supposed to bind man to man in a state of society, and, as they unfold, to display all the blessings of civilization and refinement. The succeeding work was to delineate the

growth of that more important state of mind which connects man with his Creator, and to represent the misty medium of connexion which the Pagan world had with their false gods, and the union of Jews and Christians with their true God, by means of Revelation.

His large painting of Pandora was intended to exhibit the former part, and the designs of the Mosaic doctrines from Milton . . . and others from the New Testament, the latter. (1: 282–3).

We do not know what subjects were designed to follow *The Birth of Pandora* in the sequence (1: 318–19): Barry died in 1806, before this grand scheme could be achieved or even described.

40. By David Punter, in a paper entitled 'Parts of the Body / Parts of Speech: Some Instances of Dismemberment and Healing', delivered at the conference 'The French Revolution and British Culture', University of Leicester July 1989.

41. My thanks to Marcia Pointon and Jacqueline Rose, both of whom commented most helpfully and in great detail on various drafts of this essay.

Since this essay went to press Ann Bermingham has told me of an unpublished PhD dissertation by Frank Cossa, 'Josiah Wedgwood: His Role as a Patron of Flaxman, Stubbs, and Wright of Derby' (Rutgers University, State University of New Jersey, New Brunswick, 1982). Cossa points out that originally the scheme to decorate the Great Room at the Society of Arts (eventually carried out by James Barry alone) was for eight historical subjects, to be painted by Reynolds, West, Dance, Kauffmann, Cipriani, Mortimer, Barry, and Wright, and two allegorical subjects, to be painted by Romney and Penny. Cossa suggests (p. 245) that the subject of the Corinthian Maid and the Origin of Painting may have been discussed as a possible subject for this scheme of decoration, and Bermingham comments that as 'at least six of these artists eventually produced images of the Corinthian maid, it is very likely that Cossa is correct'. For more on the Corinthian Maid in the eighteenth-century, see Ann Bermingham's essay 'The Origin of Painting and the Ends of Art: Wright of Derby's Corinthian Maid', forthcoming in John Barrell (ed.) *Painting and the Politics of Culture: New Essays on English Art 1700–1850*, Oxford University Press, 1992.

I have also learned, since the book went to press, of political tokens which circulated in the 1790s, bearing the design of a pair of knee-breeches, on fire or even exploding, with the legend PANDORA'S BREECHES. The design refers to an attempt made in 1792 to set fire to the House of Commons by placing a pair of breeches filled with combustible materials in the room below the chamber. The design is often found as the reverse of a token whose obverse represents a man hanging from a gallows, with the legend END OF PAIN: there seems to have been an attempt to pin the arson attempt on Paine (see Mark Jones in David Bindman, *The Shadow of the Guillotine: Britain and the French Revolution*, London, British Museum Publications, 1989, 116). The assumption is that these tokens were circulated by supporters of the ministry, but the breeches also appear as the reverse of a token of which the obverse is a portrait of Horne Tooke, and which may represent an example of the appropriation by radicals of ministerial and other reactionary propaganda: perhaps the exploding trousers predict an exploding of the distinction between gentlemen and *sans culottes*! Tokens bearing the design of Pandora's breeches are common and must have circulated widely, and there may have been some resonance between the design and Barry's painting, or even between the painting and Paine, if the association of Paine with Pandora is found elsewhere. On Barry's republicanism, Michael Rosenthal has pointed out to me a remark in the *New Monthly Magazine* 1823 338, that 'when he alluded to the Irish events of 1798 it was as "the late civil war, which they call a rebellion"'.

References

AR	*Asiatic Researches; or, Transactions of the Society instituted in Bengal*, etc., Calcutta 1788–1839.
Abrams	M.H. Abrams, *The Mirror and the Lamp: Romantic Theory and the Critical Tradition* (1953), New York (W.W. Norton) 1958.
Akenside	Mark Akenside, *The Pleasures of the Imagination, and Other Poems*, London (J. Dodsley) 1788.
Alison	Archibald Alison, *Essays on the Nature and Principles of Taste* (1790), 3rd edn, Edinburgh (Constable et al.) 1812.
Allentuck	Marcia Allentuck, 'Edward Francis Burney and the "Corinthian Maid"', *Burlington Magazine*, 112 (1970).
Angelo	*Reminiscences of Henry Angelo*, 2 vols, London (Henry Colburn) 1828.
Atkinson	William C. Atkinson, *Miranda: His Life and Times*, London (Venezuelan Embassy) 1950.
Bakhtin	Mikhail Bakhtin, *Rabelais and his World* (1965), tr. Hélène Iswolsky, Bloomington (Indiana University Press) 1984.
Barbier	C.P. Barbier, *William Gilpin*, Oxford (Oxford University Press) 1963.
Barrell 1980	John Barrell, *The Dark Side of the Landscape: the Rural Poor in English Painting 1730–1840*, Cambridge (Cambridge University Press) 1980.
Barrell 1982	John Barrell, 'Francis Wheatley's *Rustic Hours*', *The Antique Dealer and Collector's Guide*, December 1982.
Barrell 1983	John Barrell, *English Literature in History 1730–1780: An Equal, Wide Survey*, London (Hutchinson) 1983.
Barrell 1986	John Barrell, *The Political Theory of Painting from Reynolds to Hazlitt: 'The Body of the Public'*, New Haven and London (Yale University Press) 1986.
Barrington	[Daines Barrington], *Observations upon the Statutes, Chiefly the More Ancient*, etc. (1766), 2nd edn (with corrections and additions), London (for S. Baker and W. Sandby) 1766.
Barry 1775a	James Barry, Letter to the *Morning Chronicle*, 1 May 1775.
Barry 1775b	James Barry, *An Inquiry into the Real and Imaginary Obstructions to the Acquisition of the Arts in England*, London (T. Becket) 1775.
Barry 1809	James Barry, *The Works of James Barry*, ed. Dr Edward Fryer, 2 vols, London (Cadell and Davies) 1809.
Baskett and Snelgrove	John Baskett and Dudley Snelgrove, *The Drawings of Thomas Rowlandson in the Paul Mellon Collection* London (Barrie and Jenkins) 1977.
Bell	John Bell, *Bell's New Pantheon; or, Historical Dictionary*

of the Gods, Demi-Gods, Heroes, and Fabulous Personages of Antiquity, 2 vols, London (J. Bell) 1790.

Bentham 1843   *The Works of Jeremy Bentham*, ed. John Bowring, 11 vols, Edinburgh (William Tait) 1843.

Bentham 1948   Jeremy Bentham, *A Fragment on Government and An Introduction to the Principles of Morals and Legislation* (1776 and 1789), ed. Wilfrid Harrison, Oxford (Basil Blackwell) 1948.

Bentham 1970   Jeremy Bentham, *Of Laws in General*, ed. H.L.A. Hart, London (University of London, Athlone Press) 1970.

Bentham 1977   Jeremy Bentham, *A Comment on the Commentaries and A Fragment on Government*, eds J.H. Burns and H.L.A. Hart, London (University of London, Athlone Press) 1977.

Bentham 1983   Jeremy Bentham, *Chrestomathia* (1817), eds M.J. Smith and W.H. Burston, Oxford (Clarendon Press) 1983.

Berkeley   George Berkeley, *An Essay towards a new Theory of Vision* (1709) and *Passive Obedience* (1712), in *The Works of George Berkeley, D.D.*, 3 vols, London (for Richard Priestley) 1820.

Bhabha   Homi K. Bhabha, 'The Commitment to Theory,' *New Formations* no. 5 (Summer 1988).

Bicknell and Munro   Peter Bicknell and Jane Munro, *Gilpin to Ruskin: Drawing Masters and their Manuals, 1800–1860*, catalogue of an exhibition at the Fitzwilliam Museum, Cambridge, and at Dove Cottage and the Wordsworth Museum, Grasmere, London (Christie's) 1987.

Blackstone   William Blackstone, *Commentaries on the Laws of England* (1765–9), 4 vols, ed. Stanley N. Katz, Chicago and London (Chicago University Press) 1979.

Blackwell   Thomas Blackwell, *An Enquiry into the Life and Writings of Homer* (1735), 2nd edn, London (no publisher credited) 1736.

Boardman   John Boardman, *Greek Sculpture: The Classical Period. A Handbook*, London (Thames and Hudson) 1985.

Brewer   John Brewer, 'The Wilkites and the law, 1763–74: a study of radical notions of governance,' in Brewer and John Styles, eds, *An Ungovernable People: The English and their law in the Seventeenth and Eighteenth Centuries*, London (Hutchinson) 1980.

Bryant 1775   Jacob Bryant, *A New System, or, An Analysis of Ancient Mythology* (1774), 2nd edn, 3 vols, London (for T. Payne et al.) 1775.

Bryant 1810   Jacob Bryant, *Observations upon the Plagues inflicted upon the Egyptians* (1794), a new edition, London (for Hamilton and Ogle et al.) 1810.

Buchanan   James Buchanan, *The British Grammar*, London (for A. Millar) 1762.

Buckley   Francis Buckley, 'George Morland's Sketch Books and their Publishers', *The Print Collector's Quarterly*, vol. 20, no. 3 (1933).

Burke 1964   Edmund Burke, *Reflections on the Revolution in France* (1790), London (Dent) and New York (Dutton) 1964.

Burke 1968   Edmund Burke, *A Philosophical Enquiry into the Origin of our Ideas of the Sublime and the Beautiful* (1757–9), ed. James T. Boulton, Notre Dame, Ind., and London (University of Notre Dame Press) 1968.

Burney   Fanny Burney (Madame d'Arblay), *Memoirs of Dr Burney*, 3 vols, London (Edward Moxon) 1832.

Campbell   George Campbell, *The Philosophy of Rhetoric*, 2 vols, Edinburgh (W. Creech) 1776.

Chambers   Ephraim Chambers, *Cyclopaedia: or, an Universal Dictionary of Arts and Sciences*, (5 vols), London (for J.F. and C. Rivington et al.) 1791.

Clarke   Michael Clarke, *The Tempting Prospect: A Social History of English Watercolours*, London (British Museum) 1981.

Cleland   John Cleland, *Fanny Hill or Memoirs of a Woman of Pleasure* (1748–9), ed. Peter Wagner, Harmondsworth (Penguin Books) 1985.

Cockburn   Lord Cockburn, *An Examination of the Trials for Sedition which have hitherto occurred in Scotland*, 2 vols, Edinburgh (David Douglas) 1888.

Cohen   Ralph Cohen, *The Art of Discrimination: Thomson's The Seasons and the Language of Criticism*, London (Routledge and Kegan Paul) 1964.

Coke   Edward Coke, *The Third Part of the Institutes of the Laws of England* (1644), 6th edn, London (for Thomas Basset) 1680.

Coleridge 1956–71   *Collected Letters of S.T. Coleridge*, ed. E.L. Griggs, Oxford and New York (Clarendon Press) 1956–71.

Coleridge 1971   S.T. Coleridge, *Lectures 1795 on Politics and Religion*, eds Lewis Patton and Peter Mann, London (Routledge and Kegan Paul) and Princeton, NJ (Princeton University Press) 1971.

Coleridge 1972   S.T. Coleridge, *Lay Sermons* (1816, 1817), ed. R.J. White, London (Routledge and Kegan Paul) and Princeton (Princeton Unversity Press) 1972.

Collins 1747   William Collins, *Odes on Several Descriptive and Allegoric Subjects*, London (for A. Millar) 1747.

Collins 1979   *The Works of William Collins*, eds Richard Wendorf and Charles Ryskamp, Oxford (Clarendon Press) 1979.

Colquhoun   Patrick Colquhoun, *A Treatise on the Wealth, Power and Resources of the British Empire, in Every Quarter of the World, Including the East Indies*, etc. (1815), facsimile reprint, New York and London (Johnson Reprint) 1965.

Cooke   Thomas Cooke, *The Works of Hesiod, translated from the Greek*, London (for T. Green) 1728.

Cowper 1782   William Cowper, 'The Progress of Error', in *Poems* London (for J. Johnson) 1782.

Cowper 1785   William Cowper, *The Task*, London (for J. Johnson) 1785.

Craufurd   Quintin Craufurd, *Sketches Chiefly Relating to the History, Religion, Learning and Manners of the Hindoos*, 2nd edn enlarged, 2 vols, London (T. Cadell) 1792.

Darwin 1791   Erasmus Darwin, *The Botanic Garden*, London (Joseph Johnson) 1791.

Darwin 1803   Erasmus Darwin, *The Temple of Nature; or, the Origin
                       of Society*, London (Joseph Johnson) 1803.
Davie   Donald Davie, *Purity of Diction in English Verse*, London
                       (Routledge and Kegan Paul) 1952.
Dennis   *The Critical Works of John Dennis*, 2 vols, ed. Edward
                       Niles Hooker, Baltimore (Johns Hopkins Press) 1939
                       (vol. 1) and 1943 (vol. 2).
Diderot   Denis Diderot, *Le Neveu de Rameau*, ed. Jean Fabre,
                       Geneva (Librairie Droz) 1963.
Dinwiddy   John Dinwiddy, *Bentham*, Oxford and New York (Oxford
                       University Press) 1989.
Eade   J.C. Eade (ed.) *Projecting the Landscape*, Canberra
                       (Australian National University, Humanities Research
                       Centre) 1987.
Eagleton   Terry Eagleton, *The Function of Criticism, from 'The
                       Spectator' to Post-Structuralism*, London (Verso) 1984.
East   Edward Hyde East, *A Treatise of the Pleas of the Crown*,
                       2 vols, London (for J. Butterworth and J. Cooke) 1803.
EB   *Encyclopaedia Britannica; or, a Dictionary of the Arts and
                       Sciences ... by a Society of Gentlemen in Scotland*, 3
                       vols, Edinburgh (for A. Bell and C. Macfarquhar) 1771.
Einberg and Jones   Elizabeth Einberg and Rica Jones, *Manners and Morals:
                       Hogarth and British Painting, 1700–1760*, London (Tate
                       Gallery) 1987.
Elias   Norbert Elias, *The Civilizing Process*, (vol. 1) *The History
                       of Manners* (1939), tr. Edmund Jephcott, Oxford (Basil
                       Blackwell) 1978.
Elton 1812   Charles A. Elton, *The Remains of Hesiod translated into
                       English Verse*, London (Lackington, Allen) 1812.
Elton 1815   Charles A. Elton, *The Remains of Hesiod the Ascraean*,
                       2nd edn, London (Baldwin, Cradock and Joy) 1815.
Encyclopédie   Diderot et al., Paris, 1751–72. Reprinted in facsimile, 5
                       vols, New York (Readex Microprint) 1969, reissued New
                       York and Paris (Pergamon), no date.
Engell   James Engell, *The Creative Imagination, Enlightenment to
                       Romanticism*, Cambridge Mass. and London (Harvard
                       University Press) 1981.
Erskine   *Speeches of Thomas Lord Erskine* (1810), 2 vols, London
                       (Reeves and Turner) 1870.
Faber   George Stanley Faber, *The Origin of Pagan Idolatry*, 3
                       vols, London (F. and C. Rivingtons) 1816.
Ferenczi   Sandor Ferenczi, *Further Contributions to the Theory and
                       Technique of Psycho-Analysis*, ed. John Rickman, tr. Jane
                       Isabel Suttie, London (The Hogarth Press and the
                       Institute of Psychoanalysis; International Psycho-Ana-
                       lytic Library no. 11) 1950.
Ferguson   Adam Ferguson, *An Essay on the History of Civil Society*
                       (1767), ed. Duncan Forbes, Edinburgh (Edinburgh
                       University Press) 1966.
Ferguson, F.   Frances Ferguson, 'The Sublime of Edmund Burke, or
                       the Bathos of Experience,' in *Glyph: Johns Hopkins
                       Textual Studies*, no. 8, Baltimore and London (Johns
                       Hopkins University Press) 1981.
Fish   Stanley Fish, 'What it's like to read *L'Allegro* and *Il*

Pensoroso,' in *Is There a Text in this Class?*, Cambridge Mass. and London (Harvard University Press) 1980.

Flaxman — John Flaxman, *Lectures on Sculpture* (1829), London (Bell and Daldy) 1865.

Forster — George Forster, *Sketches of the Mythology and Customs of the Hindoos*, London (no publisher or bookseller credited) 1785.

Foster — John Foster, *Critical Essays contributed to the Eclectic Review*, ed. J.E. Ryland, 2 vols, London (Bell and Daldy) 1868.

Foster — Sir Michael Foster, *A Report of Some Proceedings on the Commission of Oyer and Terminer . . . to which is added Discourses upon a few Branches of the Crown Law*, Oxford (Clarendon Press) 1762.

Freud — Sigmund Freud, *The Standard Edition of the Complete Psychoanalytical Works of Sigmund Freud*, eds James Strachey and Anna Freud, 24 vols, London (Hogarth Press) 1953–66.

Funnell — Peter Funnell, 'Visible Appearances', *The Arrogant Connoisseur: Richard Payne Knight, 1751–1824*, eds Michael Clarke and Nicholas Penny, Manchester (Manchester University Press) 1982.

Furniss — Tom Furniss, 'Edmund Burke's Revolution: The Discourse of Aesthetics, Gender, and Political Economy in Burke's *Enquiry* and *Reflections on the Revolution in France*,' unpublished PhD dissertation, University of Southampton 1989.

Fuseli — *The Life and Writings of Henry Fuseli*, ed. John Knowles, 3 vols, London (Colburn and Bentley) 1831.

GM — *Gentleman's Magazine.*

Gerard — Alexander Gerard, *An Essay on Genius* (1774), ed. Bernhard Fabian, Munich (Wilhelm Fink) 1966.

Gilpin 1792 — William Gilpin, *Observations Relative Chiefly to Picturesque Beauty, Made in the Year 1772. On Several Parts of England; Particularly the Mountains and Lakes of Cumberland, and Westmoreland* (1789), 3rd edn, 2 vols, London (for R. Blamire) 1792.

Gilpin 1808 — William Gilpin, *Three Essays on Picturesque Beauty; on Picturesque Travel; and on Sketching Landscape: with a Poem on Landscape Painting. To these are now added Two Essays Giving an Account of the Principles and Mode in which the Author executed his own Drawings* (1792, 1804), 3rd edn, London (for T. Cadell and W. Davies) 1808.

Girouard — Mark Girouard, *Life in the English Country House* (1978) Harmondsworth (Penguin Books) 1980.

Godwin 1794 — William Godwin, *Cursory Strictures on the Charge delivered by Lord Chief Justice Eyre to the Grand Jury*, London (Daniel Eaton) 1794.

Godwin 1795 — William Godwin, *Considerations on Lord Grenville's and Mr Pitt's Bills, concerning Treasonable and Seditious Practices*, London (for Joseph Johnson) no date.

Godwin 1814 — William Godwin, 'Edward Baldwin', *The Pantheon: or Ancient History of the Gods of Greece and Rome* (1806), 4th edn, London (M.J. Godwin) 1814.

Godwin 1976　William Godwin, *Enquiry Concerning Political Justice* (1793), ed. Isaac Kramnick, Harmondsworth (Penguin Books) 1976.

Goldsmith　*The Collected Works of Oliver Goldsmith*, ed. Arthur Friedman, 5 vols, Oxford (Clarendon Press) 1966.

Goodwin　Albert Goodwin, *The Friends of Liberty: The English Democratic Movement in the Age of the French Revolution*, Cambridge Mass. (Harvard University Press) 1979.

Green　Thomas Andrew Green, *Verdict According to Conscience: Perspectives on the English Criminal Trial Jury 1200–1800*, Chicago and London (University of Chicago Press) 1985.

The Guardian　[Richard Steele, et al.], *The Guardian*, London (for Jacob Tonson) 1713.

Hale, J.　J.R. Hale, 'Art and Audience: The "Medici Venus" c. 1750–c. 1850, *Italian Studies*, vol. 31 (1976).

Hale, M.　Matthew Hale, *The History of the Pleas of the Crown*, 2 vols, London (for F. Gyles) 1736.

Halévy　Elie Halévy, *The Growth of Philosophical Radicalism*, trans. Mary Morris (1928), London (Faber and Faber) 1934.

Hammond　James Hammond, Elegies XIV and XV, in *The Works of The English Poets. With Prefaces Biographical and Critical by Samuel Johnson*, vol. 39, London (for J. Buckland et al.) 1790.

d'Hancarville　Baron d'Hancarville, *Recherches sur l'Origine, l'Esprit et les Progrès des Arts de la Grèce*, 3 vols, London (B. Appleyard) 1785.

Hans　Nicholas Hans, *New Trends in Education in the Eighteenth Century*, London (Routledge and Kegan Paul) 1951.

Hardie　Martin Hardie, *Watercolour Painting in Britain*, 3 vols, London (B.T. Batsford) 1966–8.

Hardy　Thomas Hardy, *Memoir of Thomas Hardy* (1832), in *Testaments of Radicalism: Memoirs of Working Class Politicians*, ed. David Vincent, London (Europa) 1977.

Harrington　*The Political Works of James Harrington*, ed. J.G.A. Pocock, Cambridge (Cambridge University Press) 1977.

Harris　James Harris, 'Concerning Happiness, A Dialogue' (1744), *Hermes* (1751), and *Philological Inquiries* (1780–1), in *The Works of James Harris*, London (Thomas Tegg) 1841.

Harrison, J.　J.F.C. Harrison, *Learning and Living 1790–1960: A Study in the History of the English Adult Education Movement*, London (Routledge and Kegan Paul) 1961.

Harrison, R.　Ross Harrison, *Bentham*, London, Boston, and Melbourne (Routledge and Kegan Paul) 1983.

Haskell　Francis Haskell, 'The Baron d'Hancarville: An Adventurer and Art Historian in Eighteenth-Century Europe', in *Past and Present in Art and Taste: Selected Essays*, New Haven and London (Yale University Press) 1987.

Haskell and Penny　Francis Haskell and Nicholas Penny, *Taste and the Antique: The Lure of Classical Sculpture 1500–1900*, New Haven and London (Yale University Press) 1981.

Hassell　J. Hassell, *Memoirs of the Life of George Morland*, London

	(James Cundee et al.) 1806.
Hawkins	William Hawkins, *Pleas of the Crown*, 2 vols, London (for J. Walthoe) 1716.
Hayes	John Hayes, *Rowlandson: Watercolours and Drawings*, London (Phaidon) 1972).
Hazlitt	*The Complete Works of William Hazlitt*, ed. P.P. Howe, 21 vols, London (J.M. Dent) 1930–34.
Hertz	Neil Hertz, 'Medusa's Head: Male Hysteria under Political Pressure', in *The End of the Line, Essays on Psychoanalysis and the Sublime*, New York (Columbia University Press) 1935.
Hill	Aaron Hill, 'Preface to Mr Pope' (Preface to *The Creation*, 1720), Ann Arbor, Mich. (Augustan Reprint Society, series 4, no. 2) 1949.
Hinde et al.	M. Hinde, W. Squire, J. Marshall, Thomas Cooke, *A New Royal and Universal Dictionary of Arts and Sciences; or, Complete System of Human Knowledge*, 2 vols, London (for J. Cooke) 1771–2.
Hohendahl	Peter Uwe Hohendahl, *The Institution of Criticism*, Ithaca and London (Cornell University Press) 1982.
Holcroft 1795a	Thomas Holcroft, *A Narrative of Facts Relating to a Prosecution for High Treason*, London (for H.D. Symonds) 1795.
Holcroft 1795b	Thomas Holcroft, *A Letter to the Right Honourable William Windham*, London (for H.D. Symonds) 1795.
Holdsworth	W.S. Holdsworth, *A History of English Law*, 13 vols, London (Methuen) 1903–38.
Horne Tooke	John Horne Tooke, MS Journal in his own interleaved copy of volume 1 of *The Diversions of Purley*, British Library, classmark C. 60. i. 15.
Howard	George Selby Howard, *The New Royal Cyclopaedia, and Encyclopaedia; or, Complete, Modern, and Universal Dictionary of Arts and Sciences*, 3 vols, London (for Alexander Hogg) 1788.
Hudson	J.W. Hudson, *The History of Adult Education* (1851), facsimile reprint, London (Woburn Books) 1969.
Hume 1966	David Hume, *Enquiries concerning the Human Understanding and concerning the Principles of Morals* (1748, 1751), ed. L.A. Selby-Bigge, 2nd edn, Oxford (Clarendon Press) 1966.
Hume 1978	David Hume, *A Treatise of Human Nature* (1739–40), eds L.A. Selby-Bigge and P.H. Niddich, Oxford (Oxford University Press) 1978.
Irwin	David Irwin, *English Neoclassical Art: Studies in Inspiration and Taste*, London (Faber and Faber) 1966.
Jenyns	Soame Jenyns, *The Works of Soame Jenyns*, 4 vols, London (for T. Cadell) 1790.
Johnson 1759	*The Prince of Abissinia. A Tale* [*Rasselas*], 2 vols, London (for R. and J. Dodsley and W. Johnston) 1759.
Johnson 1977	Samuel Johnson, 'Taxation no Tyranny,' in *Political Writings*, ed. Donald J. Greene, New Haven and London (Yale University Press) 1977.
Jones, S.	H. Stuart Jones, *Select Passages from Ancient Writers illustrative of the History of Greek Sculpture*, new enlarged

edition, ed. Al. N. Oikonomides, Chicago (Argonaut) 1966.

Jones, W.   *The Works of Sir William Jones*, 13 vols, London (John Stockdale and John Walker) 1807.

Jordanova   Ludmilla Jordanova, *Sexual Visions, Images of Gender in Science and Medicine between the Eighteenth and Twentieth Centuries*, New York, London (Harvester Wheatsheaf) 1989.

Junius   *Junius: including Letters by the Same Writer under other signatures* (1769ff.), ed. John Wade, 2 vols, London (Henry G. Bohn) 1850.

Kantorowicz   Ernest H. Kantorowicz, *The King's Two Bodies: A Study in Mediaeval Political Theology*, Princeton (Princeton University Press) 1957.

Kelly   Thomas Kelly, *A History of Adult Education in Great Britain*, Liverpool (Liverpool University Press) 1970.

Knight   Richard Payne Knight, *A Discourse on the Worship of Priapus* (1786), London (privately printed) 1865.

Kris   Ernst Kris and E.H. Gombrich, 'The Principles of Caricature', in Kris, *Psychoanalytic Explorations in Art*, London (George Allen and Unwin) 1953.

Kris and Gombrich   Ernst Kris and E.H. Gombrich, *Caricature*, Harmondsworth (King Penguin Books) 1940.

LCS 1796–7   *The Moral and Political Magazine of the London Corresponding Society*, vol. 1, London (John Ashley for the LCS) 1796, vol. 2, London (Evans, and H.D. Symonds) 1797.

LCS 1983   *Selections from the Papers of the London Corresponding Society 1792–1799*, ed. Mary Thale, Cambridge (Cambridge University Press) 1983.

de La Barre de Beaumarchais   [Antoine de La Barre de Beaumarchais], *The Temple of the Muses ... represented in sixty sculptures ... by Bernard Picart ... and other ... masters*, etc., Amsterdam (Zacharias Châtelain) 1733.

Lemprière   John Lemprière, *Bibliotheca Classica*, Reading (for T. Cadell) 1788.

Lieberman   David Lieberman, *The Province of Legislation Determined: Legal Theory in Eighteenth-Century Britain*. Cambridge (Cambridge University Press; Ideas in Context) 1989.

Lipking   Lawrence Lipking, *The Ordering of the Arts in Eighteenth-Century England*, Princeton (Princeton University Press) 1970.

Lonsdale   Roger Lonsdale (ed.) *The Poems of Gray, Collins and Goldsmith*, London (Longman) 1969.

Lubasz   H.M. Lubasz, 'Public Opinion Comes of Age: Reform of the Libel Law in the Eighteenth Century,' *History Today*, vol. 8 (1958).

Lyttelton   George Lyttelton, 'Possession, Eclogue IV. To Lord Cobham,' in *The Works of the English Poets. With Prefaces Biographical and Critical by Samuel Johnson*, vol. 64, London (for J. Buckland et al.) 1790.

Mack   Mary P. Mack, *Jeremy Bentham: An Odyssey of Ideas, 1748–1792*, London, Melbourne and Toronto (Heinemann) 1962.

Mackenzie — Henry Mackenzie, *The Man of Feeling* (1771), ed. Brian Vickers, London (Oxford University Press) 1967.

Macmillan — Duncan Macmillan, *Painting in Scotland: The Golden Age*, Oxford (Phaidon) 1986.

Maittaire — [Michael Maittaire], *The English Grammar; or, an Essay on the Art of Grammar Applied to and Exemplified in the English Tongue*, London (H. Clements) 1712.

Mandeville — Bernard Mandeville, *The Fable of the Bees* (1714–24), ed. Philip Harth, Harmondsworth (Penguin) 1970.

Marshall, P.H. — Peter H. Marshall, *William Godwin*, New Haven and London (Yale University Press) 1984.

Marshall, P.J. — P.J. Marshall (ed.), *The British Discovery of Hinduism in the Eighteenth Century*, Cambridge (Cambridge University Press) 1970.

Maurice 1795–8 — Thomas Maurice, *The History of Hindostan, its Arts, and its Sciences*, 3 vols, London (R. Faulder) 1795–8.

Maurice 1793–1800 — Thomas Maurice, *Indian Antiquities*, 7 vols, London (for the author) 1793–1800.

Meehan — Michael Meehan, *Liberty and Poetics in Eighteenth Century England*, London and Sydney (Croom Helm) 1986.

Middleton et. al — Erasmus Middleton, William Turnbull, Thomas Ellis, John Davison, *The New Complete Dictionary of Arts and Sciences; or, An Universal System of Useful Knowledge*, London (by authority, for the authors) 1778.

Mitter — Partha Mitter, *Much Maligned Monsters: History of European Reactions to Indian Art*, Oxford (Oxford University Press; Clarendon Press) 1977.

Moor — Edward Moor, *The Hindu Pantheon*, London (Joseph Johnson) 1810.

More — *The Complete Works of Hannah More*, 7 vols, New York (Harper) 1835.

Nicolson — Benedict Nicolson, *Joseph Wright of Derby, Painter of Light*, 2 vols, London (Routledge and Kegan Paul) and New York (Pantheon Books) 1968.

Opie — John Opie, *Lectures on Painting*, London (for Longman, Hurst, Rees and Orme) 1809.

Ousby — Ian Ousby, '"My servant Caleb": Godwin's *Caleb Williams* and the political trials of the 1790s,' *University of Toronto Quarterly*, vol. xliv, number 1 (Fall 1974).

Outram — Dorinda Outram, *The Body and the French Revolution: Sex, Class and Political Culture*, New Haven and London (Yale University Press) 1989.

Owen and Brown — Felicity Owen and David Blayney Brown, *Collector of Genius: A Life of Sir George Beaumont*, New Haven and London (Yale University Press) 1988.

Paley — William Paley, *The Principles of Moral and Political Philosophy* (1785), London (for Baldwyn et al.) 1819.

Panofskys — Dora and Erwin Panofsky, *Pandora's Box: The Changing Aspects of a Mythical Symbol*, New York (Pantheon Books for the Bollingen Foundation) 1956.

Paulson 1972 — Ronald Paulson, *Rowlandson: a New Interpretation*, London (Studio Vista) 1972.

Paulson 1975   Ronald Paulson, *Emblem and Expression: Meaning in English Art of the Eighteenth Century*, London (Thames and Hudson) 1975.

Paulson 1983   Ronald Paulson, *Representations of Revolution (1789–1820)*, New Haven and London (Yale University Press) 1983.

de Pauw   Cornelius de Pauw, *Recherches Philosophiques sur les Grecs*, 2 vols, Berlin (George Jacques Decker et Fils) 1787.

Plato   *Republic* (Loeb edition), tr. Paul Shorey, London (Heinemann), and Cambridge, Mass. (Harvard University Press) 1970.

Plutarch   *Plutarch's Lives* with an English Translation by Bernadotte Pervin, 11 vols., London (Heinemann) and Cambridge Mass. (Harvard University Press) 1914–26.

Pocock   J.G.A. Pocock, *The Machiavellian Moment: Florentine Political Thought and the Atlantic Republican Tradition*, Princeton and London (Princeton University Press) 1975.

Pope   Alexander Pope, *An Essay on Man* (1733–4), ed. Maynard Mack, London and New York (Methuen) 1950.

Postema   Gerald J. Postema, *Bentham and the Common Law Tradition*, Oxford (Clarendon Press) 1986.

Potter   John Potter, *Archaeologica Graeca: or, the Antiquities of Greece* (1697–8) 9th edn, 2 vols, London (for W. Strahan et al.) 1775.

Pressly 1981   William L. Pressly, *The Life and Art of James Barry*, New Haven and London (Yale University Press) 1981.

Pressly 1983   William L. Pressly, *James Barry, The Artist as Hero*, London (Tate Gallery) 1983.

Pugh   Simon Pugh, *Garden–Nature–Language*, Manchester (Manchester University Press) 1988.

Pyne 1806–1808   W.H. Pyne, with C. Gray and John Hill, *Microcosm: or A Picturesque Delineation of the Arts, Agriculture, Manufactures, &c. of Great Britain, in a Series of above a Thousand Groups of Small Figures for the Embellishment of Landscape*, vol. 1, London (W.H. Pyne and J.C. Nattes) 1806; vol. 2, London (William Miller) 1808.

Pyne 1971   W.H. Pyne, with C. Gray and John Hill, *Microcosm, or A Picturesque Delineation of the Arts, Agriculture and Manufactures of Great Britain in a Series of above a Thousand Groups of Small Figures for the Embellishment of Landscape* (facsimile reprint of 1845 edition of Pyne's *Microcosm*), New York (Benjamin Blom) 1971.

Radicals   Joseph O. Baylen and Norbert J. Gossman, eds, *Biographical Dictionary of Modern British Radicals*, vol. 1, 1770–1830, Hassocks, Sussex (Harvester Press) and Atlantic Highlands NJ (Humanities Press) 1979.

Reily   John Reily, *Rowlandson Drawings from the Paul Mellon Collection*, catalogue of an exhibition at the Yale Center for British Art (1977–8) and the Royal Academy (1978), New Haven (Yale Center for British Art) 1977.

Reynolds 1952   Joshua Reynolds, 'Preface' to the 'Ironical Discourse' in

Portraits by Sir Joshua Reynolds, ed. Frederick W. Hilles, London (Heinemann) 1952.

Reynolds 1975   Joshua Reynolds, *Discourses on Art*, ed. Robert R. Wark, 2nd edn, New Haven and London (Yale University Press) 1975.

Richardsons   Jonathan Richardson Senior and Junior, *An Account of Some of the Statues, Bas-Reliefs, Drawings and Pictures in Italy, etc., with Remarks*, London (for J. Knapton) 1722.

Robertson   William Robertson, *An Historical Disquisition concerning the Knowledge which the Ancients had of India* (1791) 3rd edn, London (for A. Strahan et al.) 1799.

Roe   Nicholas Roe, *Wordsworth and Coleridge, The Radical Years*, Oxford (Clarendon Press) 1988.

Roget   J.L. Roget, *A History of the 'Old Water-Colour' Society*, 2 vols, London (Longmans) 1891.

Rosenblum 1957   Robert Rosenblum, 'The Origin of Painting: A problem in the Iconography of Romantic Classicism', *Art Bulletin*, 39 (December 1957).

Rosenblum 1969   Robert Rosenblum, *Transformations in Late Eighteenth Century Art*, second printing, with corrections, Princeton NJ (Princeton University Press) 1969.

Roskill   Mark Roskill, '"Public" and "Private" Meanings: The Paintings of Van Gogh,' in *Journal of Communications* (Autumn 1979), pp. 157–69.

SHG   *Somerset House Gazette.*

ST   *A Complete Collection of State Trials*, 30 vols, eds T.B. Howell and Thomas Jones Howell, London (for Longman et al.) 1816–22.

St Clair   William St Clair, *The Godwins and the Shelleys: The biography of a family*, London and Boston (Faber and Faber) 1988.

Schiller   Johann Christoph Friedrich von Schiller, *On the Aesthetic Education of Man* (1795), eds and trs. Elizabeth M. Wilkinson and L.A. Willoughby, Oxford (Clarendon Press) 1967.

Shaftesbury 1727   *Characteristicks of Men, Manners, Opinions, Times* (1714) 4th edn, London (no publisher credited) 1727.

Shaftesbury 1914   *Second Characters, or, the Language of Forms, by the Right Honourable Anthony, Earl of Shaftesbury*, ed. Benjamin Rand, Cambridge (Cambridge University Press) 1914.

Shenstone   *The Works in Verse and Prose of William Shenstone*, 2 vols, London (R. and J. Dodsley) 1764.

Simpson   David Simpson, *Wordsworth's Historical Imagination: The Poetry of Displacement*, New York and London (Methuen) 1987.

Smith 1976a   Adam Smith, *An Enquiry into the Nature and Causes of the Wealth of Nations* (1776), eds R.H. Campbell, A.S. Skinner and W.B. Todd, Oxford (Clarendon Press) 1976.

Smith 1976b   Adam Smith, *The Theory of Moral Sentiments* (1759), eds D.D. Raphael and A.L. McFie, Oxford (Clarendon Press) 1976.

Smith 1978   Adam Smith, *Lectures on Jurisprudence*, eds R.L. Meek,
                    D.D. Raphael and P.G. Stein, Oxford (Clarendon Press)
                    1978.
Solkin 1982   David Solkin, *Richard Wilson: the Landscape of Reaction*,
                    catalogue of the Richard Wilson exhibition at the Tate
                    Gallery 1982–3, London (Tate Gallery) 1982.
Solkin 1983   David Solkin, 'The Battle of the Ciceros: Richard Wilson
                    and the Politics of Landscape in the Age of John
                    Wilkes,' *Art History*, vol. 6, no. 4, 1983, pp. 404–22.
Sonnerat   Pierre Sonnerat, *A Voyage to the East Indies and China
                    . . . Between the Years 1774 and 1781* (1782), tr. Francis
                    Magnus, 3 vols, Calcutta (vols 1 and 2 for Stuart and
                    Cooper 1788; vol. 3 for Joseph Cooper, 1789).
Spelman   Ken Spelman, *Catalogue Four, The Artist's Companion:
                    Three Centuries of Drawing Books and Manuals of
                    Instruction*, York (Ken Spelman) no date.
Spence 1755   Joseph Spence, *Polymetis: or, An Enquiry concerning the
                    Agreement between the Works of the Roman Poets, and
                    the Remains of the Antient Artists*, 2nd edn, London (for
                    R. and J. Dodsley) 1755.
Spence 1966   Joseph Spence, *Observations, Anecdotes, and Characters
                    of Books and Men, etc.*, ed. James M. Osborn, Oxford
                    (Oxford University Press) 1966.
Stallybrass and   Peter Stallybrass and Allon White, *The Politics and
    White   Poetics of Transgression*, London (Methuen) 1986.
Stryker   Lloyd Paul Stryker, *For the Defense: Thomas Erskine, The
                    Most Enlightened Liberal of his Times, 1750–1823*, Garden
                    City, NY (Doubleday) 1947.
Sunderland   John Sunderland, *John Hamilton Mortimer: His Life and
                    Works*, London (The Walpole Society) 1988.
Thelwall 1795   John Thelwall, *The Native and Constitutional Rights of
                    Britons . . . intended to have been delivered at the Bar of
                    the Old Bailey, in confutation of the late Charges of High
                    Treason*, London (for the author) 1795.
Thelwall 1796   John Thelwall, *The Tribune, A Political Publication
                    consisting chiefly of the Political Lectures of John Thelwall*,
                    3 vols, London (for the author) 1796.
Thompson   E.P. Thompson, *The Making of the English Working Class*,
                    London (Victor Gollancz) 1965.
Thomson 1730   James Thomson, *The Seasons*, London (no publisher
                    credited) 1730.
Thomson, 1981   James Thomson, *The Seasons*, ed. James Sambrook,
                    Oxford (Clarendon Press) 1981.
Thomson 1986   James Thomson, *Liberty, The Castle of Indolence, and
                    Other Poems*, ed. James Sambrook, Oxford (Clarendon
                    Press) 1986.
Tooke   Andrew Tooke, *The Pantheon, Representing the Fabulous
                    Histories of the Heathen Gods*, revised, corrected,
                    amended, etc.) London (for C. Bathurst et al.) 1778.
Trotter   Thomas Trotter, *A View of the Nervous Temperament*,
                    London (Longman, Hurst, Rees, and Orme) 1807.
Tucker   Abraham Tucker, *The Light of Nature Pursued* (1768–77),
                    2nd edn, 7 vols, London (for R. Faulder and T. Payne)
                    1805.

Turnbull	George Turnbull, *A Treatise on Ancient Painting, containing Observations on the Rise, Progress, and Decline of that Art Amongst the Greeks and Romans*, London (for the author) 1740.
Twiss	Horace Twiss, *The Public and Private Life of Lord Chancellor Eldon*, 3 vols, London (John Murray) 1844.
Universal History	*An Universal History from the Earliest Account of Time to the Present*, 23 vols., London (for J. Batley et al.) 1736–65.
Uphaus	R.W. Uphaus, 'The Ideology of Reynolds's *Discourses on Art*', *Eighteenth-Century Studies*, vol. 12, no. 1 (Fall 1978).
Veitch	G.S. Veitch, *The Genesis of Parliamentary Reform* (1913), London (Constable) 1965.
Volney	Constantin François Chasseboeuf comte de Volney, *A New Translation of Volney's Ruins; or Meditations on the Revolution of Empires* (1791) [tr. Thomas Jefferson and Joel Barlow], 2 vols, Paris (for Levrault) 1802, reprinted in facsimile New York and London (Garland) 1979.
Walker	John Walker, *A Rhetorical Grammar, or Course of Lessons in Elocution*, London (for the author) 1785.
Warburton	William Warburton, *The Divine Legation of Moses Demonstrated on the Principles of a Religious Deist* (1738–65), 4 vols, reprinted in facsimile New York (Garland) 1978.
Wark 1952	Robert R. Wark, 'James Barry', PhD dissertation, Harvard University, 1952.
Wark 1975	Robert R. Wark, *Drawings by Thomas Rowlandson in the Huntington Collection*. San Marino, Calif. (Huntington Library) 1975.
Warton 1746	Joseph Warton, *Odes on Various Subjects*, London (R. Dodsley) 1746.
Warton 1753	*The Works of Virgil, in Latin and English . . . and, Three Essays . . . by Mr. Joseph Warton*, 4 vols, London (for J. Dodsley) 1753.
Waterhouse	Ellis Waterhouse, *Gainsborough* (1958), London (Spring Books) 1966.
Webb	Daniel Webb, *Inquiry into the Beauties of Painting*, London (for R. and J. Dodsley) 1760.
Webster	Mary Webster, *Francis Wheatley*, London (Routledge and Kegan Paul) 1970.
West 1732	[Gilbert West], *Stowe, the Gardens of the Right Honourable Richard Lord Viscount Cobham*, London (Lawton Gilliver) 1732.
West 1790	Gilbert West, 'On the Abuse of Travelling', in *The Works of the English Poets. With Prefaces Biographical and Critical by Samuel Johnson*, vol. 57, London (for J. Buckland et al.) 1790.
Wilkins	Charles Wilkins, *The Bhagvat-Geeta, or Dialogues of Kreeshna and Arjoon . . . translated from the Original, in the Sanskreet . . . by Charles Wilkins*, London (for C. Nourse) 1785.
Wollstonecraft 1975	Mary Wollstonecraft, *A Vindication of the Rights of Woman* (1792), ed. Carol H. Poston, New York (W.W. Norton) 1975.

Wollstonecraft 1989   Mary Wollstonecraft, *A Vindication of the Rights of Men, in a Letter to . . . Edmund Burke* (1790), in vol. 5 of Janet Todd and Marilyn Butler (eds) *The Works of Mary Wollstonecraft*, 7 vols, London (William Pickering) 1989.

Wood   Gordon S. Wood, 'Conspiracy and the Paranoid Style: Causality and Deceit in the Eighteenth Century', *The William and Mary Quarterly*, third series, vol. xxxix, no. 3 (July 1982).

Wright   Edward Wright, *Some Observations Made in Travelling through France, Italy etc. in the years 1720, 1721 and 1722*, London (Thomas Ward and E. Wicksteed) 1730.

Index

abstract ideas, abstraction, 36, 41–3, 46–8, 52, 56, 60
accident, accidents of nature, 12, 43, 46, 51, 59, 222 n. 11
Ackermann, Rudolph, 15
Adair, James, 135
aesthetics, aesthetic inquiry, 133, 136, 140, aesthetic pleasure, the aesthetic, 68–71, 82–7, 96, 216–19; *see also* 'philosophical' and 'rhetorical' aesthetic
agriculture, 92, 95, 111
Ajax, 178
Akenside, Mark, 136, 232 nn. 19, 20
alienation, 89, 110, 116, 155
Alison, Archibald, 229, n. 6
Allan, David, 161, 234 n. 13
allegory, allegorical poetry, 26–7, 32, 34, 37, 225 n. 3
Allentuck, Marcia, 234 n. 13
analogy, in legal argument, 138–42
androgynous deities, 175–6, 236 n. 24
Angelo, Henry, 223 n. 22; 224 n. 23
Anstruther, John, 133
Apollo, 152–4, 157, 170, 173, 179–80, 181, 188
arbitrary and natural signs, 77, 170–1
aristocracy, 'patricians', 15, 68–71, 83
Aristogiton, 185
Aristotle, 52, 237 n. 24
arts, public and private functions of 13–16, 75–7, 167, 185–6 *see also* literature, painting
Asiatic Researches, 237 no. 30
Athena, *see* Minerva
Athens, 185
Atlas, 151
Attis, 216

Bacchus, 152, 157, 179, 218, 236 n. 22
Bakhtin, Mikhail, 150, 175
banditti, 114
Barbier, C. P., 239, n. 5
Barrington, Daines, 122, 133, 141
Barry, James, 11–12, 14, 15, 57–8, 61, 145–220, 233 nn. 3, 4, 9, 10; 234 nn. 13, 15; 235 n. 18; 236 nn. 22, 23, 24; 237 n.

31; 237 n. 32; 238 nn. 33, 36, 39; 239 n. 41; *Account of a Series of Pictures*, 151, 169, 190; 'Adelphi' cycle (*The Progress of Human Culture*), 149, 151–2, 162, 193, 200, 204, 233 n. 5; 234 n. 13; 237 n. 31: 238 n. 39; 239 n. 41; *The Birth of Pandora* (Luigi Schiavonetti, after James Barry; Fig. 23), 149, 157, 159, 179–81, 204, 209; *The Birth of Pandora* (etching and engraving, Fig. 29), 168, 179–81, 188, 193, 204, 214; *The Birth of Pandora* (painting, Fig. 28), 149, 151, 159, 164, 167, 174, 179–86, 188–9, 193, 208–9, 212–15, 218–20, 238 n. 39; *Crowning the Victors at Olympia* (Fig. 34), 193, 204, 208; *The Death of General Wolfe* (Fig. 38), 200, 202, 209; *The Discovery of Adam and Eve* (Fig. 43), 204; *The Education of Achilles* (Fig. 41), 204; *Elysium and Tartarus or the State of Final Retribution*, 162; 'Fragment on Pandora', 168, 172, 184, 186, 214, 238 n. 39; lecture on design, 164, 218; lecture on the history of painting, 172; *Letter to the Dilettanti Society*, 160, 162–66, 184, 190, 212–13; letter to the *Morning Chronicle*, 108, 151, 169; *Medea*-paintings, 214; *Orpheus* (Fig. 39), 200, 209; *Pandora* (drawings), 145, 149, 151, 175, 180; 'Pandora project', 145–51, 154, 156, 159, 161, 168, 170–75, 184–5; 190, 215, 232, n. 1; 233 n. 4; 238 n. 39; *Philoctetes* (etching and aquatint, Fig. 47) 209; *Philoctetes on the Island of Lemnos* (drawing, Fig. 36), 198; *Philoctetes on the Island of Lemnos* (painting, Fig. 35), 198, 202, 208–9, 212–13, 219; *Portraits of Barry and Burke in the Characters of Ulysses and a Companion* (Fig. 37), 200, 209; *The Prince of Wales as St George* (Fig. 44), 204, 214; *St Patrick and the King of Cashel* (Fig. 40), 202, 204, 219; *The Sicyonian Maid* (Fig. 24), 161, 209, 234, n. 13; 239 n. 41; *The Temptation of Adam* (Fig. 42), 204; *Venus rising from the Sea*, 209